Sports Collectors Digest

2001 Standard Catalog of

SPORTS AUTOGRAPHS

First Edition

Edited by

Tom Mortenson

© 2000 by
Krause Publications, Inc.

All rights reserved.
No portion of this publication may be reproduced or transmitted in any form or by any means, electronic or mechanical, including photocopy, recording, or any information storage and retrieval system, without permission in writing from the publisher, except by a reviewer who may quote brief passages in a critical review to be printed in a magazine or newspaper, or electronically transmitted on radio or television.

Published by

krause publications
700 East State Street • Iola, WI 54990-0001
715/445-2214 • FAX: 715/445-4087   www.krause.com

Please call or write for our free sales catalog.
Our toll-free number to place an order or obtain a free sales catalog is 800-258-0929
or please use our regular business telephone: 715-445-2214
for editorial comment and further information.

Library of Congress Catalog Number: 00-104841
ISBN: 0-87341-944-8

Printed in the United States of America

Acknowledgments

Numerous individuals have made valuable contributions which have been incorporated into *The Standard Catalog of Sports Autographs*. While all cannot be acknowledged, special appreciation is extended to the following contributors who have exhibited a special dedication by creating, revising or verifying listings and technical data, reviewing market listings, loaning items for photography or assisting in various ways.

Bob Best
Steve Bloedow
Hersh Borenstein
Kathy Briquelet
Joe Clemens
Ross Forman
Mike Gutierrez
Dan Halverson

Kevin Huard
Ross Hubbard
Tom Hultman
Kris Kandler
Tom Kessenich
Rocky Landsverk
Bert Lehman
Dave Mueller

Wendy Olson
Dean Parks
Mike Rodell
Guy Scudella
Mike Sherry
Jason Stonelake
Gordon Ullom
Corrine Zielke

Contents

Acknowledgments 3

Introduction 6

Chapter 1: Autographs Basics 7

Chapter 2: Baseball Hall of Famers 11
Players, managers and executives enshrined in Cooperstown, N.Y.

Chapter 3: Inactive Baseball Players 27
Former stars of the diamond game

Chapter 4: Active Baseball Players 44
Current stars of Major League Baseball

Chapter 5: Team Baseballs 52
Team-autographed baseballs from 1900-1999

Chapter 6: All-Star Team Baseballs 68
Team-signed All-Star Game balls

Chapter 7: Special Milestone Baseball Collectibles 70
Multi-signed collectibles associated with baseball's 500 Home Run Club, 300-Win Club and 3,000 Hit Club

Chapter 8: Baseball Negro Leagues 74
Non-Hall of Fame stars of the old Negro leagues

Chapter 9: Basketball Hall of Famers 76
Players, coaches executives and contributors to the game of basketball

Chapter 10: Inactive Basketball Players 83
Retired stars of the NBA

Chapter 11: Active Basketball Players 91
Current stars of the NBA

Chapter 12: Pro Football Hall of Famers 95
Players, coaches, executives and contributors to the professional game

Chapter 13: Inactive Football Players 106
Retired stars of the NFL

Chapter 14: Active Football Players 116
Current NFL players

Chapter 15: Hockey Hall of Famers 122
Honored players, coaches, executives and contributors to hockey

Chapter 16: Inactive Hockey Players 132
Retired hockey players

Chapter 17: Active Hockey Players 137
Current stars of the NHL

Chapter 18: Wrestlers 140
Current and retired wrestling stars

Chapter 19: Boxers 144
Current and retired greats of the ring

Chapter 20: Auto Racing 150
Current and retired racing stars

Chapter 21: Tennis 152
Current and retired tennis stars

Chapter 22: Golf 154
Current and retired golfers

Sources 156

Introduction

This premiere edition of *Sports Collectors Digest's Standard Catalog of Sports Autographs* is the result of numerous requests from collectors to publish a comprehensive sports autograph price guide.

In publishing this book, it was the author's intent to produce a book that would complement other books in the Krause Publications' standard catalog realm, most notably, the popular catalogs, *The Standard Catalog of Baseball Cards* and *The Standard Catalog of Sports Memorabilia*.

The scope of this — or any book of sports autographs — is limited because it would be impossible to list each and every single-signed or multiple-signed item ever autographed. However, it is our intention that the material listed in this catalog is interesting and relatively commonly collected.

As with any collectible, condition is often of key importance in the sale of a sports collectible. Unless noted, the condition of items priced in this book should be considered to be Excellent to Mint. Remember, any price guide is just that, a guide. The volatility of a hot market should be kept in mind whenever referring to this or any price guide. The buyer and seller ultimately determine a particular item's value.

It is hoped that this first edition will lead to bigger and better subsequent editions. Therefore, the author and publisher encourage you to offer your thoughts about this book — particularly what needs to be added, deleted or explained in more detail.

Autograph Basics

Dating back to the 19th century, autographs of famous athletes have been saved and treasured. Signatures of such celebrity athletes as Mike "King" Kelly and John L. Sullivan became physical proof that you had a brief personal encounter with a famous person.

The simple manner in which pencil signatures were obtained in those days has changed greatly. If celebrated athletes such as Kelly and Sullivan were alive today, they would probably be shocked to see how collecting autographs has evolved. They'd probably be amazed to see that athletes are paid huge sums of money just to pen their names to various items.

Even so, obtaining a signature of your childhood hero can be just as thrilling today as it was for your grandfather 50-100 years ago.

Today, the most common memorabilia which is autographed includes balls, bats, helmets, sticks, pucks, index cards, photographs and postcards, Hall of Fame plaques and postcards, equipment (shoes, skates, helmets, jerseys, trunks), programs and books, letters and documents, bank checks, and cut signatures, which have been taken from another piece of writing, such as a manuscript, letter or check.

Obtaining Autographs

Autographs can be obtained by several methods. The most personable, and perhaps memorable, experience would be acquiring the autograph from the player at the stadium or arena. This is often the best place to catch a player, and the best time to get his/her signature. But get there early, before practice; once a player is into his/her game routine he/she doesn't want to be distracted. Give yourself an edge over fans who are rude and obnoxious with their requests by being polite and courteous. Having a pen ready and keeping your request simple and fast also helps.

Some players are willing to sign in the lobby of the hotels the teams are staying at. Common sense for collecting situations should prevail. For example, if a player is having dinner or is occupied with his or her family, they should be given the courtesy to finish what they are doing before being approached for an autograph.

Card Shows and Private Signings

Another alternative is to acquire signatures at sports card shows. Show promoters often impose time or quota limitations, so if you know a player is going to be signing at a show it could be a smart move to get autograph tickets in advance and be there early.

Dealers and show promoters also hold private signings with the players, during which the player fills the mail-order requests sent to the dealer. Non-flat items which are signed sometimes require an extra fee. These private signings are usually advertised in hobby publications such as *Sports Collectors Digest* and *Tuff Stuff*. Authenticity is generally guaranteed, and most dealers also have a return policy.

Mail Requests

Direct requests can be sent to the player via the mail in care of his team's address, which is the best way, or his home, but the results can be unpredictable, due to the amount of mail the players receive. Some players also believe mail sent to their homes is an invasion of their privacy, so your request might go unheeded.

When dealing through the mail, send less valuable items; you don't want the post office to lose or damage them. Always include a self-addressed, stamped envelope or package with the required postage for its return. A courteous, creative, brief request, which distinguishes and sets off your letter from the others, will yield better results.

Specify if the item is to be personalized or dated, and don't ask the player to sign more than two items. Perhaps you can include an extra for the player to keep, but players are becoming wary of those who request several autographs, perhaps to be sold at a later date. Thus, sometimes the player, in return for the autograph, might ask for a donation to his/her favorite charity.

Auctions and Other Sources

Auctions are another source for autographed material. These events, whether by telephone, live or on the Internet, often offer quality material. Items may also turn up at antique shops and flea markets, but questions regarding authenticity, value, condition and scarcity may occur if the seller has limited knowledge of the item.

Autograph Pricing

Prices for autographed materials are set by the principles of supply and demand, based on regional interest, scarcity, condition (not faded, dirty, shellacked, smudged, scuffed, ripped), player popularity and significance of the event commemorated. Factors for autographed basketballs and footballs also include the signature form (style, placement, nickname), type of ball and writing medium used.

Multi-signed Items

Individually-signed baseballs usually have the autograph on the sweet spot, the shortest distance between two seams. Team balls, those which should include the signatures of all the key players, starters and bench players, generally reserve the sweet spot for the manager's signature.

The more complete the ball is with key players, the more valuable it is. It's also easier to pinpoint the year being represented. But having other signatures, such as those of umpires and broadcasters, detracts from the value.

Some items have just select players who have signed it. These group-signed items commemorate a particular accomplishment or event, such as the living members of hockey's 500 goal club or baseball's 3,000 hit club.

Detecting Forgeries

Forgeries are by far the most serious problem in the autograph collecting hobby today. Generally speaking, the bigger the star, the greater the chance some unscrupulous person will sell fakes of him/her.

Forgeries can sometimes be detected by uncommon breaks, peculiarities in pressure and movement in strokes, and changes in thickness in the letters. Facsimile signatures also exist; they are exact reproductions which are printed or screened on the item, often through computer-based technology. Rubber stamps and ghost writers have also been used by players to sign their mail.

Autograph collectors often find themselves authenticating a simple signature on an item rather than a handwritten letter filled with numerous samples. The act of signing one's name is routine and common, thus taking on certain characteristics indicative of this process. A person's signature becomes a personal trademark of the individual, whether it's flamboyant, careless, simple or meticulous. While parallels can be drawn between a person's handwriting and the writing that person practiced in grammar school, how one signs his/her name has less of an association. This is why collectors will often find many similarities in the handwriting of family members schooled in the same manner, yet differences in their signatures, too.

Signature Variations

The manner in which a subject signs his name depends on numerous factors such as the individual's health, age, environment, personality, temperament, even what the individual is signing and how many times he or she's signed something similar. All these factors, most of which the subject is unaware of, play important roles in the authentication of a personal signature.

It's important to consider the environmental conditions in which an item was signed. For example, Kobe Bryant can sign an item differently when he's approached by fans on his way to the arena in contrast to being mobbed while trying to enter the visiting team hotel. An Albert Belle signature acquired during his team's winter fan festival, where he agrees to sign for a specified time, will often be more meticulous than an autograph acquired from him on a crowded street corner. Too often this factor is forgotten while purchasing or authenticating an autograph.

The athlete's health can be a factor that may alter an athlete's signature. This factor is exhibited in the signatures of many individuals including Cool Papa Bell, Catfish Hunter, Ben Hogan and Muhammad Ali. An individual whose signature was once flamboyant and meticulous can suffer from an illness that can detract from the relatively easy task of signing his/her name. Numerous differences can appear such as shaky writing and lack of character definition. Depending upon the writing instrument, the ink distribution can be uneven or uncommonly heavy, all as a result of poor health.

The personality and flamboyance of an individual can alter a signature. For example, the often dynamic and flamboyant signatures of a Dennis Rodman. Professional athletes are human too and as such exhibit emotion. After winning a Super Bowl or NBC championship, the exhilaration can lead to flamboyant flourishes in some signatures.

When examining an item for authenticity, consider the writing tool used. Was the player alive when the ink, such as felt-tip, Sharpie or ballpoint pens, was available? Ballpoints became prominent in the 1940s, felt tips in the 1960s and Sharpies in the 1970s. However, whatever medium is used, never retrace the signature.

While ballplayers are used to signing balls, hats, bats, etc., authenticating a signature on a non-flat item is a study unto itself, especially if the subject is unfamiliar with signing such an item. Because of the characteristics inherent in a golf ball, basketball, cap, helmet or jersey, this task is best left to a professional authenticator.

Writing frequency is a factor that can affect a signature. Individuals differ in the frequency to which they sign their name during a given day. While athletes and other celebrities may sign their names often, an average person may go days or even weeks before signing something. And athletes who sign autographs at shows or conventions often sign their names 500 or more times. Few individuals can maintain interest, yet alone concern themselves with the consistency of the signature, even if they are being paid.

Most of us attempt to be consistent in our signature, if only to protect us from forgery. The execution of this process is the invisible combination of both the macro and micro factors, all of which can have an affect on the outcome. While minor variations are normal, significant differences are not.

How much a signature varies depends upon the individual and the environment in which it was accomplished. When you are comparing a single signature to known (authentic) examples, be sure that these exhibits exemplify all of the subtle variations of the individual in question. For example, Ty Cobb signatures exemplify variations. Early examples of Cobb's signature typically show no breaks, unless he signed "Tyrus" instead of "Ty", when a break was found between the "y" and the "r".

Comparing Cobb's signature in 1925 to that of 1960 or 1961, shows minor variations. Later signatures show a bit more slant and less roundness and flamboyance in the capitalized "C".

As an additional note, for some reason Cobb liked to use green ink, as many examples of his signature are penned in green.

As another example, Mickey Mantle's signature differed greatly from his early years with the New York Yankees in the 1950s compared to his later-in-life more flamboyant signatures of the 1980s and '90s.

To draw a conclusion on authenticity, an examiner must be able to exhibit the anomalies in known samples.

For a collector, natural changes or repeated occurrences in an individual's signature are easier to study than irregular variations. This is because natural variations occur more often.

These are three examples of Mickey Mantle's autograph (from top) his early, mid and post playing career signatures.

Autograph Basics — Chapter 1

These photos picture both authentic (top) and bogus examples of Ty Cobb's signature.

Genuine signatures can exhibit an accidental or rare variation. Because this phenomena is rather uncommon, it may require careful documentation. Examples of variations may occur when signatures are scribbled quickly on receipts. Other variations of signatures happen under extreme stress and during the declining years of ones life. Because of this, collectors must be able locate known authentic examples signed by the subject under these conditions.

Baseball Hall of Fame signature collectors often include in their files examples of Roy Campanella's signature before and after his serious automobile accident in 1958, and samples of a youthful and aging signatures of Carl Hubbell, Buck Leonard or Bill Terry.

Mechanical & Facsimile Signatures

Among the most challenging areas of autograph collecting has been the constant monitoring of the use of mechanical-generated signatures. The time constraints of busy athletes have caused some to use mechanical devices to save time. In some cases, the athlete wasn't even aware that such a signature is deemed virtually worthless to collectors.

To address the problem of answering mountains of mail, they turned to machines such as the Autopen or Signa-Signer.

These machines can easily replicate a person's signature, initials and even handwriting. While the patterns of the past can be easily identified by the tremulous strokes and the replication of a near identical signature, the machines of today have improved considerably. Entire books have been written that identify machine-generated signature and handwriting patterns for collectors. Hundreds of machine-signed letters and cards surface on the market each year.

From Lee Trevino, to Jack Kemp and Dale Murphy machine-generated signatures have proved to be cost effective for the player. A "common sense" approach to this dilemma will avoid many mistakes. Consider the popularity and work schedule of the individual, along with the content/importance of the letter or document or likelihood of an in-person signing opportunity.

Collectors will also need to be able to identify signatures created by laser copiers and pen plotters and understand the current limitations in optical scanning.

"Ghost" Signers

Hundreds of athletes have utilized "ghost" signers, to sign on their behalf. While the process was not new, it really gained popularity during the 20th century. With time a precious commodity, it allowed the athlete his/her time, while appeasing their fans.

Ghost signers have been known to be relatives, secretaries and even clubhouse personnel. It's widely known that Joe DiMaggio's sister signed many items in her brother's behalf during his playing career. So where does this leave the autograph market? Both dealer and collectors are forced to rigorously evaluate any signature acquired indirectly. To do so however, requires a strong understanding of handwriting identification. A task that is not easy and one that is being performed less and less by those entering the hobby.

Identifying the Forger

Identifying a forger can be a difficult task. A common method used involves acquiring enough examples of the party in question to construct a strong case against the individual. This is done by cutting and pasting known examples together that bear a resemblance to a particular disputed signature. In some cases, the identity of an individual was uncovered through an anomaly he had in his own handwriting, be it a unique character construction or the common addition or deletion in character pair constructions. Whatever the approach, most require a substantial amount of

This photo illustrates both authentic and forged examples (six each) of Ted Williams' signature. Can you detect any differences? Clue: examine closely the "a" in Williams.

research often without enough known examples to prove anything.

Among the things to look for in determining if an item is forged are signs of artificial aging, inconsistent writing style and form, retouching, the use of wrong writing instruments and off-scale writing (too big or too small).

If a dealer says he can't remember where the prized autograph he's offering came from, or has a story that sounds too good to be true, take a pass on it.

Certificates of Authenticity

Many items that are purchased from sources such as catalogs, mail-order and on-line dealers come with certificates of authenticity. Remember, though, that a certificate of authenticity is only as good as the reputation of the person providing it. Certificates can be forged just as easily as the autographs themselves.

This doesn't mean that they should be ignored completely. A little research can be invaluable later. Whenever possible, check out the reputation of the seller. Find out what the dealer's return policy is before buying.

Collector Terminology

Beginning collectors should become familiar with collector terminology in their area of interest. Utilize the knowledge of skilled, reputable, experienced dealers and maintain good rapport with them. They can be future sources in helping you build a collection.

Preserving Your Collection

Collections can be stored in a file cabinet or display case, with background information on the event and purchase also included. The best conditions for display cases are when effective, indirect lighting is used, so as to not damage or cause the signature to fade. Light, especially bright sunlight, can cause signatures to fade and virtually disappear in a short period of time.

Ideal temperature and humidity conditions are 65 to 70 degrees and 50 percent humidity. More valuable items can be kept in safe-deposit boxes.

Balls are best kept in cubed holders designed for their storage.

It's wise to periodically check your collection for signs of deterioration, but avoid excessive handling.

Autographed caps, jerseys and other types of equipment should be kept in cases. Restoration is best left to a professional conservator who's done that type of work before.

Insuring your valuable collection is as important as insuring other valuables and keepsakes in your home.

Official Baseballs

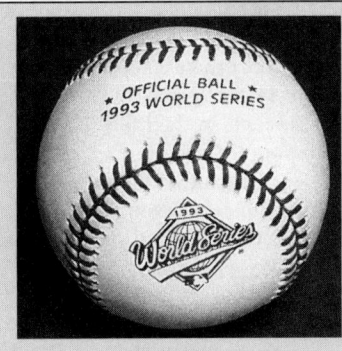

The following is a sampling of collectible baseballs and their market values without boxes.

National League Balls
Years	President	Price
1885-1902	Nicholas Young	$1,200
1903-1909	Harry Pulliam	$950
1909-1910	John Heydler	$1,200
1910-1913	Thomas Lynch	$750
1913-1918	John Tener	$700
1918-1934	John Heydler	$900
1934-1951	Ford Frick (1930s)	$330
1934-1951	Ford Frick (1940s)	$225
1951-1969	Warren Giles (1950s)	$250
	(1960s)	$175
1970-1986	Charles Feeney (1970s)	$60
	(1980s)	$50
1986-1989	Bart Giamatti	$20
1989-1994	Bill White	$15
1994-1999	Leonard Coleman	$8

American League Balls
Years	President	Price
1901-1927	Ban Johnson (1900s)	$975
1901-1927	Ban Johnson (1910s)	$825
	(1920s)	$800
1927-1931	Ernest Barnard	$800
1931-1959	William Harridge (1930s)	$500
	(1940s)	$225
	(1950s)	$300
1959-1973	Joe Cronin (1960s)	$200
	(1970s)	$175
1974-1984	Lee MacPhail (1970s)	$175
	(1980s)	$75
1984-1994	Bobby Brown	$15
1994-1999	Gene Budig	$8

World Series Balls
Years	Commissioner	Price
1978-1983	Bowie Kuhn	$20 each
1978-1983	Bowie Kuhn (Haiti)	$45 each
1984-1988	Peter Ueberroth	$20 each
	Ueberroth (Haiti)	$40 each
1989	Bart Giamatti	$20
	Giamatti (Haiti)	$35
1990-1992	Fay Vincent	$20 each
	Vincent (Haiti)	$25
1992	Without Vincent signature	$35
1993-1995	No commissioner	$20
1996	With Bud Selig signature	$150
1996	Without Selig signature	$18
1997-present	Bud Selig	$18

Commemorative Balls
Year	Ball	Price
1991	Comiskey Park Inaugural Season	$15
1994	Jacobs Field Inaugural Season	$15
1995	Cal Ripken Jr.	$15
1996	La Premiera Series	$35
1996	Mickey Mantle Day	$20
1997	Jackie Robinson (AL and NL)	$18
1997	Cleveland Indians All-Star Season	$20
2000	Atlanta All-Star Game	$17
2000	Comerica Park Inaugural	$17
2000	Pacific Bell Inaugural	$17
2000	Enron Field Inaugural	$17

Post-Season Balls
Years	President	Price
1996-1998	Gene Budig (AL Championship)	$15 each
1996-1998	Leonard Coleman (NL Championship)	$15 each
1996-1998	Gene Budig (AL Division Series)	$14 each
1996-1998	Leonard Coleman (NL Division Series)	$15 each

Major League Baseball Presidents
The following list will help date baseballs:

National League
Morgan Bulkeley	1876
William Hulbert	1877-1882
Arthur Soden	1882
Abraham Mills	1883-1884
Nicholas Young	1885-1902
Harry Pulliam	1903-1909
John Heydler	1909
Thomas Lynch	1910-1913
John Ener	1913-1918
John Heydler	1918-1934
Ford Frick	1934-1951
Warren Giles	1951-1969
Charles Feeney	1970-1986
A. Bartlett Giamatti	1986-1989
William White	1989-1994
Leonard Coleman	1994-1999

American League
Bancroft Johnson	1901-1927
Ernest Barnard	1927-1931
William Harridge	1931-1959
Joseph Cronin	1959-1973
Lee MacPhail	1974-1984
Bobby Brown	1984-1994
Gene Budig	1994-1999

Beginning in 2000, only one ball, bearing the facsimile signature of commissioner Bud Selig, is being used throughout Major League Baseball.

Baseball Hall of Fame Autographs

Hank Aaron (1934-) 1982
Cut signature $15
Single-signature ball $50
3x5 index card . . . . $20-$25
Photograph/baseball card . . . . $30-$40
HOF plaque postcard . . . . $20-$30
Perez-Steele postcards $30

Grover Cleveland Alexander
(1887-1950) 1938
Cut signature $500
Single-signature baseball $5,000
3x5 index card . . . . $450-$700
Photograph/baseball card $900
HOF plaque postcard $1,000
Perez-Steele postcards . . . . . Impossible

Walter Alston (1911-1984) 1983
Cut signature $35
Single-signature baseball $700
3x5 index card . . . . $40-$50
Photograph/baseball card $300
HOF plaque postcard . . . . . . $85-$150
Perez-Steele postcards . . . . $750-$800

Sparky Anderson (1934-) 2000
Cut signature $7
Single-signature baseball . . . . $25-$30
3x5 index card $10
Photograph/baseball card . . . . $20-$25
HOF plaque postcard $15
Perez-Steele postcards $20

Cap Anson (1852-1922) 1939
Cut signature $1,500
Single-sign. baseball $17,000
3x5 index card $1,500
Photograph/baseball card $3,500
HOF plaque postcard . . . . . Impossible
Perez-Steele postcards . . . . . Impossible

Luis Aparicio (1934-) 1984
Cut signature $7
Single-signature baseball $25
3x5 index card $10
Photograph/baseball card $20
HOF plaque postcard $15
Perez-Steele postcards $20

Luke Appling (1907-1991) 1964
Cut signature $10
Single-signature baseball $75
3x5 index card $15
Photograph/baseball card $35
HOF plaque postcard $20
Perez-Steele postcards $40

Richie Ashburn (1927-1997) 1995
Cut signature $7
Single-signature baseball $35
3x5 index card $10
Photograph/baseball card $25
HOF plaque postcard $15
Perez-Steele postcards . . . . . Impossible

Earl Averill (1902-1983) 1975
Cut signature $20
Single-signature baseball . . . $450-$500
3x5 index card $35
Photograph/baseball card $90
HOF plaque postcard $35
Perez-Steele postcards . . . . $450-$550

Frank Baker (1886-1963) 1955
Cut signature $150
Single-signature baseball $3,500
3x5 index card . . . . $300-$350
Photograph/baseball card $800
HOF plaque postcard $700
Perez-Steele postcards . . . . . Impossible

Dave Bancroft (1891-1972) 1971
Cut signature $50
Single-signature baseball $2,800
3x5 index card $75
Photograph/baseball card $250
HOF plaque postcard $600
Perez-Steele postcards . . . . . Impossible

Ernie Banks (1931-) 1977
Cut signature $10
Single-signature baseball $45
3x5 index card $15
Photograph/baseball card $35
HOF plaque postcard . . . . . . $15-$25
Perez-Steele postcards . . . . . . $30-$35

Al Barlick (1915-1995) 1989
Cut signature $7
Single-signature baseball . . . . $30-$35
3x5 index card . . . . $8-$10
Photograph/baseball card . . . . $15-$20
HOF plaque postcard . . . . $15-$20
Perez-Steele postcards $25

Edward Barrow (1868-1953) 1953
Cut signature $75
Single-signature baseball $3,300
3x5 index card $160
Photograph/baseball card $400
HOF plaque postcard . . . . . Impossible
Perez-Steele postcards . . . . . Impossible

Jake Beckley (1867-1918) 1971

Cut signature . . . .$1,200-$1,300
Single-signature baseball$4,800-$5,500
3x5 index card $1,700
Photograph/baseball card $3,500
HOF plaque postcard . . . .Impossible
Perez-Steele postcards . . . .Impossible

Cool Papa Bell (1903-1991) 1974
Cut signature $20
Single-signature baseball . .$175-$200
3x5 index card $30
Photograph/baseball card . . . .$50-$75
HOF plaque postcard $35
Perez-Steele postcards . . . . . .$35-$80

Johnny Bench (1947-) 1989
Cut signature $10
Single-signature baseball . . .$35-$40
3x5 index card $15
Photograph/baseball card . . . .$30-$35
HOF plaque postcard . . . . . .$25-$35
Perez-Steele postcards . . . . . .$35-$40

Chief Bender (1883-1954) 1953
Cut signature $100
Single-signature baseball$2,000-$3,500
3x5 index card $250
Photograph/baseball card . .$450-$500
HOF plaque postcard $1,200
Perez-Steele postcards . . . . .Impossible

Yogi Berra (1925-) 1971
Cut signature $8
Single-signature baseball . . . .$30-$35
3x5 index card $12
Photograph/baseball card . . . .$20-$25
HOF plaque postcard . . . . . .$20-$25
Perez-Steele postcards . . . . . .$25-$30

Jim Bottomley (1900-1959) 1974
Cut signature $150
Single-signature baseball $3,000
3x5 index card $300
Photograph/baseball card $400
HOF plaque postcard . . . . .Impossible
Perez-Steele postcards . . . .Impossible

Lou Boudreau (1917-) 1970
Cut signature . . . .$5-$8

Single-signature baseball $30
3x5 index card $10
Photograph/baseball card . . . .$12-$15
HOF plaque postcard . . . . . .$10-$15
Perez-Steele postcards . . . . . .$15-$25

Roger Bresnahan (1879-1944) 1945
Cut signature $500
Single-signature baseball $6,000
3x5 index card $650
Photograph/baseball card $1,200
HOF plaque postcard . . . . .Impossible
Perez-Steele postcards . . . .Impossible

George Brett (1953-) 1999
Cut signature $8
Single-signature baseball $45
3x5 index card $10
Photograph/baseball card $35
HOF plaque postcard $20
Perez-Steele postcards $35

Lou Brock (1939-) 1985
Cut signature . . . .$5-$8
Single-signature baseball . . . .$30-$35
3x5 index card . . . .$10-$12
Photograph/baseball card $20
HOF plaque postcard $15
Perez-Steele postcards $25

Dan Brouthers (1858-1932) 1945
Cut signature $1,250
Single-signature baseball$15,000-$20,000

3x5 index card $1,700
Photograph/baseball card $5,000
HOF plaque postcard . . . . .Impossible
Perez-Steele postcards . . . .Impossible

Mordecai Brown (1876-1948) 1949
Cut signature . . . .$250-$300
Single-signature baseball$3,000-$5,500
3x5 index card . . . .$350-$500
Photograph/baseball card $900
HOF plaque postcard . . . . .Impossible
Perez-Steele postcards . . . .Impossible

Morgan Bulkeley (1837-1922) 1937
Cut signature . . . .$800-$1,450
Single-signature baseball $6,000
3x5 index card $1,200
Photograph/baseball card $4,000
HOF plaque postcard . . . . .Impossible
Perez-Steele postcards . . . .Impossible

Jim Bunning (1931-) 1996
Cut signature . . . .$5-$7
Single-signature baseball $35
3x5 index card $10
Photograph/baseball card $20
HOF plaque postcard $15
Perez-Steele postcards $25

Jesse Burkett (1868-1953) 1946
Cut signature $450
Single-signature baseball $5,500
3x5 index card $600
Photograph/baseball card $1,000
HOF plaque postcard $1,500
Perez-Steele postcards . . . .Impossible

Roy Campanella (1921-1993) 1969
Cut signature . . . .$350-$400
Single-signature baseball$1,500-$2,500
3x5 index card $450
Photograph/baseball card . .$300-$800
HOF plaque postcard $325
Perez-Steele postcards . . . .$200-$250

Rod Carew (1945-) 1991
Cut signature . . . .$5-$8
Single-signature baseball . . . .$30-$40

3x5 index card . . . . $7-$9
Photograph/baseball card $20
HOF plaque postcard $20
Perez-Steele postcards $25

Max Carey (1890-1976) 1961
Cut signature $30
Single-signature baseball $750
3x5 index card $40
Photograph/baseball card $125
HOF plaque postcard . . . . $60-$75
Perez-Steele postcards . . . . . Impossible

Steve Carlton (1944-) 1994
Cut signature . . . . $5-$7
Single-signature baseball . . . . $25-$30
3x5 index card $10
Photograph/baseball card . . . . $20-$25
HOF plaque postcard $25
Perez-Steele postcards $30

Alexander Cartwright (1820-1892) 1938
Cut signature $1,000
Single-signature baseball . . . Unknown
3x5 index card $1,250
Photograph/baseball card $3,000
HOF plaque postcard . . . . . Impossible
Perez-Steele postcards . . . . . Impossible

Orlando Cepeda (1937-) 1999
Cut signature $7
Single-signature baseball $35
3x5 index card $10
Photograph/baseball card $25
HOF plaque postcard $25
Perez-Steele postcards $30

Henry Chadwick (1824-1908) 1938
Cut signature . . . . $1,000-$1,500
Single-signature baseball . . . Unknown
3x5 index card $1,200
Photograph/baseball card $3,200

HOF plaque postcard . . . . . Impossible
Perez-Steele postcards . . . . . Impossible

Frank Chance (1877-1924) 1946
Cut signature . . . . $600-$750
Single-signature baseball $5,500-$7,000
3x5 index card $750
Photograph/baseball card $2,000
HOF plaque postcard . . . . . Impossible
Perez-Steele postcards . . . . . Impossible

Happy Chandler (1898-1991) 1982
Cut signature $10
Single-signature baseball $100
3x5 index card $15
Photograph/baseball card $35
HOF plaque postcard $20
Perez-Steele postcards $35

Oscar Charleston (1896-1954) 1976
Cut signature $600
Single-signature baseball $7,000
3x5 index card . . . . $1,000-$1,750
Photograph/baseball card $3,000
HOF plaque postcard . . . . . Impossible
Perez-Steele postcards . . . . . Impossible

Jack Chesbro (1874-1931) 1946
Cut signature . . . . $600-$1,150
Single-signature baseball $10,000-$20,000
3x5 index card $750
Photograph/baseball card $2,000-$2,750
HOF plaque postcard . . . . . Impossible
Perez-Steele postcards . . . . . Impossible

Nestor Chylak (1922-1982) 1999
Cut signature $30
Single-signature baseball $50
3x5 index card . . . . $18-$20
Photograph/baseball card $25
HOF plaque postcard . . . . . Impossible
Perez-Steele postcards . . . . . Impossible

Fred Clarke (1872-1960) 1945
Cut signature $100
Single-signature baseball $1,500-$3,000
3x5 index card $200
Photograph/baseball card $400
HOF plaque postcard . . . . . $400-$500
Perez-Steele postcards . . . . . Impossible

John Clarkson (1861-1909) 1963
Cut signature . . . . $1,200-$1,845
Single-signature baseball . . . Unknown
3x5 index card $2,000
Photograph/baseball card $2,500
HOF plaque postcard . . . . . Impossible
Perez-Steele postcards . . . . . Impossible

Roberto Clemente (1934-1972) 1973
Cut signature . . . . $300-$350
Single-signature baseball $2,000-$4,000
3x5 index card $400
Photograph/baseball card . . $350-$600
HOF plaque postcard . . . . . Impossible
Perez-Steele postcards . . . . . Impossible

Ty Cobb (1886-1961) 1936
Cut signature . . . . $500-$600
Single-signature baseball $2,750-$3,000
3x5 index card $700
Photograph/baseball card $1,200
HOF plaque postcard $1,000
Perez-Steele postcards . . . . . Impossible

Mickey Cochrane (1903-1962) 1947
Cut signature . . . . $75-$100
Single-signature baseball . $750-$2,000
3x5 index card . . . . $125-$150
Photograph/baseball card $350
HOF plaque postcard $500
Perez-Steele postcards . . . . . Impossible

Eddie Collins (1887-1951) 1939
Cut signature $100
Single-signature baseball $2,250-$5,000
3x5 index card . . . . $175-$225
Photograph/baseball card $400
HOF plaque postcard $550
Perez-Steele postcards . . . . . Impossible

Jimmy Collins (1870-1943) 1945
Cut signature . . . . $500-$750
Single-signature baseball $6,000
3x5 index card . . . . $700-$950
Photograph/baseball card $1,500
HOF plaque postcard . . . . . Impossible
Perez-Steele postcards . . . . . Impossible

Earle Combs (1899-1976) 1970
Cut signature . . . . $15-$17

Single-signature baseball ..$500-$2,000
3x5 index card $40
Photograph/baseball card $350
HOF plaque postcard $100
Perez-Steele postcards .....Impossible

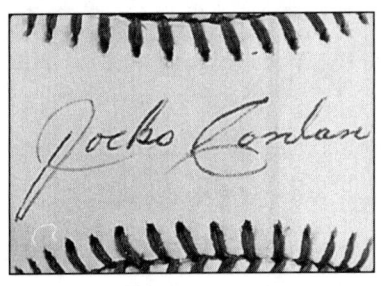

Charles Comiskey (1859-1931) 1939
Cut signature ....$350-$375
Single-signature baseball$4,500-$8,000
3x5 index card ....$450-$500
Photograph/baseball card $1,200
HOF plaque postcard .....Impossible
Perez-Steele postcards .....Impossible

Jocko Conlan (1899-1989) 1974
Cut signature $10
Single-signature baseball ..$100-$125
3x5 index card ....$15-$20
Photograph/baseball card $35
HOF plaque postcard ....$15-$20
Perez-Steele postcards ......$60-$500

Thomas Connolly (1870-1963) 1953
Cut signature $275
Single-signature baseball ..$2,345-$7,000
3x5 index card ....$250-$350
Photograph/baseball card $900
HOF plaque postcard ..$1,000-$1,200
Perez-Steele postcards .....Impossible

Roger Connor (1857-1931) 1976
Cut signature ....$1,000-$1,185
Single-signature baseball$5,600-$8,000
3x5 index card $1,700
Photograph/baseball card $2,500
HOF plaque postcard .....Impossible
Perez-Steele postcards .....Impossible

Stan Coveleski (1889-1984) 1969
Cut signature ....$15-$20
Single-signature baseball $450
3x5 index card ....$25-$30
Photograph/baseball card $80

HOF plaque postcard ....$20-$30
Perez-Steele postcards .....$325-$400

Sam Crawford (1880-1968) 1957
Cut signature ....$75-$100
Single-signature baseball$1,900-$2,500
3x5 index card $125
Photograph/baseball card $250
HOF plaque postcard .....$250-$400
Perez-Steele postcards .....Impossible

Joe Cronin (1906-1984) 1956
Cut signature $20
Single-signature baseball ..$225-$500
3x5 index card $25
Photograph/baseball card $100
HOF plaque postcard ....$35-$50
Perez-Steele postcards .....$700-$750

Candy Cummings (1848-1924) 1939
Cut signature ....$1,500-$1,750
Single-signature baseball ...Unknown
3x5 index card $1,700
Photograph/baseball card $4,500
HOF plaque postcard .....Impossible
Perez-Steele postcards .....Impossible

Ki Ki Cuyler (1899-1950) 1968
Cut signature $150
Single-signature baseball$1,500-$3,500
3x5 index card $175
Photograph/baseball card ..$400-$425
HOF plaque postcard .....Impossible
Perez-Steele postcards .....Impossible

Ray Dandridge (1913-1994) 1987
Cut signature ....$15-$20
Single-signature baseball ....$40-$50
3x5 index card $25
Photograph/baseball card ....$25-$30
HOF plaque postcard ....$15-$25
Perez-Steele postcards ......$15-$25

George Davis (1870-1940) 1998
Cut signature ....Unknown
Single-signature baseball ...Unknown
3x5 index card ....Unknown
Photograph/baseball card ..Unknown
HOF plaque postcard .....Impossible

Perez-Steele postcards .....Impossible

Leon Day (1916-1995) 1995
Cut signature $20
Single-signature baseball ...$75-$100
3x5 index card $25
Photograph/baseball card ....$30-$40
HOF plaque postcard .....Impossible
Perez-Steele postcards .....Impossible

Dizzy Dean (1911-1974) 1953
Cut signature ....$75-$80
Single-signature baseball ..$675-$800
3x5 index card ....$90-$100
Photograph/baseball card ..$250-$350
HOF plaque postcard .....$125-$150
Perez-Steele postcards .....Impossible

Ed Delahanty (1867-1903) 1945
Cut signature $1,500
Single-signature baseball ...Unknown
3x5 index card $2,000
Photograph/baseball card $4,000
HOF plaque postcard .....Impossible
Perez-Steele postcards .....Impossible

Bill Dickey (1907-1993) 1954
Cut signature $15
Single-signature baseball ..$150-$200
3x5 index card $20
Photograph/baseball card $50
HOF plaque postcard ....$35-$45
Perez-Steele postcards ......$45-$80

Martin DiHigo (1905-1971) 1977
Cut signature ....$650-$675
Single-signature baseball $4,000
3x5 index card ....$800-$1,000

Photograph/baseball card $1,500-$2,000
HOF plaque postcard .....Impossible
Perez-Steele postcards .....Impossible

Joe DiMaggio (1914-1999) 1955
Cut signature ....$30-$35
Single-signature baseball ..$300-$350
3x5 index card $60
Photograph/baseball card ..$150-$200
HOF plaque postcard .....$125-$150
Perez-Steele postcards .....$250-$300

Larry Doby (1924-) 1998
Cut signature ....$7-$10
Single-signature baseball ....$30-$35
3X5 Index card ....$10-$12
Photograph/baseball card $20
HOF plaque postcard $15
Perez-Steele postcards ....$15-$20

Bobby Doerr (1918-) 1986
Cut signature ....$5-$7
Single-signature baseball $25
3x5 index card ....$3-$7
Photograph/baseball card ....$10-$13
HOF plaque postcard ....$6-$10
Perez-Steele postcards ....$15-$20

Don Drysdale (1936-1993) 1984
Cut signature ....$25-$30
Single-signature baseball ..$125-$150
3x5 index card ....$30-$35
Photograph/baseball card ....$40-$45

HOF plaque postcard $35
Perez-Steele postcards $40

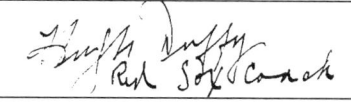

Hugh Duffy (1866-1954) 1945
Cut signature ....$300-$350
Single-signature baseball $2,200-$3,500
3x5 index card ....$350-$450
Photograph/baseball card ..$600-$750
HOF plaque postcard $900
Perez-Steele postcards .....Impossible

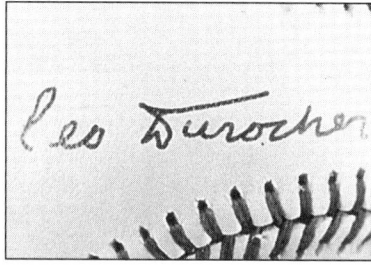

Leo Durocher (1905-1991) 1994
Cut signature ....$15-$20
Single-signature baseball ....$65-$90
3x5 index card $25
Photograph/baseball card $40
HOF plaque postcard .....Impossible
Perez-Steele postcards .....Impossible

Billy Evans (1864-1956) 1973
Cut signature $225
Single-signature baseball $2,000-$4,000
3x5 index card ....$300-$350
Photograph/baseball card ..$500-$525
HOF plaque postcard .....Impossible
Perez-Steele postcards .....Impossible

Johnny Evers (1881-1947) 1946
Cut signature $300
Single-signature baseball $3,500-$6,000
3x5 index card $400
Photograph/baseball card $1,000-$1,200
HOF plaque postcard $1,100
Perez-Steele postcards .....Impossible

Buck Ewing (1859-1906) 1939
Cut signature $1,000
Single-signature baseball $3,000
3x5 index card $2,400
Photograph/baseball card $2,500-$4,000
HOF plaque postcard .....Impossible
Perez-Steele postcards .....Impossible

Baseball Hall of Fame Autographs — Chapter 2

Red Faber (1888-1976) 1964
Cut signature $15
Single-signature baseball ..$450-$1,800
3x5 index card ....$35-$45
Photograph/baseball card ..$75-$100
HOF plaque postcard $85
Perez-Steele postcards .....Impossible

Bob Feller (1918-) 1962
Cut signature $5
Single-signature baseball ....$20-$25
3x5 index card ....$7-$10
Photograph/baseball card ..$10-$12
HOF plaque postcard ....$20-$25
Perez-Steele postcards ....$15-$35

Rick Ferrell (1905-1995) 1984
Cut signature ....$4-$5
Single-signature baseball ....$40-$60
3x5 index card ....$7-$9
Photograph/baseball card $20
HOF plaque postcard $8
Perez-Steele postcards ....$15-$30

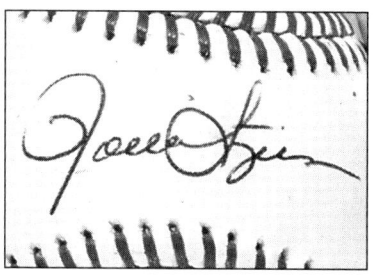

Rollie Fingers (1946-) 1992
Cut signature ....$5-$7
Single-signature baseball ....$25-$30
3x5 index card ....$8-$12
Photograph/baseball card $25
HOF plaque postcard $10
Perez-Steele postcards $25

Carlton Fisk (1947-) 2000
Cut signature ....$8-$12

Baseball Hall of Fame Autographs — Chapter 2

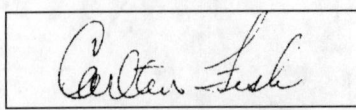

Single-signature baseball ....$35-$40
3x5 index card $10
Photograph/baseball card $25
HOF plaque postcard ......$15-$20
Perez-Steele postcards $25

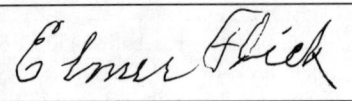

Elmer Flick (1876-1971) 1963
Cut signature ....$45-$50
Single-signature baseball$2,200-$2,500
3x5 index card ....$50-$60
Photograph baseball card ..$175-$250
HOF plaque postcard .....$300-$450
Perez-Steele postcards .....Impossible

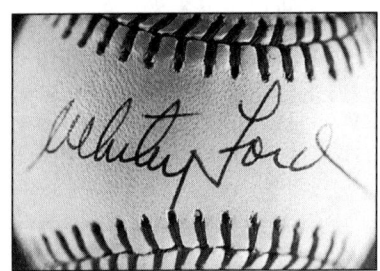

Whitey Ford (1926-) 1974
Cut signature ....$8-$10
Single-signature baseball $30
3x5 index card ....$10-$12
Photograph/baseball card $20
HOF plaque postcard ......$12-$20
Perez-Steele postcards ......$20-$30

Bill Foster (1904-1978) 1995
Cut signature $150
Single-signature baseball $5000-$7500
3x5 index card $200
Photograph/baseball card ..Unknown
HOF plaque postcard .....Impossible
Perez-Steele postcards .....Impossible

Rube Foster (1878-1930) 1981
Cut signature $2,000
Single-signature baseball $13,000
3x5 index card $3,800
Photograph/baseball card .$3,150-$5,500
HOF plaque postcard .....Impossible
Perez-Steele postcards .....Impossible

Nellie Fox (1927-1975) 1997
Cut signature ....$100-$150
Single-signature baseball $900
3x5 index card $200
Photograph/baseball card $300
HOF plaque postcard .....Impossible
Perez-Steele postcard .....Impossible

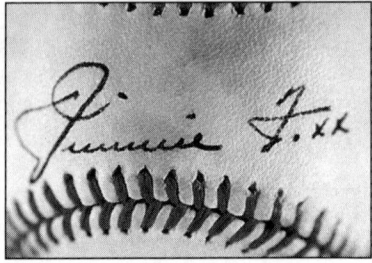

Jimmie Foxx (1907-1967) 1951
Cut signature ....$150-$200
Single-signature baseball ..$2,800-$3,000
3x5 index card ....$250-$350
Photograph/baseball card ..$500-$900
HOF plaque postcard $525
Perez-Steele postcards .....Impossible

Ford Frick (1894-1978) 1970
Cut signature ....$25-$30
Single-signature baseball ..$300-$800
3x5 index card ....$40-$50
Photograph/baseball card ...$75-$100
HOF plaque postcard $125
Perez-Steele postcards .....Impossible

Frankie Frisch (1898-1973) 1947
Cut signature ....$50-$75
Single-signature baseball$1,700-$1,800
3x5 index card ....$75-$90
Photograph/baseball card ..$100-$150
HOF plaque postcard .....$100-$150
Perez-Steele postcards .....Impossible

Pud Galvin (1855-1902) 1965
Cut signature $1,300
Single-signature baseball ....
..................$10,000-$12,000
3x5 index card $2,500
Photograph/baseball card $3,000
HOF plaque postcard .....Impossible
Perez-Steele postcards .....Impossible

Lou Gehrig (1903-1941) 1939
Cut signature $650
Single-signature baseball$5,000-$7,000
3x5 index card $800
Photograph/baseball card$2,000-$4,000
HOF plaque postcard ......Unknown

Perez-Steele postcards .....Impossible

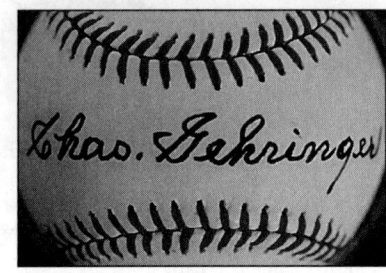

Charlie Gehringer (1903-1993) 1949
Cut signature ....$15-$20
Single-signature baseball ..$100-$150
3x5 index card $25
Photograph/baseball card ...$40-$85
HOF plaque postcard ......$25-$40
Perez-Steele postcards ......$25-$65

Bob Gibson (1935-) 1972
Cut signature ....$8-$10
Single-signature baseball ....$25-$30
3x5 index card $12
Photograph/baseball card ...$20-$25
HOF plaque postcard ......$15-$20
Perez-Steele postcards $20

Josh Gibson (1911-1947) 1972
Cut signature ....$700-$950
Single-signature baseball$4,500-$6,500
3x5 index card $800
Photograph/baseball card$1,200-$1,700
HOF plaque postcard .....Impossible
Perez-Steele postcards .....Impossible

Warren Giles (1896-1979) 1979
Cut signature $20
Single-signature baseball .$250-$1,000
3x5 index card ....$35-$45
Photograph/baseball card ...$75-$125
HOF plaque postcard .....Impossible
Perez-Steele postcards .....Impossible

Lefty Gomez (1908-1989) 1972
Cut signature ....$15-$20
Single-signature baseball ..$100-$150
3x5 index card ....$20-$25
Photograph/baseball card ....$35-$45

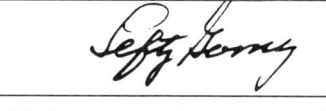

HOF plaque postcard ...... $20-$25
Perez-Steele postcards .... $40-$65

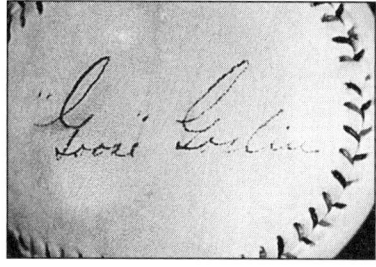

Goose Goslin (1900-1971) 1968
Cut signature .... $50-$60
Single-signature baseball .$800-$2,700
3x5 index card .... $75-$100
Photograph/baseball card $300
HOF plaque postcard ....$700-$3,000
Perez-Steele postcards ..... Impossible

Hank Greenberg (1911-1986) 1956
Cut signature .... $20-$30
Single-signature baseball ..$500-$700
3x5 index card .... $35-$75
Photograph/baseball card ...$75-$100
HOF plaque postcard .... $50-$75
Perez-Steele postcards ....$300-$325

Clark Griffith (1869-1955) 1946
Cut signature .... $130-$135
Single-signature baseball$1,000-$2,200
3x5 index card .... $150-$175
Photograph/baseball card $350
HOF plaque postcard $600
Perez-Steele postcards ..... Impossible

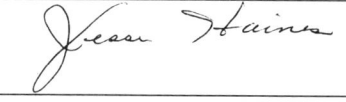

Burleigh Grimes (1893-1985) 1964
Cut signature .... $15-$20
Single-signature baseball ...$90-$200
3x5 index card .... $20-$25
Photograph/baseball card ....$50-$60
HOF plaque postcard .... $25-$30
Perez-Steele postcards .... $150-$200

Lefty Grove (1900-1975) 1947
Cut signature .... $17-$25
Single-signature baseball$1,200-$1,300
3x5 index card $40
Photograph/baseball card $200

HOF plaque postcard ..... $100-$125
Perez-Steele postcards ..... Impossible

Chick Hafey (1903-1973) 1971
Cut signature .... $40-$45
Single-signature baseball .$425-$1,500
3x5 index card $50
Photograph/baseball card ...$75-$175
HOF plaque postcard $600
Perez-Steele postcards ..... Impossible

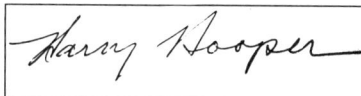

Jesse Haines (1893-1978) 1970
Cut signature .... $30-$35
Single-signature baseball ..$300-$950
3x5 index card .... $20-$40
Photograph/baseball card ...$75-$125
HOF plaque postcard $75
Perez-Steele postcards ..... Impossible

Billy Hamilton (1866-1940) 1961
Cut signature .... $500-$1,500
Single-signature baseball .$4,250-$5,500
3x5 index card $750
Photograph/baseball card .$2,150-$2,500
HOF plaque postcard ..... Impossible
Perez-Steele postcards ..... Impossible

Ned Hanlon (1857-1937) 1996
Cut signature .... Unknown
Single-signature baseball ...Unknown
3x5 index card .... Unknown
Photograph/baseball card ..Unknown
HOF plaque postcard ..... Impossible
Perez-Steele postcards ..... Impossible

Will Harridge (1883-1971) 1972
Cut signature .... $85-$90
Single-signature baseball .$875-$2,500
3x5 index card $125
Photograph/baseball card ..$225-$300
HOF plaque postcard ..... Impossible
Perez-Steele postcards ..... Impossible

Bucky Harris (1896-1977) 1975
Cut signature .... $25-$30
Single-signature baseball ..$450-$1,200
3x5 index card $40
Photograph/baseball card $200
HOF plaque postcard ..... $150-$200
Perez-Steele postcards ..... Impossible

Gabby Hartnett (1900-1972) 1955
Cut signature .... $40-$50
Single-signature baseball$1,000-$2,000

3x5 index card .... $60-$75
Photograph/baseball card ..$200-$250
HOF plaque postcard .....$200-$325
Perez-Steele postcards ..... Impossible

Harry Heilmann (1894-1951) 1952
Cut signature .... $175-$250
Single-signature baseball$2,000-$2,500
3x5 index card .... $300-$350
Photograph/baseball card ..$475-$500
HOF plaque postcard ..... Impossible
Perez-Steele postcards ..... Impossible

Billy Herman (1909-1992) 1975
Cut signature .... $4-$5
Single-signature baseball ....$50-$60
3x5 index card $7
Photograph/baseball card ....$25-$30
HOF plaque postcard .... $8-$12
Perez-Steele postcards ..... $15-$25

Harry Hooper (1887-1974) 1971
Cut signature .... $25-$30
Single-signature baseball ..$450-$1,200
3x5 index card $35
Photograph/baseball card ...$80-$150
HOF plaque postcard $115
Perez-Steele postcards ..... Impossible

Rogers Hornsby (1896-1963) 1942
Cut signature .... $200-$250
Single-signature baseball $2,500
3x5 index card $300
Photograph/baseball card ..$500-$700
HOF plaque postcard $650
Perez-Steele postcards ..... Impossible

Waite Hoyt (1899-1984) 1969
Cut signature .... $30-$40
Single-signature baseball ..$175-$450
3x5 index card $45
Photograph/baseball card ....$50-$80
HOF plaque postcard .... $30-$35

Perez-Steele postcards .....$450-$550

Cal Hubbard (1900-1977) 1976
Cut signature ....$30-$35
Single-signature baseball ..$500-$1,000
3x5 index card $40
Photograph/baseball card ..$175-$250
HOF plaque postcard $500
Perez-Steele postcards .....Impossible

Carl Hubbell (1903-1988) 1947
Cut signature ....$15-$20
Single-signature baseball ..$160-$175
3x5 index card $25
Photograph/baseball card ....$30-$35
HOF plaque postcard ....$35-$40
Perez-Steele postcards ....$60-$80

Miller Huggins (1879-1929) 1964
Cut signature ....$700-$750
Single-signature baseball$4,500-$6,000
3x5 index card $1,000
Photograph/baseball card $1,500
HOF plaque postcard .....Impossible
Perez-Steele postcards .....Impossible

William Hulbert (1832-1882) 1995
Cut signature - letter $8000
Single-signature baseball ...Unknown
3x5 index card ....Unknown
Photograph/baseball card ..Unknown
HOF plaque postcard .....Impossible
Perez-Steele postcards .....Impossible

Catfish Hunter (1946-1999) 1987
Cut signature ....$3-$5
Single-signature baseball ....$22-$28
3x5 index card ....$6-$7
Photograph/baseball card ....$12-$14
HOF plaque postcard ....$8-$12

Perez-Steele postcards ....$10-$20

Monte Irvin (1911-) 1973
Cut signature ....$5-$8
Single-signature baseball ....$20-$25
3x5 index card $10
Photograph/baseball card ....$15-$20
HOF plaque postcard ....$10-$15
Perez-Steele postcards ....$20-$25

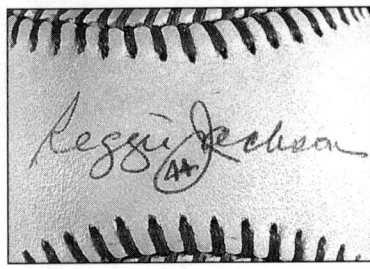

Reggie Jackson (1946-) 1993
Cut signature $10
Single-signature baseball ....$55-$60
3x5 index card $15
Photograph/baseball card ....$30-$35
HOF plaque postcard ....$25-$65
Perez-Steele postcards ....$45-$60

Travis Jackson (1903-1987) 1982
Cut signature $7
Single-signature baseball ..$140-$350
3x5 index card ....$15-$25
Photograph/baseball card ....$40-$80
HOF plaque postcard $35
Perez-Steele postcards ....$75-$80

Fergie Jenkins (1943-) 1991
Cut signature ....$3-$5
Single-signature baseball ....$22-$28
3x5 index card $7
Photograph/baseball card ....$12-$15
HOF plaque postcard ....$10-$15
Perez-Steele postcards ....$10-$15

Hugh Jennings (1869-1928) 1945
Cut signature ....$500-$825
Single-signature baseball ..$4,750-$6,000
3x5 index card $900
Photograph/baseball card$1,000-$1,500
HOF plaque postcard .....Impossible
Perez-Steele postcards .....Impossible

Ban Johnson (1864-1931) 1937
Cut signature $200
Single-signature baseball$2,700-$3,500
3x5 index card $250
Photograph/baseball card ..$500-$550
HOF plaque postcard .....Impossible
Perez-Steele postcards .....Impossible

Judy Johnson

Judy Johnson (1900-1989) 1975
Cut signature ....$10-$15
Single-signature baseball ...$75-$200
3x5 index card ....$15-$20
Photograph/baseball card ....$30-$60
HOF plaque postcard $25
Perez-Steele postcards ....$80-$90

Walter Johnson

Walter Johnson (1887-1946) 1946
Cut signature ....$400-$450
Single-signature baseball$2,950-$3,500
3x5 index card $500
Photograph/baseball card$1,000-$1,300
HOF plaque postcard ......Unknown
Perez-Steele postcards .....Impossible

Addie Joss (1880-1911) 1978
Cut signature $1,500
Single-signature baseball .$7,500-$10,000
3x5 index card $2,500
Photograph/baseball card$3,900-$4,000
HOF plaque postcard .....Impossible
Perez-Steele postcards .....Impossible

Al Kaline (1934-) 1980
Cut signature ....$5-$7
Single-signature baseball ...$25-$30

3x5 index card ....$8-$10
Photograph/baseball card $15
HOF plaque postcard ....$12-$15
Perez-Steele postcards ....$20-$25

Tim Keefe (1857-1933) 1964
Cut signature ....$600-$1,500
Single-signature baseball $7,000
3x5 index card $800
Photograph/baseball card $2,000
HOF plaque postcard .....Impossible
Perez-Steele postcards .....Impossible

Wee Willie Keeler (1872-1923) 1939
Cut signature ....$1,000-$1,400
Single-signature baseball $8,000
3x5 index card $2,000
Photograph/baseball card$3,000-$3,250
HOF plaque postcard .....Impossible
Perez-Steele postcards .....Impossible

George Kell (1922-) 1883
Cut signature ....$5-$7
Single-signature baseball ....$20-$24
3x5 index card $7
Photograph/baseball card ....$10-$12
HOF plaque postcard ....$6-$10
Perez-Steele postcards ....$10-$15

Joe Kelley (1871-1943) 1971
Cut signature ....$800-$1,100
Single-signature baseball$7,300-$8,000
3x5 index card $1,000
Photograph/baseball card$1,500-$2,250
HOF plaque postcard .....Impossible
Perez-Steele postcards .....Impossible

George Kelly (1895-1984) 1973
Cut signature ....$7-$8

Single-signature baseball ..$100-$350
3x5 index card $15
Photograph/baseball card ....$50-$75
HOF plaque postcard $30
Perez-Steele postcards .....$300-$325

Mike Kelly (1857-1894) 1945
Cut signature $2,000
Single-signature baseball $7,000
3x5 index card $3,500
Photograph/baseball card $5,000
HOF plaque postcard .....Impossible
Perez-Steele postcards .....Impossible

Harmon Killebrew (1936-) 1984
Cut signature ....$5-$8
Single-signature baseball ....$25-$32
3x5 index card $10
Photograph/baseball card $25
HOF plaque postcard ....$15-$20
Perez-Steele postcards ....$20-$30

Ralph Kiner (1922-) 1975
Cut signature ....$5-$8
Single-signature baseball $25
3x5 index card $10
Photograph/baseball card $15
HOF plaque postcard ....$15-$20
Perez-Steele postcards ....$20-$25

Chuck Klein (1904-1958) 1980
Cut signature $200
Single-signature baseball$1,500-$3,000
3x5 index card $300
Photograph/baseball card ..$400-$500
HOF plaque postcard .....Impossible
Perez-Steele postcards .....Impossible

Bill Klem (1874-1951) 1953
Cut signature ....$230-$400
Single-signature baseball$2,750-$3,500
3x5 index card $600
Photograph/baseball card .$900-$1,200
HOF plaque postcard .....Impossible
Perez-Steele postcards .....Impossible

Sandy Koufax (1935-) 1971
Cut signature $10
Single-signature baseball ....$65-$70

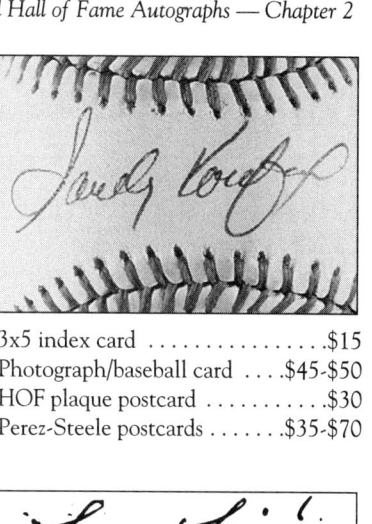

3x5 index card $15
Photograph/baseball card ....$45-$50
HOF plaque postcard $30
Perez-Steele postcards ....$35-$70

Nap Lajoie (1875-1959) 1937
Cut signature ....$225-$250
Single-signature baseball$4,500-$4,950
3x5 index card $350
Photograph/baseball card .$900-$1,000
HOF plaque postcard $750
Perez-Steele postcards .....Impossible

Kenesaw Landis (1866-1944) 1944
Cut signature ....$175-$250
Single-signature baseball$2,000-$3,500
3x5 index card $300
Photograph/baseball card ..$525-$650
HOF plaque postcard .....Impossible
Perez-Steele postcards .....Impossible

Tommy Lasorda (1927-) 1997
Cut signature $5
Single-signature baseball $30
3x5 index card ....$8-$10
Photograph/baseball card $25
HOF plaque postcard $15
Perez-Steele postcards ......$10-$25

Tony Lazzeri (1903-1946) 1991
Cut signature ....$200-$275
Single-signature baseball$1,300-$4,000
3x5 index card $450
Photograph/baseball card ..$500-$700
HOF plaque postcard .....Impossible
Perez-Steele postcards .....Impossible

Bob Lemon (1920-2000) 1976
Cut signature ....$5-$7
Single-signature baseball ....$20-$30
3x5 index card ....$7-$10
Photograph/baseball card ....$15-$20
HOF plaque postcard ....$8-$12
Perez-Steele postcards ....$12-$20

Baseball Hall of Fame Autographs — Chapter 2

Buck Leonard (1907-1997) 1972
Cut signature $10
Single-signature baseball . . . .$40-$50
3x5 index card . . . .$12-$15
Photograph/baseball card . . . .$25-$35
HOF plaque postcard $15

Perez-Steele postcards . . . .$25-$30

Freddie Lindstrom (1905-1981) 1976
Cut signature . . . .$12-$15
Single-signature baseball . .$200-$700
3x5 index card $20
Photograph/baseball card . . .$75-$100
HOF plaque postcard $40
Perez-Steele postcards . . . . .Impossible

John Lloyd (1884-1964) 1977
Cut signature $700
Single-signature baseball$5,600-$7,000
3x5 index card $750
Photograph/baseball card$1,200-$2,500
HOF plaque postcard . . . . .Impossible
Perez-Steele postcards . . . . .Impossible

Ernie Lombardi (1908-1977) 1986
Cut signature . . . .$35-$50
Single-signature baseball .$525-$1,200
3x5 index card . . . .$50-$60
Photograph/baseball card . .$225-$300
HOF plaque postcard . . . . .Impossible
Perez-Steele postcards . . . . .Impossible

Al Lopez (1908-) 1977
Cut signature $15

Single-signature baseball . . . .$75-$85
3x5 index card $15
Photograph/baseball card . . . .$30-$35
HOF plaque postcard $30
Perez-Steele postcards . . . . . .$50-$75

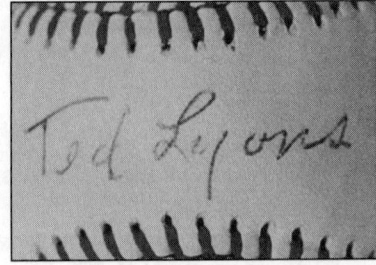

Ted Lyons (1900-1986) 1955
Cut signature . . . .$8-$12
Single-signature baseball . .$125-$225
3x5 index card $15
Photograph/baseball card . . . .$45-$75
HOF plaque postcard . . . .$30-$35
Perez-Steele postcards . . . . .$200-$250

Connie Mack (1862-1956) 1937
Cut signature . . . .$100-$125
Single-signature baseball $1,000
3x5 index card . . . .$150-$200
Photograph/baseball card . .$350-$400
HOF plaque postcard $600
Perez-Steele postcards . . . . .Impossible

Larry MacPhail (1890-1975) 1978
Cut signature $60
Single-signature baseball .$785-$1,700
3x5 index card $175
Photograph/baseball card . .$300-$400
HOF plaque postcard . . . . .Impossible
Perez-Steele postcards . . . . .Impossible

Lee MacPhail (1917-) 1998
Cut signature $5
Single-signature baseball $20
3x5 index card $8
Photograph . . . .$12-$15
HOF plaque postcard $12
Perez-Steele postcard $20

Mickey Mantle (1931-1995) 1974

Cut signature . . . .$50-$60
Single-signature baseball . .$175-$250
3x5 index card $75
Photograph/baseball card $125
HOF plaque postcard $125
Perez-Steele postcards . . . . .$125-$350

Heinie Manush (1901-1971) 1964
Cut signature . . . .$25-$40
Single-signature baseball . .$1,500-$2,200
3x5 index card $60
Photograph/baseball card . .$200-$300
HOF plaque postcard . . . . .$250-$300
Perez-Steele postcards . . . . .Impossible

Rabbit Maranville (1891-1954) 1954
Cut signature . . . .$140-$150
Single-signature baseball$1,600-$2,000
3x5 index card $250
Photograph/baseball card . .$350-$425
HOF plaque postcard . . . . .Impossible
Perez-Steele postcards . . . . .Impossible

Juan Marichal (1938-) 1983
Cut signature . . . .$6-$8
Single-signature baseball $25
3x5 index card $10
Photograph/baseball card . . . .$15-$18
HOF plaque postcard $12
Perez-Steele postcards . . . .$10-$20

Rube Marquard (1889-1980) 1971
Cut signature . . . .$10-$15
Single-signature baseball . .$450-$700
3x5 index card $20
Photograph/baseball card . .$100-$150
HOF plaque postcard $45
Perez-Steele postcards . . . . .Impossible

Eddie Mathews (1931-) 1978

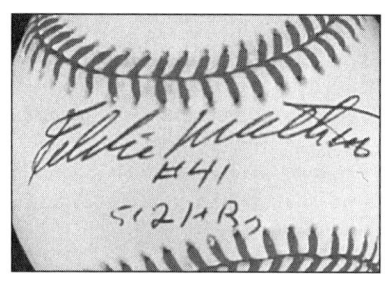

Cut signature . . . .$8-$10
Single-signature baseball . . . .$25-$38
3x5 index card $10
Photograph/baseball card . . . .$20-$25
HOF plaque postcard $15
Perez-Steele postcards . . . .$15-$25

Christy Mathewson (1880-1925) 1936
Cut signature . . . .$900-$1,200
Single-sign. baseball .$11,500-$13,000
3x5 index card $1,400
Photograph/baseball card .$2,900-$3,000
HOF plaque postcard . . . . .Impossible
Perez-Steele postcards . . . .Impossible

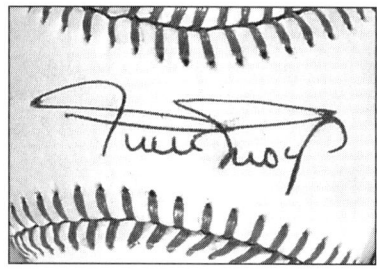

Willie Mays (1931-) 1979
Cut signature . . . .$10-$15
Single-signature baseball . . . .$45-$50
3x5 index card $20
Photograph/baseball card . . . .$25-$35
HOF plaque postcard $30
Perez-Steele postcards . . . .$35-$65

Joe McCarthy (1887-1978) 1957
Cut signature . . . .$25-$35
Single-signature baseball ..$650-$1,000
3x5 index card $40
Photograph/baseball card ..$100-$150
HOF plaque postcard . . . .$50-$80
Perez-Steele postcards . . . .Impossible

Tom McCarthy (1864-1922) 1946
Cut signature . . . .$1,500-$1,675
Single-signature baseball$4,000-$4,250
3x5 index card $2,000
Photograph/baseball card$4,000-$4,250
HOF plaque postcard . . . . .Impossible
Perez-Steele postcards . . . .Impossible

Willie McCovey (1938-) 1986
Cut signature . . . .$4-$5
Single-signature baseball $30
3x5 index card $8
Photograph/baseball card . . . .$20-$25
HOF plaque postcard $12
Perez-Steele postcards . . . .$10-$25

Joe McGinnity (1871-1929) 1946
Cut signature . . . .$800-$1,250
Single-signature baseball$5,000-$9,000
3x5 index card $1,500
Photograph/baseball card$4,000-$5,000
HOF plaque postcard . . . . .Impossible
Perez-Steele postcards . . . .Impossible

Bill McGowan (1871-1954) 1992
Cut signature $300
Single-signature baseball $5,000
3x5 index card $400
Photograph/baseball card $2,000
HOF plaque postcard . . . . .Impossible
Perez-Steele postcards . . . .Impossible

John McGraw (1873-1934) 1937
Cut signature . . . .$450-$500
Single-signature baseball$3,500-$6,000
3x5 index card $650
Photograph/baseball card$1,250-$1,500
HOF plaque postcard . . . . .Impossible
Perez-Steele postcards . . . .Impossible

Bid McPhee (1859-1943) 2000
Cut signature . . . .$75-$100
Single-signature baseball$2,000-$2,500
3x5 index card $150
Photograph/baseball card ..$350-$400
HOF plaque postcard . . . . .Impossible
Perez-Steele postcards . . . .Impossible

Bill McKechnie (1886-1965) 1962
Cut signature . . . .$60-$75
Single-signature baseball$1,500-$2,000
3x5 index card $150
Photograph/baseball card ..$300-$350
HOF plaque postcard $300
Perez-Steele postcards . . . .Impossible

Ducky Medwick (1911-1975) 1968
Cut signature . . . .$20-$25
Single-signature baseball .$500-$1,700
3x5 index card $45
Photograph/baseball card ..$150-$200
HOF plaque postcard $125
Perez-Steele postcards . . . .Impossible

Johnny Mize (1913-1993) 1981
Cut signature . . . .$8-$10
Single-signature baseball . . . .$35-$60
3x5 index card . . . .$10-$12
Photograph/baseball card . . . .$30-$35
HOF plaque postcard . . . .$15-$20
Perez-Steele postcards . . . .$25-$40

Joe Morgan (1943-) 1990
Cut signature . . . .$8-$10
Single-signature baseball . . . .$25-$30
3x5 index card . . . .$10-$12
Photograph/baseball card . . . .$20-$30
HOF plaque postcard . . . .$15-$20
Perez-Steele postcards . . . .$20-$25

Stan Musial (1920-) 1969
Cut signature . . . .$10-$12
Single-signature baseball $50
3x5 index card $15
Photograph/baseball card . . . .$30-$35

HOF plaque postcard $25
Perez-Steele postcards . . . .$30-$80

Hal Newhouser (1921-1998) 1992
Cut signature . . . .$3-$5
Single-signature baseball . . . .$22-$27
3x5 index card $7
Photograph/baseball card $12
HOF plaque postcard $8
Perez-Steele postcards . . . .$15-$20

Kid Nichols (1869-1953) 1949
Cut signature . . . .$150-$200
Single-signature baseball . .$3,200-$4,000
3x5 index card $300
Photograph/baseball card . .$475-$500
HOF plaque postcard $1,000
Perez-Steele postcards . . . . .Impossible

Phil Niekro (1939-) 1997
Cut signature $7
Single-signature baseball $25
3x5 index card $10
Photograph/baseball card . . . .$15-$20
HOF plaque postcard $15
Perez-Steele postcards $20

James O'Rourke (1852-1919) 1945
Cut signature . . . .$1,500-$1,750
Single-signature baseball$5,200-$10,000
3x5 index card $2,500
Photograph/baseball card$3,500-$3,700
HOF plaque postcard . . . . . .Impossible
Perez-Steele postcards . . . . .Impossible

Mel Ott (1909-1958) 1951
Cut signature . . . .$200-$300
Single-signature baseball$2,500-$3,500
3x5 index card $300
Photograph/baseball card . .$500-$725
HOF plaque postcard $650
Perez-Steele postcards . . . . .Impossible

Satchel Paige (1906-1982) 1971
Cut signature . . . .$35-$45
Single-signature baseball . .$900-$990
3x5 index card . . . .$80-$125
Photograph/baseball card . .$200-$235

HOF plaque postcard $140
Perez-Steele postcards $3,500

Jim Palmer (1945-) 1990
Cut signature $7
Single-signature baseball . . . .$25-$30
3x5 index card $10
Photograph/baseball card . . . .$15-$20
HOF plaque postcard . . . .$12-$20
Perez-Steele postcards . . . . . .$15-$25

Herb Pennock (1894-1948) 1948
Cut signature $175
Single-signature baseball$1,625-$2,500
3x5 index card $200
Photograph/baseball card $350
HOF plaque postcard . . . . . .Impossible
Perez-Steele postcards . . . . .Impossible

Gaylord Perry (1938-) 1991
Cut signature . . . .$5-$7
Single-signature baseball . . . .$20-$25
3x5 index card $10
Photograph/baseball card . . . .$15-$20
HOF plaque postcard $10
Perez-Steele postcards $15

Tony Perez (1943-) 2000
Cut signature $7
Single-signature baseball . . . .$25-$30
3x5 index card $10
Photograph/baseball card . . . .$15-$20
HOF plaque postcard $15
Perez-Steele postcards $20

Ed Plank (1875-1926) 1946
Cut signature . . . .$1,500-$1,775
Single-signature baseball $8,000

3x5 index card $2,200
Photograph/baseball card$3,200-$3,500
HOF plaque postcard . . . . . .Impossible
Perez-Steele postcards . . . . .Impossible

Charles Radbourne (1854-1897) 1948
Cut signature . . . .$1,425-$2,000
Single-signature baseball $7,500
3x5 index card $2,500
Photograph/baseball card$3,200-$3,500
HOF plaque postcard . . . . . .Impossible
Perez-Steele postcards . . . . .Impossible

Pee Wee Reese (1918-1999) 1984
Cut signature . . . .$7-$10
Single-signature baseball . . . .$50-$60
3x5 index card $15
Photograph/baseball card . . . .$30-$40
HOF plaque postcard . . . .$20-$30
Perez-Steele postcards . . . . . .$15-$35

Sam Rice (1890-1974) 1963
Cut signature . . . .$25-$50
Single-signature baseball . .$625-$1,500
3x5 index card $60
Photograph/baseball card . .$125-$150
HOF plaque postcard . . . . . .$100-$135
Perez-Steele postcards . . . . .Impossible

Branch Rickey (1881-1965) 1967
Cut signature . . . .$175-$225
Single-signature baseball$1,100-$2,500
3x5 index card $300
Photograph/baseball card . .$525-$750
HOF plaque postcard . . . . . .Impossible
Perez-Steele postcards . . . . .Impossible

Eppa Rixey (1891-1963) 1963
Cut signature . . . .$70-$85
Single-signature baseball .$800-$3,500
3x5 index card $100
Photograph/baseball card . .$250-$350
HOF plaque postcard . . . . . .Impossible
Perez-Steele postcards . . . . .Impossible

Phil Rizzuto (1918-) 1994
Cut signature . . . .$5-$7
Single-signature baseball $25
3x5 index card $10

Baseball Hall of Fame Autographs — Chapter 2

Photograph/baseball card . . . .$12-$18
HOF plaque postcard $12
Perez-Steele postcards $35

Robin Roberts (1926-) 1976
Cut signature . . . .$5-$7
Single-signature baseball $25
3x5 index card $10
Photograph/baseball card $15
HOF plaque postcard $10
Perez-Steele postcards . . . .$15-$20

Brooks Robinson (1937-) 1983
Cut signature . . . .$5-$7
Single-signature baseball . . . .$25-$30
3x5 index card $10
Photograph/baseball card . . . .$15-$20
HOF plaque postcard $10
Perez-Steele postcards . . . . . .$12-$20

Frank Robinson (1935-) 1982
Cut signature . . . .$4-$5
Single-signature baseball $30
3x5 index card $8
Photograph/baseball card $20
HOF plaque postcard . . . .$12-$20
Perez-Steele postcards $25

Jackie Robinson (1919-1972) 1962
Cut signature . . . .$150-$200

Single-signature baseball$2,200-$2,500
3x5 index card $300
Photograph/baseball card . .$575-$700
HOF plaque postcard . . . . .$600-$700
Perez-Steele postcards . . . .Impossible

Wilbert Robinson (1863-1934) 1945
Cut signature . . . .$700-$750
Single-signature baseball$4,225-$6,000
3x5 index card $750
Photograph/baseball card $2,000
HOF plaque postcard . . . . .Impossible
Perez-Steele postcards . . . .Impossible

Joe Rogan (1889-1967) 1998
Cut signature $2,500
Single-signature baseball$5,000-$10,000
3x5 index card $2,500
Photograph $3,000
HOF plaque postcard . . . . .Impossible
Perez-Steele postcards . . . .Impossible

Edd Roush (1893-1988) 1962
Cut signature . . . .$9-$12
Single-signature baseball . . .$80-$160
3x5 index card $10
Photograph/baseball card . . . .$45-$75
HOF plaque postcard . . . .$30-$80
Perez-Steele postcards . . . . . .$65-$80

Red Ruffing (1904-1986) 1967
Cut signature . . . .$20-$35
Single-signature baseball . .$195-$500
3x5 index card $40
Photograph/baseball card . . .$70-$125
HOF plaque postcard $100
Perez-Steele postcards . . . . .$350-$400

Amos Rusie (1871-1942) 1977
Cut signature . . . .$700-$1,100
Single-signature baseball . .$5,000-$6,500
3x5 index card $750
Photograph/baseball card . .$2,000-$2,300
HOF plaque postcard . . . . .Impossible
Perez-Steele postcards . . . .Impossible

Babe Ruth (1895-1948) 1936
Cut signature . . . .$550-$800
Single-signature baseball . .$4,500-$5,500
3x5 index card $1,000
Photograph/baseball card . .$2,500-$3,000
HOF plaque postcard $4,500
Perez-Steele postcards . . . .Impossible

Nolan Ryan (1947-) 1999
Cut signature . . . .$7-$10
Single-signature baseball . . . .$55-$60
3x5 index card $15
Photograph/baseball card . . . .$35-$40
HOF plaque postcard . . . .$30-$45
Perez-Steele postcards . . . . . .$45-$60

Ray Schalk (1892-1970) 1955
Cut signature . . . .$35-$45
Single-signature baseball . .$600-$1,700
3x5 index card . . . .$75-$85
Photograph/baseball card . .$225-$350
HOF plaque postcard . . . . .$300-$450
Perez-Steele postcards . . . .Impossible

Mike Schmidt (1949-) 1995
Cut signature . . . .$5-$10
Single-signature baseball . . . .$40-$60
3x5 index card $15
Photograph/baseball card . . . .$35-$55
HOF plaque postcard $40

Perez-Steele postcards $35

Red Schoendienst (1923-) 1989
Cut signature . . . .$5-$7
Single-signature baseball $25
3x5 index card $10
Photograph/baseball card . . . .$15-$20
HOF plaque postcard $15
Perez-Steele postcards . . . .$15-$20

Frank Selee (1859-1909) 1999
Cut signature $550
Single-signature baseball $850
3x5 index card $600
Photograph/baseball card . .$700-$800
HOF plaque postcard . . . . .Impossible
Perez-Steele postcards . . . . .Impossible

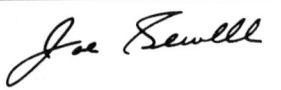

Tom Seaver (1944-) 1992
Cut signature . . . .$7-$10
Single-signature baseball . . . .$40-$45
3x5 index card $15
Photograph/baseball card $35
HOF plaque postcard $30
Perez-Steele postcards . . . .$35-$40

Joe Sewell (1898-1990) 1977
Cut signature . . . .$8-$10
Single-signature baseball . . .$80-$125
3x5 index card $12
Photograph/baseball card . . . .$30-$35
HOF plaque postcard $20
Perez-Steele postcards . . . .$35-$60

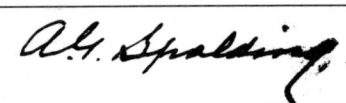

Al Simmons (1902-1956) 1953
Cut signature . . . .$90-$180
Single-signature baseball . .$950-$2,800

3x5 index card . . . .$225-$325
Photograph/baseball card $500
HOF plaque postcard $800
Perez-Steele postcards . . . . .Impossible

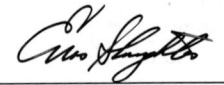

George Sisler (1893-1973) 1939
Cut signature . . . .$25-$40
Single-signature baseball . .$550-$1,200
3x5 index card . . . .$50-$60
Photograph/baseball card . .$135-$175
HOF plaque postcard $125
Perez-Steele postcards . . . . .Impossible

Enos Slaughter (1916-) 1985
Cut signature $5
Single-signature baseball . . . .$20-$25
3x5 index card $7
Photograph/baseball card . . . .$12-$15
HOF plaque postcard . . . .$8-$10
Perez-Steele postcards . . . . . .$12-$20

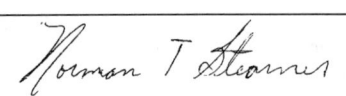

Duke Snider (1926-) 1980
Cut signature . . . .$5-$8
Single-signature baseball . . . .$25-$30
3x5 index card $10
Photograph/baseball card . . . .$20-$25
HOF plaque postcard . . . .$15-$20
Perez-Steele postcards . . . . . .$15-$25

Warren Spahn (1921-) 1973
Cut signature . . . .$5-$8
Single-signature baseball . . . .$20-$25
3x5 index card $10
Photograph/baseball card . . . .$15-$20
HOF plaque postcard $10
Perez-Steele postcards . . . . . .$20-$30

Al Spalding (1850-1915) 1939

Cut signature . . . .$750-$1,250
Single-signature baseball$6,000-$12,000
3x5 index card $1,750
Photograph/baseball card$1,800-$2,200
HOF plaque postcard . . . . .Impossible
Perez-Steele postcards . . . . .Impossible

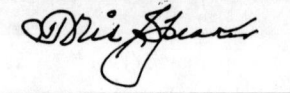

Tris Speaker (1888-1958) 1937
Cut signature . . . .$125-$200
Single-signature baseball$2,900-$3,000
3x5 index card . . . .$225-$275
Photograph/baseball card . .$500-$700
HOF plaque postcard $600
Perez-Steele postcards . . . . .Impossible

Willie Stargell (1940-) 1988
Cut signature . . . .$5-$8
Single-signature baseball . . . .$25-$30
3x5 index card $10
Photograph/baseball card . . . .$15-$20
HOF plaque postcard $10
Perez-Steele postcards . . . . . .$12-$20

Turkey Stearns (1901-1979) 2000
Cut signature . . . .$200-$250
Single-signature baseball . . .$400-$500
3x5 index card . . . .$$300
Photograph/baseball card . .$500-$700
HOF plaque postcard . . . . .Impossible
Perez-Steele postcards . . . . .Impossible

Casey Stengel (1890-1975) 1966
Cut signature . . . .$20-$40

Single-signature baseball ..$480-$1,000
3x5 index card ....$90-$100
Photograph/baseball card $150
HOF plaque postcard $100
Perez-Steele postcards .....Impossible

Don Sutton (1945-) 1998
Cut signature ....$5-$8
Single-signature baseball $25
3x5 index card $10
Photograph/baseball card ....$15-$20
HOF plaque postcard ....$12-$20
Perez-Steele postcards ....$20-$25

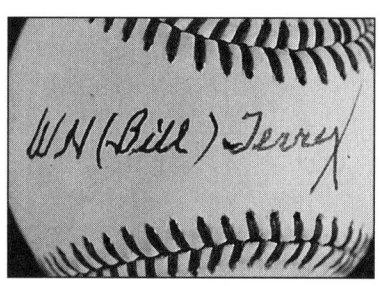

Bill Terry (1898-1989) 1954
Cut signature $15
Single-signature baseball ..$160-$175
3x5 index card $20
Photograph/baseball card ...$45-$50
HOF plaque postcard ....$25-$30
Perez-Steele postcards ....$65-$80

Sam Thompson (1860-1922) 1974
Cut signature ....$1,200-$2,125
Single-signature baseball$8,000-$10,000
3x5 index card $3,250
Photograph/baseball card $6,000
HOF plaque postcard .....Impossible
Perez-Steele postcards .....Impossible

Joe Tinker (1880-1948) 1946
Cut signature ....$300-$350
Single-signature baseball $6,000
3x5 index card ....$375-$400
Photograph/baseball card .$900-$1,200
HOF plaque postcard $1,000
Perez-Steele postcards .....Impossible

Pie Traynor (1899-1972) 1948
Cut signature ....$50-$100
Single-signature baseball$1,175-$1,200
3x5 index card ....$125-$175
Photograph/baseball card $300
HOF plaque postcard $450
Perez-Steele postcards .....Impossible

Dazzy Vance (1891-1961) 1955
Cut signature ....$70-$200
Single-signature baseball$1,500-$3,200
3x5 index card ....$250-$300
Photograph/baseball card ..$650-$750
HOF plaque postcard $600
Perez-Steele postcards .....Impossible

Arky Vaughan (1912-1952) 1985
Cut signature ....$150-$175
Single-signature baseball$1,525-$3,500
3x5 index card $250
Photograph/baseball card ..$500-$650
HOF plaque postcard .....Impossible
Perez-Steele postcards .....Impossible

William Veeck (1914-1986) 1991
Cut signature ....$15-$45
Single-signature baseball ..$550-$2,000
3x5 index card $75
Photograph/baseball card ..$250-$325
HOF plaque postcard .....Impossible
Perez-Steele postcards .....Impossible

Rube Waddell (1876-1914) 1946
Cut signature ....$1,000-$1,400
Single-signature baseball$7,000-$12,500
3x5 index card $1,500
Photograph/baseball card $4,500
HOF plaque postcard .....Impossible
Perez-Steele postcards .....Impossible

Honus Wagner (1874-1955) 1936
Cut signature ....$200-$275
Single-signature baseball $4,000
3x5 index card $350
Photograph/baseball card ..$750-$800
HOF plaque postcard $1,200
Perez-Steele postcards .....Impossible

Bobby Wallace (1873-1960) 1953
Cut signature ....$175-$225

Single-signature baseball$3,000-$4,500
3x5 index card $300
Photograph/baseball card ..$625-$700
HOF plaque postcard $800
Perez-Steele postcards .....Impossible

Ed Walsh (1881-1959) 1946
Cut signature ....$125-$150
Single-signature baseball$2,725-$3,600
3x5 index card $200
Photograph/baseball card ..$350-$400
HOF plaque postcard $350
Perez-Steele postcards .....Impossible

Lloyd Waner (1906-1982) 1967
Cut signature ....$15-$20
Single-signature baseball $500
3x5 index card $25
Photograph/baseball card $150
HOF plaque postcard $30
Perez-Steele postcards $3,500

Paul Waner (1903-1965) 1952
Cut signature ....$50-$100
Single-signature baseball$2,300-$2,500
3x5 index card $125
Photograph/baseball card ..$200-$300
HOF plaque postcard $350
Perez-Steele postcards .....Impossible

Monte Ward (1860-1925) 1964
Cut signature ....$1,000-$1,450
Single-signature baseball$8,350-$12,000
3x5 index card $1,500
Photograph/baseball card$3,000-$3,250
HOF plaque postcard .....Impossible
Perez-Steele postcards .....Impossible

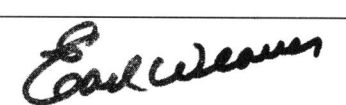

Earl Weaver (1930-) 1996
Cut signature ....$5-$7
Single-signature baseball $25
3x5 index card $10
Photograph/baseball card $15

HOF plaque/postcard $10
Perez-Steele postcards $15

George Weiss (1895-1972) 1971
Cut signature . . . . $40-$45
Single-signature baseball . $675-$3,500
3x5 index card . . . . $75-$100
Photograph/baseball card . . $250-$300
HOF plaque postcard . . . . . Unknown
Perez-Steele postcards . . . . . Impossible

Mickey Welch (1859-1941) 1973
Cut signature . . . . $1,700-$2,000
Single-signature baseball $5,800-$8,500
3x5 index card $2,750
Photograph/baseball card $4,000
HOF plaque postcard . . . . . Impossible
Perez-Steele postcards . . . . . Impossible

Willie Wells (1905-1989) 1997
Cut signature . . . . $10-$12
Single-signature baseball $35
3x5 index card $15
Photograph $30
HOF plaque postcard . . . . . Impossible
Perez-Steele postcards . . . . . Impossible

Zack Wheat (1888-1972) 1959
Cut signature . . . . $20-$50
Single-signature baseball . $975-$1,600
3x5 index card $80
Photograph/baseball card . . $175-$200
HOF plaque postcard . . . . . $200-$350
Perez-Steele postcards . . . . . Impossible

Hoyt Wilhelm (1923-) 1985
Cut signature $5
Single-signature baseball $20
3x5 index card $8
Photograph/baseball card . . . $12-$16
HOF plaque postcard . . . . . . $10-$15
Perez-Steele postcards $15

Billy Williams (1938-) 1987
Cut signature . . . . $5-$7
Single-signature baseball $25
3x5 index card $10
Photograph/baseball card . . . . $15-$20
HOF plaque postcard $10
Perez-Steele postcards . . . . . . $12-$20

Smoky Joe Williams (1885-1946) 1999
Cut signature . . . . $400-$450
Single-signature baseball . . $600-$800
3x5 index card $450
Photograph/baseball card . . $500-$600
HOF plaque postcard . . . . . Impossible
Perez-Steele postcards . . . . . Impossible

Ted Williams (1918-) 1966
Cut signature . . . . $25-$35
Single-signature baseball . . $175-$200
3x5 index card $50
Photograph/baseball card . . . $85-$100
HOF plaque postcard $75
Perez-Steele postcards . . . . . $90-$300

Vic Willis (1876-1947) 1995
Cut signature $1,500
Single-signature baseball . . . Unknown
3x5 index card $425
Photograph/baseball card $750
HOF plaque postcard . . . . . Impossible
Perez-Steele postcards . . . . . Impossible

Hack Wilson (1900-1948) 1979
Cut signature . . . . $235-$300
Single-signature baseball $2,400-$3,000
3x5 index card $450
Photograph/baseball card . . $675-$800
HOF plaque postcard . . . . . Impossible
Perez-Steele postcards . . . . . Impossible

George Wright (1847-1937) 1937
Cut signature . . . . $800-$900
Single-signature baseball $5,725-$8,500
3x5 index card $1,200
Photograph/baseball card $2,750
HOF plaque postcard . . . . . Impossible
Perez-Steele postcards . . . . . Impossible

Harry Wright (1835-1895) 1953
Cut signature . . . . $1,200-$1,600
Single-signature baseball $5,000
3x5 index card $2,000
Photograph/baseball card $3,500
HOF plaque postcard . . . . . Impossible
Perez-Steele postcards . . . . . Impossible

Early Wynn (1920-1999) 1972
Cut signature . . . . $7-$10
Single-signature baseball . . . $25-$30
3x5 index card . . . . $10-$12
Photograph/baseball card . . . $20-$25
HOF plaque postcard $15
Perez-Steele postcards . . . . . $20-$25

Carl Yastrzemski (1939-) 1989
Cut signature . . . . $8-$10
Single-signature baseball . . . $35-$45
3x5 index card $15
Photograph/baseball card $30
HOF plaque postcard $20
Perez-Steele postcards . . . . . $20-$30

Tom Yawkey (1903-1976) 1980
Cut signature . . . . $70-$100
Single-signature baseball $1,050-$2,000
3x5 index card . . . . $125-$175
Photograph/baseball card . . $325-$400
HOF plaque postcard . . . . . Impossible
Perez-Steele postcards . . . . . Impossible

Cy Young (1867-1955) 1937
Cut signature . . . . $175-$300
Single-signature baseball . . $3,400-$3,500
3x5 index card $350
Photograph/baseball card . . $700-$825
HOF plaque postcard $1,000
Perez-Steele postcards . . . . . Impossible

Ross Youngs (1897-1927) 1972
Cut signature . . . . $1,000-$1,150
Single-signature baseball $7,000
3x5 index card $1,500
Photograph/baseball card $2,500
HOF plaque postcard . . . . . Impossible
Perez-Steele postcards . . . . . Impossible

Robin Yount (1955-) 1999
Cut signature . . . . $5-$7
Single-signature baseball . . . $25-$30
3x5 index card $15
HOF plaque postcard $20
Perez-Steele postcards . . . . . $20-$25

Inactive Baseball Player Autographs

* Indicates player is deceased

Cal Abrams *
Ball $24
Photo $12
3x5 index card $5

Joe Adcock *
Ball ....$35-$40
Photo $25
3x5 index card ....$10-$12

Tommie Agee
Ball $20
Photo $10
3x5 index card $4

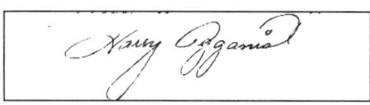

Harry Agganis *
Ball $250
Photo $200
3x5 index card ....$90-$100

Willie Aikens
Ball $17
Photo $10
3x5 index card $5

Danny Ainge
Ball $16
Photo $12
3x5 index card ....$4-$6

Dick Allen
Ball ....$25-$30
Photo $15

3x5 index card $5

Sandy Alomar Sr.
Ball $20
Photo $15
3x5 index card $5

Felipe Alou
Ball $25
Photo $15
3x5 index card $5

Jesus Alou
Ball $20
Photo $10
3x5 index card $4

Matty Alou
Ball $23
Photo $13
3x5 index card ....$5-$6

Sandy Amoros *
Ball $75
Photo $30
3x5 index card ....$12-$15

Joaquin Andujar
Ball $18
Photo $10
3x5 index card ....$4-$5

Johnny Antonelli
Ball $21
Photo $13
3x5 index card $5

Tony Armas
Ball $19
Photo $11
3x5 index card $5

Alan Ashby
Ball $17
Photo $9
3x5 index card $4

Bobby Avila
Ball $25
Photo $17
3x5 index card $5

Ed Bailey
Ball $20
Photo $10
3x5 index card ....$4-$5

Bob Bailor
Ball $15
Photo $8
3x5 index card $4

Harold Baines
Ball $25
Photo $15
3x5 index card $5

Dusty Baker
Ball $25
Photo $15
3x5 index card $5

Chris Bando
Ball $14
Photo $8
3x5 index card ....$3-$4

Sal Bando
Ball $20
Photo $12
3x5 index card $5

Floyd Bannister
Ball $14
Photo $8
3x5 index card $4

George Bamberger
Ball $23
Photo $12
3x5 index card $5

Steve Barber
Ball $21
Photo $12
3x5 index card $5

Jesse Barfield
Ball $19
Photo $10
3x5 index card ....$4-$5

Len Barker
Ball $18
Photo $9
3x5 index card $4

Kevin Bass
Ball $16
Photo ....$9-$12
3x5 index card $4

Earl Battey
Ball $21
Photo $12
3x5 index card $4

Don Baylor
Ball $24
Photo $14
3x5 index card $4

Glenn Beckert
Ball $18
Photo $10
3x5 index card .... $4-$5

Mark Belanger *
Ball $25
Photo $15
3x5 index card $5

Bo Belinsky
Ball .... $25-$30
Photo .... $15-$20
3x5 index card $6

Buddy Bell
Ball $20
Photo $12
3x5 index card $4

George Bell
Ball $20
Photo $11
3x5 index card $4

Gus Bell *
Ball .... $45-$50
Photo .... $20-$25
3x5 index card .... $8-$10

Johnny Berardino *
Ball .... $40-$50
Photo .... $20-$25
3x5 index card .... $8-$10

Moe Berg *
Ball $200
Photo .... $60-$75
3x5 index card .... $20-$30

Dale Berra
Ball $20
Photo $10
3x5 index card $5

Joe Black
Ball $20
Photo .... $10-$12
3x5 index card $5

Ewell Blackwell *
Ball $45
Photo $20
3x5 index card .... $10-$12

Paul Blair
Ball $20
Photo $12

3x5 index card $5

Johnny Blanchard
Ball $21
Photo $11
3x5 index card .... $4-$5

Steve Blass
Ball $18
Photo $9
3x5 index card .... $4-$5

Ron Blomberg
Ball $18
Photo $9
3x5 index card .... $4-$5

Vida Blue
Ball .... $25-$30
Photo .... $15-$20
3x5 index card $6

Bert Blyleven
Ball $22
Photo $12
3x5 index card $5

Mike Boddicker
Ball $22
Photo $12
3x5 index card $5

Wade Boggs
Ball .... $30-$35
Photo .... $25-$30
3x5 card $10

Frank Bolling
Ball $20
Photo $12
3x5 index card $5

Milt Bolling
Ball $18
Photo $10
3x5 index card .... $4-$5

Bobby Bonds
Ball $25
Photo $12
3x5 index card $6

Bob Boone
Ball $23

Photo $14
3x5 index card $5

Ray Boone
Ball $30
Photo $20
3x5 index card .... $4-$5

Frenchy Bordagaray *
Ball $19
Photo $9
3x5 index card $5

Lyman Bostock Jr. *
Ball $45
Photo $25
3x5 index card .... $10-$15

Jim Bouton
Ball $21
Photo $10
3x5 index card .... $4-$5

Larry Bowa
Ball $20
Photo $10
3x5 index card .... $4-$5

Clete Boyer
Ball $23
Photo $12
3x5 index card $5

Ken Boyer *
Ball .... $290-$325
Photo .... $70-$90
3x5 index card .... $35-$45

Ralph Branca
Ball $22
Photo .... $12-$15
3x5 index card .... $5-$6

Ken Brett
Ball $19
Photo $11
3x5 index card ....$4-$5

Rocky Bridges
Ball $24
Photo $10
3x5 index card ....$5-$6

Nelson Briles
Ball ....$19-$20
Photo ....$9-$12
3x5 index card $4

Greg Brock
Ball $17
Photo $8
3x5 index card $4

Hubie Brooks
Ball $18
Photo ....$10-$15
3x5 index card $4

Tom Browning
Ball $24
Photo $15
3x5 index card ....$5-$6

Tom Brunansky
Ball $16
Photo ....$8-$10
3x5 index card $4

Billy Bruton *
Ball ....$30-$40
Photo ....$20-$25
3x5 index card ....$10-$12

Bill Buckner
Ball $25
Photo $15
3x5 index card ....$5-$6

Don Buford
Ball $20
Photo ....$15-$20
3x5 index card ....$4-$5

Bob Buhl
Ball $18
Photo ....$10-$12
3x5 index card ....$4-$5

Al Bumbry
Ball $18
Photo $10
3x5 index card $4

Lew Burdette
Ball ....$24-$28
Photo ....$15-$20
3x5 index card ....$5-$6

Smoky Burgess *
Ball ....$30-$40
Photo ....$20-$25
3x5 index card ....$12-$15

Jeff Burroughs
Ball $19
Photo $10
3x5 index card $4

Brett Butler
Ball $24
Photo $12
3x5 index card $5

Enos Cabell
Ball $22
Photo $11
3x5 index card ....$4-$5

Mike Caldwell
Ball $18
Photo $10
3x5 index card $4

Johnny Callison
Ball $19
Photo $9
3x5 index card $4

Bert Campaneris
Ball $20
Photo $11
3x5 index card ....$4-$5

Bill Campbell
Ball $19
Photo $9
3x5 index card ....$4-$5

Dave Campbell
Ball $22
Photo $11
3x5 index card ....$4-$5

John Candelaria
Ball $19
Photo $10
3x5 index card ....$4-$5

Bernie Carbo
Ball $20
Photo $10
3x5 index card ....$4-$5

Chico Carrasquel
Ball $22
Photo $10
3x5 index card $5

Jose Cardenal
Ball $24
Photo $15
3x5 index card $5

Gary Carter
Ball $28
Photo ....$15-$18
3x5 index card ....$8-$10

Joe Carter
Ball $25
Photo $15
3x5 index card ....$7-$8

Rico Carty
Ball $25
Photo $15
3x5 index card ....$7-$8

Dave Cash
Ball $22
Photo $11
3x5 index card ....$4-$5

Norm Cash *
Ball $200
Photo ....$45-$60
3x5 index card ....$15-$20

Phil Cavarretta
Ball $30
Photo $15
3x5 index card ....$6-$7

Cesar Cedeno
Ball $28
Photo $14
3x5 index card ....$5-$6

Rick Cerone
Ball ....$18-$20
Photo $8
3x5 index card $4

Bob Cerv
Ball $18
Photo $10
3x5 index card $4

Ron Cey
Ball $24
Photo $13
3x5 index card $5

Chris Chambliss
Ball $24
Photo $15
3x5 index card ....$5-$6

Dean Chance
Ball ....$22-$24
Photo ....$10-$12
3x5 index card ....$4-$5

Spud Chandler *
Ball ....$40-$50
Photo ....$25-$30
3x5 index card ....$12-$15

Joe Charboneau
Ball $22
Photo $14
3x5 index card $5

Eddie Cicotte *
Ball ....$1,000-$1,400
Photo ....$450-$500
3x5 index card ....$200-$250

Jack Clark
Ball $23
Photo $13
3x5 index card $5

Donn Clendenon
Ball ....$20-$24
Photo ....$11-$15
3x5 index card ....$5-$6

Harlond Clift *
Ball $45
Photo $23
3x5 index card ....$12-$15

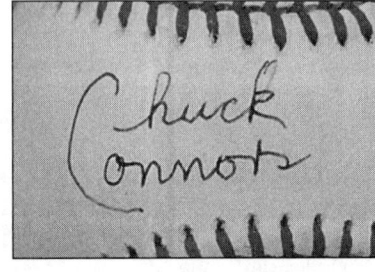

Rocky Colavito
Ball $30
Photo ....$19-$24
3x5 index card ....$10-$12

Nate Colbert
Ball $22
Photo $13
3x5 index card ....$4-$5

Gerry Coleman
Ball ....$22-$24
Photo $13
3x5 index card ....$5-$6

Joe Collins *
Ball ....$30-$40
Photo $20
3x5 index card ....$9-$11

Dave Concepcion
Ball $25
Photo $15
3x5 index card $5

Tony Conigliaro *
Ball ....$150-$200
Photo ....$80-$100
3x5 index card ....$40-$60

Gene Conley
Ball ....$18-$20
Photo ....$12-$15
3x5 index card ....$4-$5

Chuck Connors *
Ball $150
Photo $35
3x5 index card ....$15-$20

Cecil Cooper
Ball ....$20-$24
Photo ....$13-$15
3x5 index card $5

Wes Covington
Ball ....$55-$60
Photo ....$30-$40
3x5 index card ....$15-$18

Roger Craig
Ball $24
Photo $13

3x5 index card ....$4-$5

Roger Cramer *
Ball ....$150-$200
Photo ....$40-$50
3x5 index card ....$25-$40

Del Crandall
Ball $22
Photo $12
3x5 index card $5

Warren Cromartie
Ball $17
Photo $9
3x5 index card $4

Jose Cruz
Ball $23
Photo $14
3x5 index card $5

Frank Crosetti
Ball $30
Photo $20
3x5 index card ....$6-$8

Mike Cuellar
Ball $24
Photo $12
3x5 index card $5

Babe Dahlgren *
Ball $40
Photo ....$20-$25
3x5 index card ....$12-$15

Kal Daniels
Ball $18
Photo $9
3x5 index card $4

Alvin Dark
Ball $23
Photo $11
3x5 index card ....$4-$5

Ron Darling
Ball $20
Photo ....$10-$12
3x5 index card ....$4-$5

Darren Daulton
Ball $23
Photo $11
3x5 index card $5

Alvin Davis
Ball $20
Photo $10
3x5 index card $4

Chili Davis
Ball $23

Photo $11
3x5 index card $5

Glenn Davis
Ball $21
Photo $12
3x5 index card $4

Tommy Davis
Ball $25
Photo .... $15-$20
3x5 index card .... $5-$6

Willie Davis
Ball .... $15-$20
Photo .... $8-$12
3x5 index card .... $4-$5

Andre Dawson
Ball $30
Photo .... $18-$24
3x5 index card .... $10-$12

Paul "Daffy" Dean *
Ball .... $125-$150
Photo .... $75-$100
3x5 index card .... $20-$25

Doug DeCinces
Ball $20
Photo $10
3x5 index card $4

Rick Dempsey
Ball $22
Photo $12
3x5 index card $4

John Denny
Ball $22
Photo $12
3x5 index card $4

Bucky Dent
Ball .... $24-$30
Photo .... $15-$20
3x5 index card .... $6-$8

Bob Dernier
Ball $15
Photo .... $8-$10
3x5 index card $4

Dom DiMaggio
Ball $35
Photo $20
3x5 index card $7

Al Downing
Ball $24
Photo $14
3x5 index card $5

Dave Dravecky
Ball $23
Photo $13
3x5 index card $5

Charlie Dressen *
Ball .... $35-$40
Photo .... $20-$25
3x5 index card $7

Walt Dropo
Ball $20
Photo $10
3x5 index card $4

Ryne Duren
Ball $20
Photo .... $9-$12
3x5 index card $4

Leon Durham
Ball $15
Photo $9
3x5 index card $4

Duffy Dyer
Ball $17
Photo $8
3x5 index card $4

Len Dykstra
Ball .... $28-$30
Photo $20
3x5 index card $6

Dennis Eckersley
Ball .... $30-$35
Photo .... $20-$25
3x5 index card .... $8-$10

Jim Eisenreich
Ball .... $18-$20
Photo $10
3x5 card $4

Bob Elliot *
Ball $50
Photo $35
3x5 index card .... $10-$12

Dock Ellis
Ball $20
Photo $11
3x5 index card $4

Woody English *
Ball $50
Photo .... $30-$35
3x5 index card .... $10-$12

Del Ennis *
Ball $30
Photo $18
3x5 index card .... $7-$9

Carl Erskine
Ball $26
Photo .... $12-$15
3x5 index card $5

Nick Esasky
Ball $17
Photo $9
3x5 index card $4

Darrell Evans
Ball $22
Photo $12
3x5 index card .... $4-$5

Dwight Evans
Ball $25
Photo $12
3x5 index card $5

Hoot Evers *
Ball .... $30-$35
Photo .... $20-$25
3x5 index card .... $8-$10

Elroy Face
Ball $22
Photo $10
3x5 index card .... $4-$5

Ferris Fain
Ball $20
Photo $12
3x5 index card $5

Dick Farrell *
Ball $40
Photo $30
3x5 index card .... $10-$12

Chico Fernandez
Ball $24
Photo $12

Inactive Baseball Player Autographs — Chapter 3

3x5 index card $5

Wes Ferrell *
Ball ....$45-$50
Photo ....$25-$30
3x5 index card ....$12-$14

Boo Ferriss
Ball ....$15-$18
Photo ....$8-$10
3x5 index card $4

Cecil Fielder
Ball $25
Photo $15
3x5 index card $6

Mark Fidrych
Ball $24
Photo $11
3x5 index card $5

Ed Figueroa
Ball $15
Photo ....$8-$10
3x5 index card $4

Mike Flanagan
Ball $22
Photo $12
3x5 index card $5

Elbie Fletcher *
Ball ....$30-$40
Photo ....$25-$30
3x5 index card ....$12-$15

Curt Flood *
Ball ....$35-$40
Photo ....$20-$25
3x5 index card $12

Dan Ford

Ball $20
Photo $13
3x5 index card $4

George Foster
Ball $24
Photo $12
3x5 index card $5

Julio Franco
Ball $20
Photo $10
3x5 index card $5

Terry Francona
Ball $21
Photo $11
3x5 index card $5

Tito Francona
Ball ....$20-$24
Photo ....$10-$15
3x5 index card $5

Jim Fregosi
Ball $23
Photo $12
3x5 index card $5

Bill Freehan
Ball $21
Photo $11
3x5 index card ....$4-$5

Bob Friend
Ball $20
Photo ....$12-$15
3x5 index card ....$4-$5

Carl Furillo *
Ball $400
Photo $90
3x5 index card ....$50-$60

Gary Gaetti
Ball $19
Photo $12
3x5 card $5

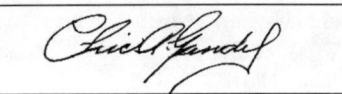

Chick Gandel *
Ball ....$1,000-$1,500
Photo $500
3x5 index card $250

Oscar Gamble
Ball $20
Photo $12
3x5 index card $5

Jim Gantner
Ball ....$15-$18
Photo ....$9-$12
3x5 index card $4

Joe Garagiola
Ball ....$25-$30
Photo ....$17-$20
3x5 index card ....$6-$7

Mike Garcia *
Ball ....$45-$50
Photo ....$30-$35
3x5 index card ....$15-$20

Phil Garner
Ball $23
Photo $13
3x5 index card $5

Ralph Garr
Ball $17
Photo $12
3x5 index card $4

Ned Garver
Ball $22
Photo ....$12-$15
3x5 index card ....$4-$5

Steve Garvey
Ball $25
Photo $14

3x5 index card . . . . $5-$6

Cito Gaston
Ball $25
Photo $13
3x5 index card $5

Jim Gentile
Ball $21
Photo $10
3x5 index card . . . . $4-$5

Cesar Geronimo
Ball $23
Photo . . . . $12-$15
3x5 index card $5

Kirk Gibson
Ball . . . . $28-$30
Photo $18
3x5 index card . . . . $5-$6

Jim Gilliam *
Ball . . . . $50-$60
Photo . . . . $30-$40
3x5 index card . . . . $12-$15

Al Gionfriddo
Ball $15
Photo $9
3x5 index card $4

Dan Gladden
Ball $18
Photo $9
3x5 index card $4

Joe Gordon *
Ball . . . . $65-$70
Photo . . . . $40-$45
3x5 index card . . . . $18-$20

Sid Gordon *
Ball . . . . $60-$65
Photo . . . . $35-$40
3x5 index card . . . . $15-$18

Goose Gossage
Ball $25
Photo $14
3x5 index card . . . . $5-$6

Mudcat Grant
Ball $21
Photo $11
3x5 index card . . . . $

Pete Gray
Ball $30
Photo . . . . $18-$20
3x5 index card . . . . $8-$9

Mike Greenwell
Ball $19
Photo $9
3x5 index card . . . . $4-$5

Bobby Grich
Ball $22
Photo $10
3x5 index card . . . . $4-$5

Ken Griffey Sr.
Ball $28
Photo $17
3x5 index card . . . . $6-$7

Charlie Grimm *
Ball . . . . $125-$150
Photo . . . . $45-$50
3x5 index card $25

Dick Groat
Ball $23
Photo $12
3x5 index card $5

Jerry Grote
Ball $22
Photo $11
3x5 index card $4

Kelly Gruber
Ball $23
Photo $13
3x5 index card . . . . $5-$6

Pedro Guerrero
Ball $22
Photo $13
3x5 index card . . . . $4-$5

Ron Guidry
Ball $28
Photo $15
3x5 index card . . . . $6-$7

Don Gullett
Ball $19
Photo $9
3x5 index card $4

Randy Gumpert
Ball $18
Photo $9
3x5 index card $4

Harvey Haddix *
Ball $55
Photo $24
3x5 index card $10

Fred Haney *
Ball . . . . $120-$130
Photo . . . . $45-$50
3x5 index card . . . . $15-$20

Mel Harder
Ball $28
Photo . . . . $16-$18
3x5 index card . . . . $5-$6

Tommy Harper
Ball $21
Photo $11
3x5 index card $4

Bud Harrelson
Ball $20
Photo $10
3x5 index card . . . . $4-$5

Bob Hazle *
Ball . . . . $30-$35
Photo . . . . $18-$20
3x5 index card . . . . $9-$12

Richie Hebner
Ball $22
Photo $13
3x5 index card $4

Jim Hegan *
Ball . . . . $45-$50
Photo $25
3x5 index card . . . . $15-$18

Mike Hegan
Ball $19
Photo $9
3x5 index card $4

Dave Henderson
Ball $20
Photo $10

3x5 index card $4

George Hendrick
Ball $21
Photo $12
3x5 index card $4

Ellie Hendricks
Ball $17
Photo $8
3x5 index card $4

Tom Henke
Ball $22
Photo $11
3x5 index card $4

Tommy Henrich
Ball $22
Photo $11
3x5 index card $5

Keith Hernandez
Ball $28
Photo ....$18-$20
3x5 index card ....$7-$10

Orel Hershiser
Ball $22
Photo $13
3x5 index card ....$4-$5

Whitey Herzog
Ball $28
Photo $15
3x5 index card $6

Ted Higuera
Ball $23
Photo $11
3x5 index card $5

Larry Hisle
Ball $21
Photo $10
3x5 index card ....$4-$5

Butch Hobson
Ball $16
Photo $8
3x5 index card $4

Gil Hodges *
Ball $1,450

Photo ....$400-$500
3x5 index card $200

Billy Hoeft
Ball ....$20-$25
Photo ....$15-$18
3x5 index card ....$4-$5

Tommy Holmes
Ball $24
Photo $14
3x5 index card ....$4-$5

Bob Horner
Ball $22
Photo $11
3x5 index card ....$4-$5

Willie Horton
Ball $21
Photo $11
3x5 index card ....$4-$5

Charlie Hough
Ball $20
Photo $10
3x5 index card $4

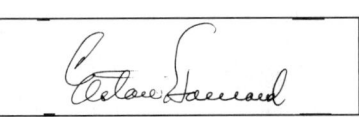

Ralph Houk
Ball $24
Photo $13
3x5 index card $5

Elston Howard *
Ball $500
Photo ....$90-$125
3x5 index card ....$75-$90

Frank Howard
Ball $25
Photo $11
3x5 index card $5

Steve Howe
Ball $18
Photo $9
3x5 index card $4

Roy Howell
Ball $18
Photo $9
3x5 index card $4

Al Hrabosky
Ball $25
Photo ....$14-$20
3x5 index card $5

Kent Hrbek
Ball $25
Photo $13
3x5 index card $5

Randy Hundley
Ball $17
Photo $9
3x5 index card $4

Fred Hutchinson *
Ball $100
Photo $40
3x5 index card ....$20-$25

Bo Jackson
Ball $30
Photo $20
3x5 index card ....$7-$10

Joe Jackson *
Ball ....$25,000-$30,000
Photo ....$10,000-$15,000
3x5 index card ....$8,000-$12,000

Joey Jay
Ball ....$30-$35
Photo ....$20-$25
3x5 index card $7

Jackie Jensen *
Ball $150
Photo $50
3x5 index card ....$20-$25

Inactive Baseball Player Autographs — Chapter 3

Sam Jethroe
Ball $24
Photo $12
3x5 index card $5

Tommy John
Ball $25
Photo $15
3x5 index card $5

Davey Johnson
Ball ....$25-$30
Photo ....$12-$20
3x5 index card ....$5-$6

Alex Johnson
Ball $17
Photo $8
3x5 index card $4

Howard Johnson
Ball $24
Photo $13
3x5 index card ....$4-$5

Jay Johnstone
Ball $25
Photo $14
3x5 index card $5

Cleon Jones
Ball ....$19-$24
Photo ....$10-$15
3x5 index card ....$4-$5

Jim Kaat
Ball $25
Photo $14
3x5 index card $5

Don Kessinger
Ball $19
Photo $10
3x5 index card ....$4-$5

Jimmy Key
Ball $25
Photo $13
3x5 index card $5

Dave Kingman
Ball $25
Photo $13
3x5 index card $5

Ron Kittle
Ball $19
Photo $9
3x5 index card $4

Ted Kluszewski *
Ball $300
Photo $75
3x5 index card $35

Ray Knight
Ball $25
Photo $14
3x5 index card ....$4-$5

Mark Koenig *
Ball $35
Photo ....$20-$25
3x5 index card ....$6-$8

John Kruk
Ball $25
Photo ....$15-$18
3x5 index card $5

Jerry Koosman
Ball $22
Photo $10
3x5 index card $4

Tony Kubek
Ball $35
Photo $22
3x5 index card $8

Whitey Kurowski *
Ball ....$20-$24
Photo ....$15-$20
3x5 index card $5

Harvey Kuenn *
Ball $200
Photo ....$45-$60
3x5 index card ....$15-$20

Ed Kranepool
Ball $20
Photo $10
3x5 index card ....$4-$5

Clem Labine
Ball $24
Photo ....$12-$15
3x5 index card $5

Ken Landreaux
Ball $17
Photo $8
3x5 index card $4

Don Larsen
Ball $26
Photo ....$15-$20
3x5 index card ....$6-$8

Tony LaRussa
Ball $24
Photo $13
3x5 index card $5

Vance Law
Ball $18
Photo $9
3x5 index card $4

Vern Law
Ball $24
Photo ....$12-$15
3x5 index card $5

Bill Lee
Ball $26
Photo ....$16-$20
3x5 index card $6

Ron LeFlore
Ball $23
Photo $12
3x5 index card $5

Mark Lemke
Ball $18
Photo $9
3x5 card $4

Jeffrey Leonard

Ball $19
Photo $9
3x5 index card ....$4-$5

Phil Linz
Ball ....$20-$25
Photo ....$12-$15
3x5 index card $5

Johnny Logan
Ball $19
Photo $9
3x5 index card $4

Mickey Lolich
Ball $20
Photo $10
3x5 index card $4

Sherm Lollar *
Ball $60
Photo ....$28-$34
3x5 index card ....$15-$20

Vic Lombardi
Ball $20
Photo $8
3x5 index card $4

Jim Lonborg
Ball $23
Photo ....$11-$15
3x5 index card $4

Dale Long *
Ball $40
Photo ....$25-$30
3x5 index card ....$8-$10

Ed Lopat *
Ball $40
Photo ....$20-$25
3x5 index card $12

Stan Lopata
Ball $18
Photo $9
3x5 index card $4

Davey Lopes
Ball $22
Photo $12
3x5 index card ....$4-$5

Greg Luzinski
Ball ....$20-$25
Photo ....$12-$15
3x5 index card $5

Sparky Lyle
Ball $22
Photo $12
3x5 index card $5

Fred Lynn
Ball $25
Photo $14
3x5 index card ....$5-$6

Garry Maddox
Ball $24
Photo $14
3x5 index card $5

Bill Madlock
Ball $23
Photo $12
3x5 index card $5

Sal Maglie *
Ball ....$60-$75
Photo ....$28-$35
3x5 index card ....$10-$12

Frank Malzone
Ball $22
Photo $12
3x5 index card $5

Rick Manning
Ball $18
Photo $9
3x5 index card $4

Felix Mantilla
Ball $20
Photo $10
3x5 index card ....$4-$5

Marty Marion
Ball $25
Photo ....$15-$18
3x5 index card $5

Roger Maris *
Ball ....$700-$900
Photo ....$275-$350
3x5 index card ....$50-$75

Mike A. Marshall
Ball $18
Photo $9
3x5 index card $4

Mike G. Marshall
Ball ....$100-$125
Photo ....$50-$60
3x5 index card ....$15-$20

Billy Martin *
Ball $200
Photo ....$70-$100
3x5 index card ....$35-$45

Dennis Martinez
Ball $24
Photo $13
3x5 index card $5

Don Mattingly
Ball $45
Photo ....$25-$30
3x5 index card ....$9-$12

John Matlack
Ball $17
Photo $9
3x5 index card $4

Gary Matthews
Ball $22
Photo $11
3x5 index card ....$4-$5

Gene Mauch
Ball $25
Photo ....$10-$15
3x5 index card $5

Carlos May
Ball $17
Photo $8
3x5 index card $4

Lee May
Ball $19
Photo $10
3x5 index card $4

Rudy May
Ball $20
Photo $10
3x5 index card ....$4-$5

John Mayberry
Ball $20
Photo $10
3x5 index card $4

Lee Maye
Ball $18
Photo ....$9-$12
3x5 index card $4

Bill Mazeroski
Ball $30
Photo ....$18-$20
3x5 index card ....$6-$8

Lee Mazzilli
Ball $17
Photo $9
3x5 index card $4

Bake McBride
Ball $22
Photo $11
3x5 index card $5

Al McBean
Ball $28
Photo $18
3x5 index card ....$6-$7

Tim McCarver
Ball ....$27-$30
Photo ....$15-$20
3x5 index card ....$6-$8

Willie McGee
Ball $23
Photo ....$14-$18
3x5 index card ....$5-$6

Mickey McDermott
Ball $17
Photo $9

3x5 index card $4

Oddibe McDowell
Ball $17
Photo $8
3x5 index card $4

Gil McDougald
Ball ....$20-$25
Photo ....$10-$12
3x5 index card $5

Sam McDowell
Ball $18
Photo $9
3x5 index card $4

Tug McGraw
Ball $25
Photo ....$14-$18
3x5 index card ....$5-$6

Denny McLain
Ball $25
Photo $12
3x5 index card $5

Roy McMillan *
Ball $30
Photo ....$18-$20
3x5 index card $8

Dave McNally
Ball $22
Photo $10
3x5 index card ....$4-$5

Hal McRae
Ball $23
Photo $13
3x5 index card ....$4-$5

Kevin McReynolds
Ball $19
Photo $10
3x5 index card ....$4-$5

Bill Melton
Ball ....$22-$24
Photo ....$12-$15
3x5 index card $5

Gene Michael
Ball $17
Photo $8
3x5 index card $4

Felix Millan
Ball $23
Photo ....$12-$15
3x5 index card ....$5-$6

Don Mincher
Ball $21
Photo ....$16-$18
3x5 index card ....$4-$5

Minnie Minoso
Ball $28
Photo $20
3x5 index card ....$6-$7

Kevin Mitchell
Ball $24
Photo $13
3x5 index card ....$4-$5

Wilmer Mizell *
Ball ....$28-$30
Photo ....$15-$20
3x5 index card ....$7-$8

Paul Molitor
Ball $45
Photo ....$25-$30
3x5 index card ....$9-$10

Rick Monday
Ball $23
Photo $13
3x5 index card $5

Don Money
Ball $21
Photo $12
3x5 index card ....$4-$5

Wally Moon
Ball $19
Photo $10
3x5 index card $4

Charlie Moore
Ball $19
Photo $10
3x5 index card $4

Terry Moore *
Ball ....$40-$45
Photo $25
3x5 index card $12

Keith Moreland
Ball $18
Photo $9
3x5 index card $4

Jack Morris
Ball $22
Photo $11
3x5 index card ....$4-$5

Omar Moreno
Ball $25
Photo $15
3x5 index card $5

Manny Mota
Ball $27
Photo ....$15-$20
3x5 index card $6

Van Lingle Mungo *
Ball ....$90-$125
Photo ....$45-$50
3x5 index card ....$15-$20

Thurman Munson *
Ball $1,100
Photo $450
3x5 index card $150

Bobby Murcer
Ball $25
Photo $12
3x5 index card $5

Dale Murphy
Ball $28
Photo $17
3x5 index card ....$6-$7

Eddie Murray
Ball ....$45-$50
Photo ....$27-$30
3x5 index card ....$12-$15

Danny Murtaugh *
Ball ....$90-$120
Photo ....$40-$70
3x5 index card ....$15-$20

Graig Nettles
Ball $25
Photo $13
3x5 index card $5

Don Newcombe
Ball $25
Photo $12
3x5 index card $5

Bobo Newsom *
Ball ....$90-$125
Photo $45
3x5 index card $15

Joe Niekro
Ball $21
Photo ....$11-$15
3x5 index card ....$4-$5

Gary Nolan
Ball $17
Photo $8
3x5 index card $4

Irv Noren
Ball $20
Photo ....$10-$15
3x5 index card ....$4-$5

Joe Nuxhall
Ball $17
Photo $9
3x5 index card $4

Lefty O'Doul *
Ball ....$250-$300
Photo $175
3x5 index card $40

Blue Moon Odom
Ball $20
Photo $9
3x5 index card ....$4-$5

Ben Oglivie
Ball $19
Photo $9
3x5 index card $4

Tony Oliva
Ball $23
Photo $14
3x5 index card $5

Al Oliver
Ball $19
Photo $13
3x5 index card $4

Gene Oliver
Ball $19
Photo $12
3x5 index card $4

Claude Osteen
Ball $24
Photo $12
3x5 index card ....$4-$5

Amos Otis
Ball $22
Photo $12
3x5 index card $4

Ed Ott
Ball $19
Photo $9
3x5 index card $4

Mickey Owen
Ball $21
Photo $10
3x5 index card ....$4-$5

Andy Pafko
Ball ....$22-$25
Photo ....$12-$15
3x5 index card $5

Dave Parker
Ball ....$25-$27
Photo ....$13-$15
3x5 index card ....$5-$6

Wes Parker
Ball $22
Photo $11
3x5 index card $4

Mel Parnell
Ball $24
Photo $12
3x5 index card $5

Camilo Pascual
Ball $26
Photo ....$14-$18
3x5 index card ....$5-$6

Alejandro Pena
Ball $22
Photo $11
3x5 index card ....$4-$5

Tony Pena
Ball $24
Photo $13
3x5 index card $5

Terry Pendleton
Ball $20
Photo $10
3x5 index card ....$4-$5

Joe Pepitone
Ball ....$25-$30
Photo ....$15-$20
3x5 index card ....$7-$8

Jim Perry
Ball $20
Photo ....$10-$15
3x5 index card ....$4-$5

Johnny Pesky
Ball $21
Photo $11
3x5 index card $4

Rico Petrocelli
Ball ....$15-$17
Photo $8
3x5 index card $4

Billy Pierce
Ball $21
Photo $12

3x5 index card ....$4-$5

Jimmy Piersall
Ball $24
Photo $14
3x5 index card $5

Lou Piniella
Ball $24
Photo $14
3x5 index card $4

Vada Pinson *
Ball $45
Photo ....$25-$30
3x5 index card $15

Juan Pizzaro
Ball ....$28-$30
Photo ....$18-$20
3x5 index card $7

Johnny Podres
Ball $24
Photo ....$13-$15
3x5 index card $5

Darrell Porter
Ball $23
Photo $12
3x5 index card $5

Boog Powell
Ball ....$23-$25
Photo ....$13-$15
3x5 index card $6

Vic Power
Ball $25
Photo ....$15-$18
3x5 index card ....$6-$7

Kirby Puckett
Ball $50
Photo $34
3x5 index card ....$10-$12

Pedro Ramos
Ball $23
Photo $13
3x5 index card ....$4-$5

Willie Randolph
Ball $25
Photo $13
3x5 index card $5

Vic Raschi *
Ball ....$100-$120
Photo $35
3x5 index card ....$10-$12

Dick Radatz
Ball $19
Photo $9
3x5 index card $4

Tim Raines
Ball $25
Photo $14
3x5 card $5

Jeff Reardon
Ball $22
Photo $11
3x5 index card ....$4-$5

Jimmy Reese *
Ball $35
Photo $20
3x5 index card ....$9-$10

Pete Reiser *
Ball ....$60-$75
Photo ....$35-$40

3x5 index card . . . . $12-$15

Allie Reynolds *
Ball $100
Photo . . . . $35-$40
3x5 index card . . . . $12-$15

Harold Reynolds
Ball $20
Photo $10
3x5 index card $4

Dusty Rhodes
Ball $24
Photo . . . . $12-$15
3x5 index card $5

Jim Rice
Ball $30
Photo . . . . $15-$20
3x5 index card . . . . $7-$9

J.R. Richard
Ball $23
Photo $14
3x5 index card . . . . $4-$5

Bobby Richardson
Ball $20
Photo $10
3x5 index card $4

Bill Rigney
Ball . . . . $25-$30
Photo . . . . $18-$25
3x5 index card $7

Dave Righetti
Ball $20
Photo $10
3x5 index card $4

Billy Ripken
Ball $18
Photo $9
3x5 index card $4

Mickey Rivers
Ball $21
Photo $11
3x5 index card $4

Eddie Robinson
Ball $24
Photo $15
3x5 index card $5

Preacher Roe
Ball $25

Photo $14
3x5 index card $5

Bob "Buck" Rodgers
Ball $19
Photo $10
3x5 index card $4

Steve Rogers
Ball $20
Photo $10
3x5 index card . . . . $4-$5

Cookie Rojas
Ball $21
Photo . . . . $12-$15
3x5 index card . . . . $4-$5

Red Rolfe*
Ball . . . . $50-$60
Photo . . . . $35-$40
3x5 index card . . . . $12-$14

Pete Rose
Ball $40
Photo $25
3x5 index card . . . . $10-$14

Al Rosen
Ball $25
Photo $16
3x5 index card $5

Johnny Roseboro
Ball $20
Photo $10
3x5 index card . . . . $4-$5

Joe Rudi
Ball $24
Photo $13
3x5 index card $5

Bill Russell
Ball $21
Photo $11
3x5 index card $4

Chris Sabo
Ball $24
Photo $12
3x5 index card . . . . $4-$5

Deion Sanders
Ball $40
Photo $25
3x5 index card . . . . $7-$10

Johnny Sain
Ball $25
Photo $13
3x5 index card $5

Ryne Sandberg
Ball $35
Photo $23
3x5 index card . . . . $10-$12

Manny Sanguillen
Ball $28
Photo $17
3x5 index card $6

Ron Santo
Ball . . . . $25-$30
Photo . . . . $15-$20
3x5 index card $6

Hank Sauer
Ball . . . . $19-$24
Photo . . . . $9-$12
3x5 index card $5

Steve Sax
Ball $20
Photo $10
3x5 index card . . . . $4-$5

Herb Score
Ball $23
Photo $14
3x5 index card $5

George Scott
Ball $23
Photo $12
3x5 index card $5

Mike Scott
Ball ....$19-$25
Photo ....$12-$15
3x5 index card ....$4-$6

Bobby Shantz
Ball $21
Photo $10
3x5 index card ....$4-$6

Kevin Seitzer
Ball $20
Photo $10
3x5 index card ....$4-$5

Chris Short *
Ball $40
Photo $30
3x5 index card ....$10-$12

Ruben Sierra
Ball $22
Photo ....$11-$15
3x5 card $5

Roy Sievers
Ball $21
Photo $11
3x5 index card ....$4-$5

Ken Singleton
Ball $20
Photo $10
3x5 index card $4

Ted Simmons
Ball $25
Photo $16
3x5 index card $5

Sibby Sisti
Ball ....$18-$20
Photo ....$10-$12
3x5 index card $4

Bill "Moose" Skowron
Ball $24
Photo $12
3x5 index card $5

Don Slaught
Ball $18
Photo $9

3x5 index card $4

Roy Smalley Jr.
Ball $20
Photo $11
3x5 index card $4

Roy Smalley Sr.
Ball $19
Photo $9
3x5 index card $4

Lee Smith
Ball $24
Photo $15
3x5 index card $5

Lonnie Smith
Ball $19
Photo $9
3x5 index card $4

Ozzie Smith
Ball ....$28-$30
Photo ....$18-$20
3x5 index card ....$6-$7

Reggie Smith
Ball $22
Photo $12
3x5 index card ....$4-$5

Cory Snyder
Ball $18
Photo $9
3x5 index card $4

Billy Southworth*
Ball ....$60-$75
Photo ....$35-$40
3x5 index card ....$15-$20

Eddie Stanky *
Ball $30
Photo ....$17-$20
3x5 index card ....$7-$8

Bob Stanley
Ball ....$16-$18
Photo ....$8-$9
3x5 index card $4

Fred Stanley

Ball $21
Photo $10
3x5 index card ....$4-$5

Rusty Staub
Ball $23
Photo $12
3x5 index card $5

Terry Steinbach
Ball $21
Photo $12
3x5 index card ....$4-$5

Vern Stephens*
Ball ....$150-$175
Photo ....$90-$100
3x5 index card $25

Dave Stewart
Ball $24
Photo $12
3x5 index card $5

Dave Stieb
Ball $22
Photo $11
3x5 index card ....$4-$5

Steve Stone
Ball $25
Photo ....$13-$18
3x5 index card $5

Mel Stottlemyre
Ball $24
Photo $12
3x5 index card $5

Billy Sunday *
Ball ....$400-$500
Photo ....$300-$350
3x5 index card ....$90-$100

Rick Sutcliffe
Ball $22
Photo $12
3x5 index card ....$4-$5

Bruce Sutter
Ball $23
Photo $12
3x5 index card $5

Ron Swoboda
Ball $20
Photo $10
3x5 index card $4

Frank Tanana
Ball $21
Photo $12
3x5 index card $4

Danny Tartabull
Ball $20
Photo $10
3x5 index card $4

Birdie Tebbetts *
Ball $24
Photo ....$13-$15
3x5 index card ....$5-$6

Johnny Temple *
Ball $28
Photo $15
3x5 index card $6

Ralph Terry
Ball $23
Photo $12
3x5 index card ....$4-$5

Chuck Tanner
Ball $25
Photo ....$18-$20
3x5 index card $5

Kent Tekulve
Ball $23
Photo $12
3x5 index card $5

Garry Templeton
Ball $24
Photo $12
3x5 index card $5

Gene Tenace
Ball $24
Photo $12
3x5 index card $5

Wayne Terwilliger
Ball $18
Photo $9
3x5 index card $4

Mickey Tettleton
Ball $24
Photo $12
3x5 index card $5

Bob Tewksbury
Ball $17
Photo $9

3x5 index card $4

Frank J. Thomas
Ball $19
Photo $9
3x5 index card $4

Gorman Thomas
Ball $24
Photo $12
3x5 index card $5

Bobby Thomson
Ball $25
Photo $15
3x5 index card ....$5-$6

Andre Thornton
Ball $24
Photo $17
3x5 index card $5

Faye Throneberry *
Ball $25
Photo $17
3x5 index card $6

Marv Throneberry *
Ball $50
Photo $25
3x5 index card ....$8-$10

Luis Tiant
Ball $25
Photo $12
3x5 index card $5

Frank Torre
Ball $21
Photo $10

3x5 index card ....$4-$5

Joe Torre
Ball ....$28-$30
Photo ....$15-$20
3x5 index card ....$6-$8

Alan Trammell
Ball $26
Photo $16
3x5 index card ....$5-$6

Tom Tresh
Ball $21
Photo $11
3x5 index card ....$4-$5

Manny Trillo
Ball $21
Photo $12
3x5 index card $4

Virgil Trucks
Ball $24
Photo $14
3x5 index card $5

Bob Turley
Ball $21
Photo $12
3x5 index card $4

Bob Uecker
Ball ....$35-$40
Photo ....$20-$25
3x5 index card $8

Del Unser
Ball $17
Photo $8
3x5 index card $4

Elmer Valo *
Ball $26
Photo $14
3x5 index card $5

Johnny VanderMeer *
Ball ....$28-$30
Photo ....$15-$20
3x5 index card $6

Andy Van Slyke
Ball $24

Photo $14
3x5 index card $5

Mickey Vernon
Ball $22
Photo $11
3x5 index card ....$4-$5

Frank Viola
Ball $23
Photo $12
3x5 index card $5

Bill Virdon
Ball ....$18-$20
Photo ....$9-$12
3x5 index card ....$4-$5

Pete Vuckovich
Ball $23
Photo $14
3x5 index card $5

Dixie Walker *
Ball ....$35-$45
Photo ....$25-$30
3x5 index card $10-12

Harry Walker *
Ball ....$25-$30
Photo ....$15-$20
3x5 index card ....$5-$6

Rube Walker *
Ball ....$30-$35
Photo ....$18-$20
3x5 index card $7

Bucky Walters *
Ball ....$40-$60
Photo ....$25-$30
3x5 index card ....$12-$15

Bill Wambganss*
Ball ....$150-$200
Photo ....$75-$100
3x5 index card ....$40-$50

Claudell Washington
Ball $17

Photo ....$8-$10
3x5 index card $4

Bob Watson
Ball $18
Photo $9
3x5 index card $4

Bob Welch
Ball $21
Photo $12
3x5 index card $4

Lou Whitaker
Ball $25
Photo $15
3x5 index card $5

Bill White
Ball $25
Photo $13
3x5 index card $5

Roy White
Ball $21
Photo $10
3x5 index card $4

Dick Williams
Ball $25
Photo $15
3x5 index card $5

Ken Williams *
Ball $200
Photo ....$100-$125
3x5 index card $40

Mitch Williams
Ball $20
Photo $10
3x5 index card $4

Maury Wills
Ball ....$27-$30
Photo ....$13-$18
3x5 index card ....$5-$6

Mookie Wilson

Ball $22
Photo $10
3x5 index card ....$4-$5

Dave Winfield
Ball $40
Photo ....$20-$25
3x5 index card $10

Smoky Joe Wood*
Ball ....$125-$150
Photo $75
3x5 index card $35

Wilbur Wood
Ball $20
Photo ....$10-$15
3x5 index card ....$4-$5

Gene Woodling
Ball $20
Photo $10
3x5 index card ....$4-$5

Jimmy Wynn
Ball $21
Photo $11
3x5 index card ....$4-$5

Steve Yeager
Ball $18
Photo $9
3x5 index card $4

Rudy York *
Ball ....$150-$200
Photo $100
3x5 index card ....$50-$60

Gus Zernial
Ball $22
Photo $10
3x5 index card ....$4-$5

Don Zimmer
Ball $25
Photo $15
3x5 index card $5

Active Baseball Player Autographs

Jeff Abbott
Ball $22
Photo $12
3x5 card $5

Bobby Abreu
Ball $24
Photo $15
3x5 card $6

Rick Aguilera
Ball $23
Photo $13
3x5 card $6

Luis Alicia
Ball $20
Photo $12
3x5 card $5

Roberto Alomar
Ball $28
Photo $15
3x5 card $6

Sandy Alomar Jr.
Ball $23
Photo $13
3x5 card $5

Moises Alou
Ball $26
Photo $14
3x5 card $7

Wilson Alvarez
Ball $20
Photo $10
3x5 card $5

Brady Anderson
Ball $22
Photo $12
3x5 card $5

Garret Anderson
Ball $23
Photo $14
3x5 card $5

Shane Andrews
Ball $22
Photo $12
3x5 card $5

Rich Ankiel
Ball $30
Photo $17
3x5 card $7

Kevin Appier
Ball $22
Photo $13
3x5 card $6

Paul Assenmacher
Ball $19
Photo $11
3x5 card $5

Rich Aurilia
Ball $20
Photo $12
3x5 card $5

Brad Ausmus
Ball $21
Photo $12
3x5 card $5

Steve Avery
Ball $21
Photo $13
3x5 card $5

Carlos Baerga
Ball $22
Photo $12
3x5 card $5

Jeff Bagwell
Ball $30
Photo $22
3x5 card $8

Michael Barrett
Ball $23
Photo $13
3x5 card $5

Rod Beck
Ball $20
Photo $11
3x5 card $5

Tim Belcher
Ball $19
Photo $10
3x5 card $5

Derek Bell
Ball $23
Photo $14
3x5 card $6

Jay Bell
Ball $23
Photo $14
3x5 card $6

Albert Belle
Ball $40
Photo $24
3x5 card $9

Ronnie Belliard
Ball $24
Photo $13
3x5 card $6

Adrian Beltre
Ball $20
Photo $9
3x5 card $5

Alan Benes
Ball $22
Photo $13
3x5 card ....$6-$7

Andy Benes
Ball $23
Photo $14
3x5 card $6

Mike Benjamin
Ball $20
Photo $10
3x5 card $5

Jason Bere
Ball $21
Photo $10
3x5 card $5

Dante Bichette
Ball $24
Photo $13
3x5 card $6

Craig Biggio
Ball $25
Photo $15
3x5 card $6

Barry Bonds
Ball $60
Photo $35
3x5 card $12

Bobby Bonilla
Ball $28

Active Baseball Player Autographs — Chapter 4

Photo $17
3x5 card $7

Aaron Boone
Ball $21
Photo $10
3x5 card $5

Bret Boone
Ball $23
Photo $12
3x5 card $6

Mike Bordick
Ball $22
Photo $12
3x5 card $6

Jeff Brantley
Ball $23
Photo $13
3x5 card $6

Rico Brogna
Ball $18
Photo $9
3x5 card $5

Scott Brosius
Ball $24
Photo $13
3x5 card $6

Kevin Brown
Ball $26
Photo $15
3x5 card $7

Jay Buhner
Ball $28
Photo $15
3x5 card $7

Jeromy Burnitz
Ball $25
Photo $15
3x5 card $7

John Burkett
Ball $25
Photo $15
3x5 card $7

Ellis Burks
Ball $20
Photo $11

3x5 card $5

Paul Byrd
Ball $24
Photo $13
3x5 card $6

Ken Caminiti
Ball $26
Photo $15
3x5 card $6

Jose Canseco
Ball $35
Photo $28
3x5 card $8

Mike Caruso
Ball $21
Photo $12
3x5 card $5

Sean Casey
Ball $28
Photo $15
3x5 card $7

Vinny Castilla
Ball $25
Photo $15
3x5 card $6

Jeff Cirillo
Ball $24
Photo $15
3x5 card $6

Tony Clark
Ball $27
Photo $15
3x5 card $6

Will Clark
Ball $35
Photo $22
3x5 card $7

Royce Clayton
Ball $24
Photo $13
3x5 card $6

Roger Clemens
Ball $50
Photo $30

3x5 card $10

David Cone
Ball $25
Photo $15
3x5 card $6

Jeff Conine
Ball $23
Photo $13
3x5 card $6

Wil Cordero
Ball $24
Photo $13
3x5 card $6

Marty Cordova
Ball $23
Photo $13
3x5 card $5

Craig Counsell
Ball $21
Photo $12
3x5 card $5

Jose Cruz Jr.
Ball $28
Photo $17
3x5 card $7

Chad Curtis
Ball $20
Photo $10
3x5 card $5

Johnny Damon
Ball $21
Photo $12
3x5 card $5

Eric Davis
Ball $24
Photo $15
3x5 card $6

Russ Davis
Ball $23
Photo $11
3x5 card $6

Carlos Delgado
Ball $27
Photo $18
3x5 card $8

Delino DeShields
Ball $25
Photo $15
3x5 card $6

Jason Dickson
Ball $21
Photo $12
3x5 card $5

Gary DiSarcina
Ball $21
Photo $12
3x5 card $5

J. D. Drew
Ball $35
Photo $20
3x5 card $8

Shawon Dunston
Ball $20
Photo $10
3x5 card $5

Ray Durham
Ball $25
Photo $17
3x5 card $6

Damion Easley
Ball $25
Photo $15
3x5 card $6

Jim Edmonds
Ball $25
Photo $15
3x5 card $6

Cal Eldred
Ball $18
Photo $9
3x5 card $5

Juan Encaracion
Ball $20
Photo $9
3x5 card $5

Darin Erstad
Ball $25
Photo $16
3x5 card $6

Tony Fernandez
Ball $22
Photo $15
3x5 card $5

Darrin Fletcher
Ball $20
Photo $11
3x5 card $5

Cliff Floyd
Ball $26
Photo $14
3x5 card $6

Andy Fox
Ball $23
Photo $14
3x5 card $5

John Franco
Ball $24
Photo $12
3x5 card $6

Travis Fryman
Ball $25
Photo $16
3x5 card $6

Andres Galarraga
Ball $26
Photo $16
3x5 card $7

Ron Gant
Ball $24
Photo $14
3x5 card $6

Freddy Garcia
Ball $21
Photo $11
3x5 card $5

Nomar Garciaparra
Ball $40
Photo $25
3x5 card $8

Jason Giambi
Ball $23
Photo $12
3x5 card $6

Brian Giles
Ball $24
Photo $12
3x5 card $5

Doug Glanville
Ball $22
Photo $11
3x5 card $5

Troy Glaus
Ball $22
Photo $11
3x5 card ....$6-$7

Tom Glavine
Ball $30
Photo $20
3x5 card $6

Tom Goodwin
Ball $22
Photo $12
3x5 card $5

Wayne Gomes
Ball $20
Photo $9
3x5 card $5

Alex Gonzalez
Ball $30
Photo $20
3x5 card $7

Juan Gonzalez
Ball $29
Photo $18
3x5 card $7

Luis Gonzalez
Ball $24
Photo $12
3x5 card $5

Tom Gordon
Ball $18
Photo $14
3x5 card $5

Mark Grace
Ball $25
Photo $13
3x5 card $6

Shawn Green
Ball $24
Photo $12
3x5 card $6

Willie Greene
Ball $21
Photo $12
3x5 card $5

Rusty Greer
Ball $22
Photo $12
3x5 card $5

Ben Grieve
Ball $30
Photo $18
3x5 card ....$7-$8

Ken Griffey Jr.

Ball $45
Photo $30
3x5 card $14

Mark Grudzielanek
Ball $20
Photo $10
3x5 card $5

Marquis Grissom
Ball $25
Photo $18
3x5 card $7

Vladamir Guerrero
Ball $35
Photo $22
3x5 card $9

Jose Guillen
Ball $22
Photo $12
3x5 card $5

Ricky Gutierrez
Ball $19
Photo $11
3x5 card $5

Tony Gwynn
Ball $38
Photo $25
3x5 card $10

Darryl Hamilton
Ball $20
Photo $10
3x5 card $5

Mike Hampton
Ball $24
Photo $13
3x5 card $6

Erik Hanson
Ball $25
Photo $15
3x5 card $7

Pete Harnisch
Ball $16
Photo $10
3x5 card $5

Charlie Hayes
Ball $24
Photo $12
3x5 card $6

Todd Helton
Ball $20
Photo $10
3x5 card $5

Rickey Henderson
Ball $35

Photo $25
3x5 card $8

Livian Hernandez
Ball $22
Photo $12
3x5 card $5

Orlando Hernandez
Ball $30
Photo $18
3x5 card $7

Bobby Higginson
Ball $20
Photo $13
3x5 card $5

Ken Hill
Ball $24
Photo $13
3x5 card $6

Sterling Hitchcock
Ball $20
Photo $10
3x5 card $5

Trevor Hoffman
Ball $25
Photo $15
3x5 card $6

Chris Hoiles
Ball $21
Photo $11
3x5 card $5

Todd Hollandsworth
Ball $25
Photo $14
3x5 card $6

Dave Hollins
Ball $21
Photo $11
3x5 card $5

Brian Hunter
Ball $22
Photo $12
3x5 card $5

Butch Huskey
Ball $24
Photo $14
3x5 card $6

Hideki Irabu

Ball $25
Photo $13
3x5 card $6

Mike Jackson
Ball $22
Photo $11
3x5 card $5

John Jaha
Ball $24
Photo $13
3x5 card $6

Stan Javier
Ball $21
Photo $12
3x5 card $5

Gregg Jefferies
Ball $25
Photo $20
3x5 card $6

Geoff Jenkins
Ball $26
Photo $14
3x5 card $7

Derek Jeter
Ball $55
Photo $35
3x5 card $12

Jose Jimenez
Ball $24
Photo $13
3x5 card $6

Charles Johnson
Ball $23
Photo $12
3x5 card $6

Randy Johnson
Ball $35
Photo $22
3x5 card $8

Andrew Jones
Ball $35
Photo $22
3x5 card $8

Chipper Jones

Active Baseball Player Autographs — Chapter 4

Ball $40
Photo $25
3x5 card $9

Wally Joyner
Ball $22
Photo $11
3x5 card $5

David Justice
Ball $35
Photo $21
3x5 card $7

Gabe Kapler
Ball $27
Photo $15
3x5 card $6

Eric Karros
Ball $26
Photo $16
3x5 card $6

Takashi Kashiwada
Ball $24
Photo $13
3x5 card $6

Roberto Kelly
Ball $22
Photo $11
3x5 card $5

Jason Kendall
Ball $28
Photo $16
3x5 card $7

Darryl Kile
Ball $23
Photo $13
3x5 card $5

Chuck Knoblauch
Ball $26
Photo $14
3x5 card $6

Paul Konerko
Ball $19
Photo $10
3x5 card $5

Mark Langston
Ball $22
Photo $11
3x5 card $5

Ray Lankford
Ball $25
Photo $15
3x5 card $6

Mike Lansing
Ball $22
Photo $14
3x5 card $5

Barry Larkin
Ball $25
Photo $14
3x5 card $6

Matt Lawton
Ball $22
Photo $11
3x5 card $5

Ricky Ledee
Ball $20
Photo $10
3x5 card $5

Derek Lee
Ball $23
Photo $13
3x5 card $5

Travis Lee
Ball $30
Photo $18
3x5 card $7

Al Leiter
Ball $23
Photo $13
3x5 card $5

Jim Leyritz
Ball $20
Photo $10
3x5 card $5

Mike Lieberthal
Ball $24
Photo $15
3x5 card $6

Kerry Lightenberg
Ball $22
Photo $13
3x5 card $5

Keith Lockhart
Ball $19
Photo $9
3x5 card $5

Kenny Lofton
Ball $30
Photo $20
3x5 card $7

Rich Loiselle
Ball $21
Photo $11
3x5 card $5

Javier Lopez
Ball $28
Photo $16
3x5 card $6

Mark Loretta
Ball $20
Photo $12
3x5 card $5

Greg Maddux
Ball $60
Photo $35
3x5 card $10

Dave Magadan
Ball $19
Photo $10
3x5 card $5

Eli Marrero
Ball $22
Photo $11
3x5 card $5

Edgar Martinez
Ball $25

Photo $15
3x5 card $6

Pedro Martinez
Ball $40
Photo $24
3x5 card $11

Tino Martinez
Ball $35
Photo $20
3x5 card $7

Brent Mayne
Ball $21
Photo $11
3x5 card $5

Quinton McCracken
Ball $22
Photo $11
3x5 card $5

Fred McGriff
Ball $26
Photo $15
3x5 card $6

Mark McGwire
Ball $150
Photo $100
3x5 card $15

Mark McLemore
Ball $21
Photo $11
3x5 card $5

Brian McRae
Ball $24
Photo $12
3x5 card $6

Pat Meares
Ball $21
Photo $11
3x5 card $5

Orlando Merced
Ball $22
Photo $11
3x5 card $5

Kent Mercker
Ball $21

Photo $11
3x5 card $5

Jose Mesa
Ball $24
Photo $14
3x5 card $6

Kevin Millwood
Ball $25
Photo $14
3x5 card $6

Raul Mondesi
Ball $30
Photo $24
3x5 card $7

Mickey Morandini
Ball $22
Photo $13
3x5 card $5

Hal Morris
Ball $21
Photo $12
3x5 card $5

Matt Morris
Ball $23
Photo $13
3x5 card $5

Bill Mueller
Ball $24
Photo $14
3x5 card $5

Mike Mussina
Ball $28
Photo $18
3x5 card $7

Tim Naehring
Ball $19
Photo $10
3x5 card $5

Charles Nagy
Ball $24
Photo $15
3x5 card $6

Denny Neagle
Ball $24
Photo $14
3x5 card $6

Robb Nen
Ball $23
Photo $14
3x5 card $5

Phil Nevin
Ball $23
Photo $14

3x5 card $5

Hideo Nomo
Ball $29
Photo $18
3x5 card $7

Jose Offerman
Ball $26
Photo $18
3x5 card $6

Chad Ogea
Ball $21
Photo $12
3x5 card $5

Troy O'Leary
Ball $23
Photo $12
3x5 card $5

John Olerud
Ball $27
Photo $17
3x5 card $6

Paul O'Neill
Ball $28
Photo $15
3x5 card $6

Magglio Ordonez
Ball $25
Photo $13
3x5 card $6

David Ortiz
Ball $22
Photo $12
3x5 card ....$

Donovan Osborne
Ball $21
Photo $11
3x5 card $5

Rafael Palmeiro
Ball $30
Photo $20
3x5 card $7

Dean Palmer
Ball $23
Photo $12
3x5 card $5

Chan Ho Park
Ball $23
Photo $13
3x5 card $5

Troy Percival
Ball $21
Photo $12
3x5 card $5

Andy Pettitte
Ball $32
Photo $19
3x5 card $7

Mike Piazza
Ball $38
Photo $25
3x5 card $7

Jorge Posada
Ball $23
Photo $13
3x5 card $5

Manny Ramirez
Ball $30
Photo $18
3x5 card $7

Joe Randa
Ball $20
Photo $10
3x5 card $5

Pokey Reese
Ball $25
Photo $14
3x5 card $6

Edgar Renteria
Ball $22
Photo $12
3x5 card $5

Cal Ripken Jr.
Ball $75
Photo $40
3x5 card $12

Mariano Rivera
Ball $28
Photo $15

3x5 card $6

John Rocker
Ball $30
Photo $20
3x5 card $7

Alex Rodriguez
Ball $60
Photo $35
3x5 card $12

Ivan Rodriguez
Ball $28
Photo $17
3x5 card $7

Scott Rolen
Ball $30
Photo $18
3x5 card $6

Bret Saberhagen
Ball $24
Photo $14
3x5 card $6

Tim Salmon
Ball $28
Photo $20
3x5 card $6

Rey Sanchez
Ball $20
Photo $12
3x5 card $5

Reggie Sanders
Ball $22
Photo $13
3x5 card $5

Benito Santiago
Ball $24

Photo $14
3x5 card $5

Jason Schmidt
Ball $20
Photo $11
3x5 card $5

Richie Sexson
Ball $24
Photo $14
3x5 card $6

Jeff Shaw
Ball $22
Photo $12
3x5 card $5

Gary Sheffield
Ball $28
Photo $16
3x5 card $6

Heathcliff Slocumb
Ball $22
Photo $13
3x5 card $5

John Smiley
Ball $21
Photo $12
3x5 card $5

John Smoltz
Ball $32
Photo $20
3x5 card $7

J.T. Snow
Ball $24
Photo $14
3x5 card $6

Paul Sorrento
Ball $20
Photo $12
3x5 card $5

Sammy Sosa
Ball $125
Photo $75
3x5 card $15

Shane Spencer
Ball $20
Photo $12

3x5 card $5

Ed Sprague
Ball $21
Photo $12
3x5 card $5

Kevin Stocker
Ball $20
Photo $10
3x5 card $5

B. J. Surhoff
Ball $23
Photo $13
3x5 card $5

Bill Swift
Ball $21
Photo $12
3x5 card $5

Greg Swindell
Ball $18
Photo $9
3x5 card $5

Kevin Tapani
Ball $22
Photo $13
3x5 card $5

Fernando Tatis
Ball $25
Photo $15
3x5 card $6

Eddie Taubensee
Ball $23
Photo $12
3x5 card $5

Miguel Tejada
Ball $24
Photo $14
3x5 card $5

Frank E. Thomas
Ball $45
Photo $25
3x5 card $8

Jim Thome
Ball $25
Photo $15

3x5 card $6

Ugueth Urbina
Ball $22
Photo $11
3x5 card $5

John Valentin
Ball $18
Photo $10
3x5 card $6

Jose Valentin
Ball $20
Photo $12
3x5 card $5

Greg Vaughn
Ball $28
Photo $17
3x5 card $6

Mo Vaughn
Ball $35
Photo $20
3x5 card $7

Robin Ventura
Ball $30
Photo $18
3x5 card $6

Fernando Vina
Ball $24
Photo $15
3x5 card $6

Omar Vizquel
Ball $24
Photo $15
3x5 card $6

Billy Wagner
Ball $26
Photo $15
3x5 card $6

Tim Wakefield
Ball $23
Photo $13
3x5 card $5

Matt Walbeck
Ball $21
Photo $10
3x5 card $5

Larry Walker
Ball $35
Photo $20
3x5 card $7

Walt Weiss
Ball $21
Photo $11
3x5 card $5

David Wells
Ball $28
Photo $17
3x5 card $6

John Wetteland
Ball $25
Photo $14
3x5 card $6

Rondell White
Ball $25
Photo $14
3x5 card $5

Mark Whiten
Ball $23
Photo $12
3x5 card $5

Bernie Williams
Ball $45
Photo $25
3x5 card $8

Matt Williams
Ball $35
Photo $25
3x5 card $7

Scott Williamson
Ball $27
Photo $18
3x5 card $6

Dan Wilson
Ball $21
Photo $12
3x5 card $5

Kerry Wood
Ball $40
Photo $20
3x5 card $8

Jaret Wright
Ball $22
Photo $13
3x5 card $5

Dmitri Young
Ball $21
Photo $11
3x5 card $5

Kevin Young
Ball $23
Photo $14
3x5 card $5

Todd Zeile
Ball $22
Photo $14
3x5 card $5

Autographed Team Baseballs

Key signatures follow each team name

1920 Boston (AL) - Barrow, Hendryx, Hooper, Pennock, Hoyt ....$800-$1250
1920 Boston (NL) - Maranville, Powell, Mann . ...$600-$900
1920 Brooklyn - Robinson, Konetchy, Myers, Wheat, Grimes, Marquard ....$1200-$1750
1920 Chicago (AL) - Collins, Risberg, Weaver, Leibold, Felsch, Jackson, Schalk, Faber, Williams, Kerr, Cicotte ....$ uncertain
1920 Chicago (NL) - Hollocher, Flack, Robertson, Alexander ....$900-$1400
1920 Cincinnati - Daubert, Roush ...$450-$700
1920 Cleveland - Wambsganss, Chapman, Gardner, Smith, Speaker, Jamieson, O'Neill, Sewell, Coveleski ....$1300-$2000
1920 Detroit - Jennings, Heilmann, Cobb, Veach ....$1700-$2500
1920 New York (AL) - Huggins, Pratt, Ruth, Mays, Shawkey ....$2200-$3400
1920 New York (NL) - McGraw, Kelly, Bancroft, Frisch, Youngs, Toney, Nehf, Barnes $1700-$2750
1920 Philadelphia (AL) - Mack .....$600-$850
1920 Philadelphia (NL) - Stengel, Williams, Meusel, Wheat, Rixey ....$800-$1300
1920 Pittsburgh - Carey, McKechnie, Traynor, Cooper ....$675-$1000
1920 St. Louis (AL) - Sisler, Tobin, Jacobson, Williams, Shocker ....$425-$675
1920 St. Louis (NL) - Rickey, Fournier, Hornsby, Stock, Doak, Haines ....$1150-$1750
1920 Washington - Griffith, Judge, Harris, Rice, Milan, Johnson ....$1300-$2000
1921 Boston (AL) - Duffy, McInnis, Pratt, Leibold, Menosky, Jones, Pennock ...$550-$875
1921 Boston (NL) - Barbare, Boeckel, Southworth, Powell, Cruise, Oeschger .....$400-$600
1921 Brooklyn - Robinson, Schmandt, Johnston, Griffith, Wheat, Grimes ....$800-$1200
1921 Chicago (AL) - Sheely, Collins, Hooper, Strunk, Schalk, Faber ....$725-$1100
1921 Chicago (NL) - Evers, Grimes, Flack, Maisel, Barber, Alexander ....$1200-$1800
1921 Cincinnati - Daubert, Groh, Bressler, Roush, Duncan, Rixey, Marquard ....$550-$825
1921 Cleveland - Speaker, Sewell, Gardner, Jamieson, ONeill, Coveleski ....$725-$1200
1921 Detroit - Cobb, Blue, Heilmann, Veach, Bassler, Jones ....$800-$1200
1921 New York (AL) - Huggins, Ward, Baker, Meusel, Ruth, Mays, Hoyt ....$3000-$6000
1921 New York (NL) - McGraw, Kelly, Bancroft, Frisch, Youngs, Meusel, Snyder, Stengel, Nehf ... .$2000-$3000
1921 Philadelphia (AL) - Mack, Witt, T. Walker ....$500-$775
1921 Philadelphia (NL) - Konetchy, Williams, Meusel, Bruggy, Stengel ....$400-$600
1921 Pittsburgh - Cuthsaw, Maranville, Carey, Bigbee, Traynor, Cuyler, Cooper ....$800-$1200
1921 St. Louis (AL) - Sisler, Tobin, Jacobson, Williams, Severeid, Shocker ....$425-$625
1921 St. Louis (NL) - Rickey, Fournier, Hornsby, Stock, Smith, Mann,McHenry, Clemons, Dillhoefer, Haines, Doak ....$1075-$1600
1921 Washington - Judge, Harris, Shanks, Rice, Gharrity, Goslin, Johnson .....$1000-$1500
1922 Boston (AL) - Duffy, Burns, Pratt, Harris, Pennock ....$500-$750
1922 Boston (NL) - Marquard ......$400-$575

1922 Brooklyn - Johnston, Robinson, Myers, Wheat, DeBerry, Ruether, Vance, Grimes, T. Griffith ....$1000-$1500
1922 Chicago (AL) - Sheely, Collins, Hooper, Mostil, Schalk, Evers, Faber ....$1200-$1750
1922 Chicago (NL) - Grimes, Hollocher, Friberg, Miller, O'Farrell, Hartnett, Alexander$800-$1200
1922 Cincinnati - Daubert, Pinelli, Harper, Duncan, Hargrave, Roush, Rixey ....$450-$700
1922 Cleveland - Speaker, McGinnis, Sewell, Uhle, Jamieson, O'Neill, Coveleski ..$675-$1000
1922 Detroit - Cobb, Blue, Rigney, Heilmann, Veach, Bassler ....$800-$1200
1922 New York (AL) - Pipp, Meusel, Ruth, Schang, Baker, Bush, Shawkey, Hoyt, Huggins .. ..$2000-$3000
1922 New York (NL) - McGraw, Kelly, Frisch, Bancroft, Youngs, Stengel, Meusel, Snyder, Jackson, Nehf ....$2000-$3000
1922 Philadelphia (AL) - Mack, Hauser, Galloway, Rommel, Miller ....$500-$750
1922 Philadelphia (NL) - Walker, Williams, Lee, Henline ....$325-$500
1922 Pittsburgh - McKechnie, Tierney, Carey, Maranville, Traynor, Russell, Bigbee, Gooch, Cuyler, Cooper ....$1100-$1600
1922 St. Louis (AL) - Sisler, McManus, Tobin, Jacobson, Williams, Severeid, Shocker $400-$650
1922 St. Louis (NL) - Rickey, Hornsby, Toporcer, Stock, Smith, Schultz, Bottomley, Haines ....$1350-$2000
1922 Washington - Harris, Rice, Goslin, Johnson ....$900-$1400
1923 Boston (AL) - Burns, Flagstead, Harris, Ehmke, Chance ....$900-$1400
1923 Boston (NL) - McInnis, Southworth, Powell, Marquard ....$375-$550
1923 Brooklyn - Robinson, Fournier, Johnston, Wheat, Grimes, Vance ....1100-$1600
1923 Chicago (AL) - Collins, Hooper, Falk, Schalk, Faber, Lyons ....$750-$1200
1923 Chicago (NL) - Grimes, Friberg, Statz, Miller, O'Farrell, Hartnett, Alexander, Aldridge . ...$800-$1000
1923 Cincinnati - Roush, Duncan, Hargrave, Luque, Rixey ....$400-$600
1923 Cleveland - Speaker, Sewell, Summa, Jamieson, Uhle, Coveleski ....$800-$1200
1923 Detroit - Cobb, Rigney, Heilmann, Manush, Daus ....$900-$1500
1923 New York (AL) - Huggins, Pipp, Ruth, Witt, Meusel, Gehrig, Pennock, Hoyt ....$2500-$3750
1923 New York (NL) - McGraw, Kelly, Frisch, Bancroft, Youngs, Jackson, Stengel, Terry, Wilson, Ryan ....$2100-$3150
1923 Philadelphia (AL) - Mack, Hauser ....$475-$700
1923 Philadelphia (NL) - Holke, Tierney, Mokan, Henline ....$300-$450
1923 Pittsburgh - McKechnie, Grimm, Maranville, Traynor, Barnhart, Carey, Cuyler, Morrison ....$1000-$1500
1923 St. Louis (AL) - McManus, Tobin, Jacobson, Williams, Severeid, Shocker ....$350-$525
1923 St. Louis (NL) - Rickey, Bottomley, Hornsby, Myers, Smith, Haines ....$1200-$1800
1923 Washington - Judge, Harris, Rice, Leibold, Goslin, Ruel, Johnson ....$900-$1400
1924 Boston (AL) - Harris, Boone, Flagstead, Ruffing ....$350-$525
1924 Boston (NL) - Stengel, Bancroft, Marquard ....$700-$900
1924 Brooklyn - Robinson, Fournier, High,

Brown, Wheat, Grimes, Vance ....$1000-$1500
1924 Chicago (AL) - Evers, Sheely, Collins, Hooper, Mostil, Falk, Schalk, Thurston, Lyons, Faber ....$1300-$1800
1924 Chicago (NL) - Grantham, Heathcote, Hartnett, Alexander ....$725-$1200
1924 Cincinnati - Critz, Pinelli, Walker, Roush, Mays, Rixey ....$400-$600
1924 Cleveland - Speaker, Burns, Sewell, Jamieson, Myatt, Shaute, Coveleski ..$800-$1000
1924 Detroit - Cobb, Blue, Pratt, Heilmann, Manush, Bassler, Gehringer ......$1000-$1550
1924 New York (AL) - Huggins, Dugan, Ruth, Meusel, Combs, Gehrig, Pennock, Hoyt ....$3000-$4500
1924 New York (NL) - McGraw, Kelly, Frisch, Jackson, Youngs, Wilson, Snyder, Terry, Lindstrom, Bentley ....$1900-$2900
1924 Philadelphia (AL) - Miller, Simmons, Lamar ....$600-$1000
1924 Philadelphia (NL) - Holke, Wrightstone, Williams ....$300-$450
1924 Pittsburgh - McKechnie, Maranville, Traynor, Carey, Cuyler, Cooper ...$800-$1225
1924 St. Louis (AL) - Sisler, McManus, Robertson, Jacobson, Williams, Severeid ....$400-$600
1924 St. Louis (NL) - Rickey, Bottomley, Hornsby, Blades, Hafey ....$1300-$1800
1924 Washington - Harris, Judge, Rice, Goslin, Johnson ....$1000-$1500
1925 Boston (AL) - Prothro, Boone, Carlyle, Ruffing ....$300-$500
1925 Boston (NL) - Bancroft, Burrus, Welsh, Felix, Stengel, Marquard ....$600-$900
1925 Brooklyn - Robinson, Fournier, Stock, Cox, Brown, Wheat, Taylor, Vance, Grimes ....$900-$1500
1925 Chicago (AL) - Collins, Sheely, Hooper, Falk, Schalk, Lyons, Faber, Bender ..$900-$1500
1925 Chicago (NL) - Maranville, Grimm, Freigau, Jahn, Hartnett, Alexander ..$800-$1200
1925 Cincinnati- Walker, Roush, Hargrave, Rixey ....$350-$575
1925 Cleveland - Speaker, Burns, Sewell, McNulty, Buckeye ....$550-$925
1925 Detroit - Cobb, Blue, Heilmann, Wingo, Manush, Gehringer ....$900-$1300
1925 New York (AL) - Huggins, Gehrig, Ruth, Hoyt, Pennock, Durocher ......$2750-$4175
1925 New York (NL) - McGraw, Terry, Kelly, Jackson, Lindstrom, Youngs, Meusel, Frisch, Wilson ....$1800-$2700
1925 Philadelphia (AL) - Mack, Hale, Miller, Simmons, Lamar, Cochrane, Foxx, Rommel, Grove ....$1400-$2100
1925 Philadelphia (NL) - Hawks, Williams, Harper ....$300-$475
1925 Pittsburgh - McKechnie, Grantham, Wright, Traynor, Cuyler, Carey, Barnhart, Smith, Meadows ....$800-$1200
1925 St. Louis (AL) - Sisler, Rice, Jacobson, Williams ....$375-$600
1925 St. Louis (NL) - Rickey, Bottomley, Hornsby, Hafey, Mueller, Blades, Haines ....$1300-$2000
1925 Washington - Harris, Judge, Rice, Goslin, Johnson, Coveleski ....$1000-$1500
1926 Boston (AL) - Jacobson, Ruffing ....$300-$475
1926 Boston (NL) - Bancroft, J. Smith, Brown . ...$325-$525
1926 Brooklyn - Robinson, Herman, Wheat, Maranville, Carey, Grimes, Vance .$1200-$1800
1926 Chicago - McCarthy, Adams, Wilson,

1926 St. Louis Cardinals

Stephenson, Hartnett, Alexander . . .$900-$1400
1926 Chicago (AL) - Collins, Barrett, Mostil, Falk, Schalk, Lyons, Faber . . . .$600-$900
1926 Cincinnati - Walker, Roush, Donahue, Rixey . . . .$325-$575
1926 Cleveland - Speaker, Burns, J. Sewell, Summa, Uhle . . . .$600-$900
1926 Detroit - Cobb, Gehringer, Heilmann, Manush, Fothergill . . . .$800-$1200
1926 New York (AL) - Huggins, Gehrig, Lazzeri, Ruth, Combs, Meusel, Pennock, Hoyt . . . .$3500-$5000
1926 New York (NL) - McGraw, Kelly, Frisch, Jackson, Lindstrom, Youngs, Terry, Ott . . . .$1800-$2750
1926 Philadelphia (AL) - Mack, French, Simmons, Cochrane, Foxx . . . .$1300-$2100
1926 Philadelphia (NL) - Williams, Leach, Mokan, Wilson . . . .$250-$400
1926 Pittsburgh - McKechnie, Grantham, Wright, Traynor, Waner, Carey, Cuyler, Smith, Cronin, Kremer, Meadows . . . .$800-$1200
1926 St. Louis (AL) - Sisler, Miller, Rice, Shang . . . .$350-$500
1926 St. Louis (NL) - Hornsby, Bottomley, Bell, Southworth, Douthit, Blades, Hafey, Rhem, Haines, Alexander . . . .$1600-$2300
1926 Washington - Harris, Myer, Rice, McNeely, Goslin, Johnson, Coveleski . . . .$800-$1200
1927 Boston (AL) - Tobin, Ruffing . .$300-$450
1927 Boston (NL) - Bancroft, High, Richbourg, Brown . . . .$300-$450
1927 Brooklyn - Robinson, Carey, Vance . . . .$800-$1200
1927 Chicago (AL) - Schalk, Clancy, Metzler, Falk, Lyons, Faber . . . .$350-$550
1927 Chicago (NL) - McCarthy, Grimm, Webb, Wilson, Stephenson, Hartnett, Root .$500-$800
1927 Cincinnati - Hargrave, Kelly, Rixey . . . .$300-$450
1927 Cleveland - Burns, Fonseca, J. Sewell, Jamieson, Miller . . . .$300-$450
1927 Detroit - Gehringer, Heilmann, Manush, Fothergill, Collins . . . .$375-$625
1927 New York (AL) - Gehrig, Lazzeri, Ruth, Combs, Meusel, Hoyt, Moore, Pennock . . . .$8000-$16000
1927 New York (NL) - McGraw, Terry, Hornsby, Jackson, Lindstrom, Harper, Roush, Grimes . . . .$1800-$2700
1927 Philadelphia (AL) - Mack, Dykes, Hale, Cobb, Simmons, French, Cochrane, Collins, Wheat, Foxx, Grove . . . .$2200-$3300
1927 Philadelphia (NL) - Wrightstone, Thompson, Leach . . . .$275-$400
1927 Pittsburgh - Harris, Grantham, Traynor, P. Waner, L. Waner, Barnhart, Cuyler, Groh, Cronin, Kremer . . . .$700-$1000

1927 St. Louis (AL) - Sisler, Miller, Williams, Schang . . . .$400-$650
1927 St. Louis (NL) - Bottomley, Frisch, Maranville, Haines, Alexander . . . .$1200-$1750
1927 Washington - Harris, Judge, Rice, Speaker, Goslin, Ruel, Lisenbee, Hadley, Johnson, Coveleski . . . .$1200-$1800
1928 Boston (AL) - Myer, Williams, Ruffing . . . .$300-$475
1928 Boston (NL) - Hornsby, Sisler, Richbourg . . . .$800-$1200
1928 Brooklyn - Robinson, Bissonette, Bancroft, Hendrick, Herman, Carey, Lopez, Vance . . . .$1000-$1400
1928 Chicago (AL) - Schalk, Kamm, Metzler, Lyons, Walsh, Faber . . . .$500-$775
1928 Chicago (NL) - McCarthy, Cuyler, Wilson, Stephenson, Hartnett . . . .$450-$725
1928 Cincinnati - Kelly, Allen, Rixey .$300-$425
1928 Cleveland - Fonseca, Sewell, Hodapp, Jamieson . . . .$300-$425
1928 Detroit - Gehringer, Heilmann, Rice . . . .$325-$500
1928 New York (AL) - Huggins, Gehrig, Lazzeri, Koenig, Ruth, Combs, Dickey, Pipgras, Hoyt, Pennock, Coveleski . . . .$3500-$5000
1928 New York (NL) - McGraw, Terry, Jackson, Lindstrom, Ott, Welsh, ODoul, Hogan, Roush, Benton, Fitzsimmons, Hubbell . . . .$1300-$1750
1928 Philadelphia (AL) - Mack, Bishop, Hale, Cobb, Miller, Simmons, Cochrane, Foxx, Speaker, Collins, Grove, Quinn . . . .$2000-$3000
1928 Philadelphia (NL) - Whitney, Klein, Leach . . . .$300-$500
1928 Pittsburgh - Grantham, Wright, Traynor, P. Waner, L. Waner, Brickell, Grimes . . .$500-$750
1928 St. Louis (AL) - Manush, Crowder . . . .$300-$450
1928 St. Louis (NL) - McKechnie, Bottomley, Frisch, Maranville, Hafey, Haines, Alexander . . . .$1200-$1800
1928 Washington - Harris, Judge, Reeves, Rice, Barnes, Goslin, Cronin, Sisler, Jones . .$500-$750
1929 Boston (AL) - Rothrock, Ruffing . . . .$250-$350
1929 Boston (NL) - Sisler, Maranville, Richbourg, Clark, Evers . . . .$700-$1200
1929 Brooklyn - Robinson, Bancroft, Gilbert, Herman, Frederick, Bressler, Carey, Vance . . . .$850-$1300
1929 Chicago (AL) - Shires, Reynolds, Lyons, Faber . . . .$275-$450
1929 Chicago (NL) - McCarthy, Hornsby, Cuyler, Wilson, Hartnett, Malone . . . .$800-$1200
1929 Cincinnati - Kelly, Dressen, Swanson, Gooch, Rixey . . . .$275-$425
1929 Cleveland - Fonseca, Hodapp, Sewell, Falk, Averill, Sewell, Ferrell . . . .$300-$500
1929 Detroit - Harris, Alexander, Gehringer, Heilmann, Rice, Johnson . . . .$300-$500
1929 New York (AL) - Huggins, Gehrig, Lazzeri, Ruth, Combs, Dickey, Wells, Hoyt, Pennock . . . .$2800-$4250
1929 New York (NL) - McGraw, Terry, Jackson, Lindstrom, Ott, Roush, Hubbell . . .$1000-$1600
1929 Philadelphia (AL) - Mack, Foxx, Miller, Haas, Simmons, Cochrane, Cronin, Collins, Earnshaw, Grove . . . .$800-$1200
1929 Philadelphia (NL) - Hurst, Thompson, Thevenow, Whitney, Klein, Sothern, O'Doul . . . .$300-$450
1929 Pittsburgh - Grantham, Bartell, Traynor, P. Waner, L. Waner, Comorosky, Grimes $500-$800
1929 St. Louis (AL) - Kress, Schulte, Manush,

1931 Philadelphia Athletics

Ferrell . . . .$325-$550
1929 St. Louis (NL) - McKechnie, Bottomley, Frisch, Orsatti, Douthit, Hafey, Wilson, Johnson, Haines, Alexander . . . .$900-$1400
1929 Washington - Johnson, Judge, Myer, Cronin, Rice, Goslin . . . .$1300-$1850
1930 Boston (AL) - Webb, Ruffing . .$225-$350
1930 Boston (NL) - McKechnie, Sisler, Maranville, Grimes . . . .$450-$750
1930 Brooklyn - Robinson, Bissonette, Wright, Herman, Frederick, Lopez, Vance . . .$650-$1200
1930 Chicago (AL) - Watwood, Jolley, Reynolds, Lyons, Appling, Faber . . . .$250-$400
1930 Chicago (NL) - McCarthy, Grimm, Cuyler, Wilson, Hartnett, Hornsby, Kelly . . .$900-$1450
1930 Cincinnati - Durocher, Cuccinello, Heilmann, Walker, Kelly, Rixey . . . .$900-$1450
1930 Cleveland - Morgan, Hodapp, J. Sewell, Porter, Averill, Jamieson, L. Sewell, Ferrell . . . .$300-$475
1930 Detroit - Harris, Alexander, Gehringer, McManus, Stone, Hoyt, Greenberg ..$300-$475
1930 New York (AL) - Gehrig, Lazzeri, Chapman, Ruth, Hoyt, Combs, Ruffing, Gomez, Pennock, Dickey . . . .$2500-$3750
1930 New York (NL) - McGraw, Terry, Jackson, Lindstrom, Ott, Leach, Hogan, Bancroft, Roush, Hubbell . . . .$1200-$1800
1930 Philadelphia (AL) - Mack, Foxx, Dykes, Miller, Simmons, Cochrane, Collins, Grove . . . .$700-$1000
1930 Philadelphia (NL) - Hurst, Whitney, O'Doul, Davis, Alexander, Klein . . . . .$500-$700
1930 Pittsburgh - Grantham, Bartell, Traynor, P. Waner, L. Waner, Comorosky . . . . . .$450-$700
1930 St. Louis (AL) - Kress, Goslin, Ferrell, Manush . . . .$375-$575
1930 St. Louis (NL) - Street, Bottomley, Frisch, Gelbert, Adams, Watkins, Douthit, Hafey, Wilson, Grimes, Haines, Dean . . . .$700-$1000
1930 Washington - Johnson, Judge, Myer, Cronin, Rice, Manush, Goslin, Marberry . . . .$1500-$2250
1931 Boston (AL) - Webb . . . .$200-$300
1931 Boston (NL) - Maranville, Schulmerich, Berger, McKechnie . . . .$300-$500
1931 Brooklyn - O'Doul, Lopez, Lombardi, Vance, Robinson . . . .$800-$1200
1931 Chicago (AL) - Blue, Appling, Faber, Lyons . . . .$250-$375
1931 Chicago (NL) - Grimm, Hornsby, English, Cuyler, Wilson, Taylor, Hartnett, Herman . . . .$750-$1200
1931 Cincinnati - Hendrick, Cuccinello, Stripp, Roush, Heilmann, Rixey . . . .$325-$500
1931 Cleveland - Morgan, Porter, Averill . . . .$250-$375
1931 Detroit - Alexander, Gehringer, Rogell,

1932 New York Yankees

Stone, Hoyt, Harris ....$300-$500
1931 New York (AL) - Gehrig, Lazzeri, Sewell, Ruth, Combs, Chapman, Dickey, Ruffing, Gomez, Pennock, McCarthy ....$3000-$4500
1931 New York (NL) - Terry, Jackson, Lindstrom, Ott, Leach, Hogan, Walker, Hubbell, McGraw ....$1000-$1500
1931 Philadelphia (AL) - Mack, Foxx, Simmons, Cochrane, Grove, Earnshaw, Hoyt ..$700-$1000
1931 Philadelphia (NL) - Hurst, Mallon, Arlett, Klein, Davis ....$300-$450
1931 Pittsburgh - Grantham, Traynor, Waner, Waner ....$425-$700
1931 St. Louis (AL) - Melillo, Kress, Schulte, Goslin, Ferrell ....$300-$450
1931 St. Louis (NL) - Bottomley, Frisch, Hafey, Hallahan, Grimes, Haines ....$550-$900
1931 Washington - Cronin, Rice, West, Manush, Crowder, Marberry, Johnson ....$1200-$1800
1932 Boston (AL) - Alexander, Jolley, Morris .. ..$225-$350
1932 Boston (NL) - Maranville, Berger, Worthington, McKechnie ....$300-$450
1932 Brooklyn - Kelly, Wright, Stripp, Wilson, Taylor, O'Doul, Lopez, Clark, Vance, Hoyt, Carey ....$600-$950
1932 Chicago (AL) - Appling, Lyons, Faber ....$325-$500
1932 Chicago (NL) - Grimm, Herman, Cuyler, Moore, Stephenson, Hartnett, Hornsby, Warneke, Grimes ....$700-$1000
1932 Cincinnati - Hendrick, Durocher, Herman, Lombardi, Hafey, Heilmann, Frey ....$450-$750
1932 Cleveland - Cissell, Porter, Averill, Vosmik ....$250-$375
1932 Detroit - Gehringer, Walker, Harris ....$300-$500
1932 New York (AL) - Gehrig, Lazzeri, Sewell, Ruth, Combs, Dickey, Ruffing, Gomez, Allen, Pennock, McCarthy ....$1750-$4000
1932 New York (NL) - Terry, Ott, Lindstrom, McGraw, Hogan, Jackson, Jo-Jo Moore, Hoyt, Hubbell ....$900-$1325
1932 Philadelphia (AL) - Cramer, Haas, Simmons, Cochrane, Grove, Mack ...$500-$750
1932 Philadelphia (NL) - Hurst, Bartell, Klein, Davis, Lee, Davis ....$300-$425
1932 Pittsburgh - Vaughn, Traynor, Waner, Waner ....$525-$750
1932 St. Louis (AL) - Burns, Scharien, Goslin, Ferrell ....$300-$450
1932 St. Louis (NL) - Watkins, Martin, Orsatti, Frisch, Bottomley, Medwick, Dean, Haines ....$500-$700
1932 Washington - Cronin, Reynolds, Manush, Rice, Crowder, Johnson ....$1200-$1800
1933 Boston (AL) - Hodapp, Johnson, Ferrell .. ..$250-$375

1933 Boston (NL) - Maranville, Moore, Cantwell, McKechnie ....$300-$450
1933 Brooklyn - Wright, Frederick, Wilson, Lopez, Mungo, Carey ....$700-$1000
1933 Chicago (AL) - Appling, Swanson, Simmons, Lyons, Faber ....$375-$575
1933 Chicago (NL) - Grimm, Stephenson, Hartnett, Cuyler, Bush, Grimes, Billy Herman ....$400-$600
1933 Cincinnati - Bottomley, Hafey, Lombardi, Durocher, Rixey ....$400-$600
1933 Cleveland - Averill, Johnson ..$800-$1200
1933 Detroit - Greenberg, Gehringer, Harris ... .$375-$600
1933 New York (AL) - Gehrig, Lazzeri, Sewell, Ruth, Combs, Chapman, Dickey, Gomez, Allen, Ruffing, Pennock, McCarthy ......$2800-$4200
1933 New York (NL) - Terry, Ott, Jackson, Hubbell ....$750-$1000
1933 Philadelphia (AL) - Foxx, Higgins, Cochrane, Grove, Mack ....$400-$600
1933 Philadelphia (NL) - Klein, Fullis, Schulmerich, Davis ....$300-$450
1933 Pittsburgh - Piet, Vaughan, Traynor, Waner, Lindstrom, Waner, Hoyt .....$575-$900
1933 St. Louis (AL) - West, Ferrell, Hornsby .. ..$450-$675
1933 St. Louis (NL) - Collins, Frisch, Durocher, Martin, Medwick, Hornsby, Haines, Dean, Vance, Grimes ....$900-$1500
1933 Washington - Kuhel, Myer, Cronin, Goslin, Manush, Rice, Crowder, Whitehill ...$475-$725
1934 Boston (AL) - Harris, Reynolds, Johnson, R. Ferrell, W. Ferrell, Grove, Pennock $375-$525
1934 Boston (NL) - McKechnie, Jordan, Maranville, Frankhouse ....$325-$450
1934 Brooklyn - Stengel, Leslie, Stripp, Boyle, Koenecke, Lopez, Mungo ....$250-$500
1934 Chicago (AL) - Appling, Simmons, Conlan ....$400-$575
1934 Chicago (NL) - Grimm, Billy Herman, Hack, Cuyler, Klein, Hartnett ....$325-$600
1934 Cincinnati - Bottomley, Hafey, Lombardi . ...$300-$525
1934 Cleveland - Johnson, Trosky, Hale, Knickerbocker, Averill, Vosmik, Harder ..$775-$1250
1934 Detroit - Cochrane, Greenberg, Gehringer, Fox, Goslin, Rowe, Bridges ....$525-$800
1934 New York (AL) - McCarthy, Gomez, Lazzeri, Dickey, Gehrig, Ruffing, Grimes, Ruth, Combs ....$2600-$3900
1934 New York (NL) - Terry, Jackson, Ott, Hubbell ....$400-$575
1934 Philadelphia (AL) - Mack, Foxx, Higgins, Cramer, Johnson ....$300-$500
1934 Philadelphia (NL) - Chiozza, Bartell, J. Moore, Allen, Todd ....$200-$300
1934 Pittsburgh - Traynor, Vaughan, P. Waner, L. Waner, Lindstrom, Hoyt, Grimes ....`$550-$875
1934 St. Louis (AL) - Hornsby, West, Hemsley . ...$400-$675
1934 St. Louis (NL) - Frisch, Collins, Durocher, Martin, Orsatti, Medwick, Davis, Dean, Haines, Grimes, Vance ....$575-$900
1934 Washington - Cronin, Manush .$275-$450
1935 Boston (AL) - Cronin, Cooke, R. Johnson, R. Ferrell, W. Ferrell, Grove ......$300-$500
1935 Boston (NL) - McKechnie, Lee, Ruth, Maranville ....$1000-$1500
1935 Brooklyn - Stengel, Leslie, Stripp, Lopez .. ..$300-$475
1935 Chicago (AL) - Appling, Simmons, Conlan, Lyons, Stratton ....$375-$575
1935 Chicago (NL) - Grimm, Herman, Lee, Klein, Demaree, Galan, Hartnett, Cuyler, Lindstrom, Hack ....$500-$750
1935 Cincinnati - Bottomley, Herman, Lombardi, Cuyler, Hafey, Derringer ....$350-$575
1935 Cleveland - Johnson, Averill ..$700-$1200
1935 Detroit - Cochrane, Greenberg, Gehringer, Goslin ....$500-$750
1935 New York (AL) - McCarthy, Gehrig, Lazzeri, Dickey, Combs, Ruffing, Gomez ....$1300-$2000
1935 New York (NL) - Terry, Jackson, Ott, Leiber, Hubbell ....$475-$800
1935 Philadelphia (AL) - Mack, Foxx, Moses, Cramer ....$300-$450
1935 Philadelphia (NL) - Moore, Allen ....$500-$1000
1935 Pittsburgh - Traynor, Vaughan, P. Waner, L. Waner, Hoyt ....$500-$700
1935 St. Louis (AL) - Hornsby, West, Solters, Andrews ....$450-$675
1935 St. Louis (NL) - Frisch, Collins, Durocher, Martin, Medwick, Haines, P. Dean, D. Dean ....$350-$575
1935 Washington - Harris, Myer, Travis, Powell, Manush, Bolton ....$250-$375
1936 Boston (AL) - Cronin, Foxx, R. Ferrell, Hanush, Grove ....$400-$600
1936 Boston (NL) - McKechnie, Jordan, Cuccinello, Lopez ....$250-$350
1936 Brooklyn - Stengel, Hassett, Stripp, Bordagaray, Lindstrom ....$275-$425
1936 Chicago (AL) - Appling, Lyons, Stratton . $250-$400
1936 Chicago (NL) - Grimm, Herman, Demaree, Hartnett, Klein, French ....$300-$450
1936 Cincinnati - Scarsella, Cuyler, Lombardi, Hafey ....$275-$450
1936 Cleveland - Trosky, Hale, Weatherly, Averill, Sullivan, Allen ....$200-$325
1936 Detroit - Cochrane, Gehringer, Simmons, Goslin, Greenberg ....$400-$575
1936 New York (AL) - McCarthy, Gehrig, Lazzeri, DiMaggio, Dickey, Ruffing, Gomez ....$1150-$1750
1936 New York (NL) - Terry, Jackson, Ott, Moore, Mancuso, Hubbell ....$450-$700
1936 Philadelphia (AL) - Mack, Finney, Moses . ...$250-$375
1936 Philadelphia (NL) - Camilli, Klein, Moore ....$200-$300
1936 Pittsburgh - Traynor, Suhr, Vaughan, P. Waner, L. Waner, Hoyt ....$425-$700
1936 St. Louis (AL) - Hornsby, Bottomley, Clift, Bell ....$450-$725
1936 St. Louis (NL) - Frisch, Mize, Durocher, Martin, Alston, Dean, Haines ......$425-$675
1936 Washington - Harris, Travis, Chapman, Stone ....$200-$350
1937 Boston (AL) - Foxx, Cronin, Higgins, Chapman, Cramer, Doerr, Ferrell, Grove ....$450-$550
1937 Boston (NL) - Lopez, McKechnie ....$200-$350
1937 Brooklyn - Hassett, Manush, Phelps, Hoyt, Grimes ....$350-$500
1937 Chicago (AL) - Appling, Stratton, Lyons . ...$250-$425
1937 Chicago (NL) - Herman, Demaree, Hartnett, Carleton, Grimm ....$275-$400
1937 Cincinnati - Wallace, Hafey, Cuyler, Lombardi ....$350-$500
1937 Cleveland - Campbell, Sotters, Pytlak, Feller, Averill ....$225-$375
1937 Detroit - Greenberg, Gehringer, Goslin,

1936 New York Yankees

Cochrane . . . . $400-$700
1937 New York (AL) - Gehrig, Lazzeri, DiMaggio, Dickey, Gomez, Ruffing, McCarthy . . . . $1450-$2500
1937 New York (NL) - Bartell, Ott, Ripple, Moore, Hubbell, Melton, Terry . . . . . $400-$600
1937 Philadelphia (AL) - Moses, Johnson, Mack $225-$375
1937 Philadelphia (NL) - Camilli, Whitney, Klein . . . . $200-$300
1937 Pittsburgh - Vaughan, Waner, Waner, Todd, Traynor, Hoyt . . . . $425-$650
1937 St. Louis (AL) - Clift, Bell, West, Vosmik, Hornsby, Bottomley . . . . $425-$650
1937 St. Louis (NL) - Mize, Durocher, Padgett, Medwick, Martin, Frisch, Dean, Haines $375-$600
1937 Washington (AL) - Travis, Lewis, Stone, Almada, Simmons, R. Ferrell, Harris . $300-$425
1938 Boston (AL) - Foxx, Doerr, Cronin, Higgins, Chapman, Cramer, Vosmik, Grove . . . . $550-$900
1938 Boston (NL) - Stengel, Lopez, MacFayden . . . . $350-$575
1938 Brooklyn - Grimes, Durocher, Phelps, Cuyler, Manush, Hoyt . . . . $2000-$2750
1938 Chicago (AL) - Hayes, Appling, Steinbacher, Walker, Stratton . . . . $250-$450
1938 Chicago (NL) - Herman, Hack, Reynolds, Hartnett, Garbark, Lee, Grimm, Dean, Lazzeri . . . . $800-$1000
1938 Cincinnati - McKechnie, McCormick, Berger, Lombardi, Derringer, Vander Meer . . . . $250-$400
1938 Cleveland - Trosky, Averill, Heath, Pytlak, Boudreau, Feller . . . . $250-$400
1938 Detroit - Cochrane, Greenberg, Gehringer, Walker, Bridges . . . . $400-$700
1938 New York (AL) - McCarthy, Gehrig, DiMaggio, Dickey, Ruffing, Gomez . . $900-$1200
1938 New York (NL) - Terry, Ott, Moore, Danning, Hubbell . . . . $350-$550
1938 Philadelphia (AL) - Mack, Moses, Johnson $400-$600
1938 Philadelphia (NL) - Weintraub $250-$325
1938 Pittsburgh - Traynor, Vaughan, Waner, Waner, Rizzo, Manush, Brown . . . . . . $700-$1000
1938 St. Louis (AL) - McQuinn, Kress, Almada . . . . $200-$300
1938 St. Louis (NL) - Frisch, Mize, Slaughter, Medwick, Martin . . . . $400-$650
1938 Washington - Harris, Myer, Travis, Case, Simmons, Ferrell, Goslin, Ferrell . . . . $300-$475
1939 Boston (AL) - Cronin, Foxx, Doerr, Williams, Cramer, Grove . . . . $450-$650
1939 Boston (NL) - Stengel, Hassett, Cuccinello, Lopez, Simmons . . . . $300-$450
1939 Brooklyn - Durocher, Lazzeri . . . . $250-$450

1939 Chicago (AL) - Kuhel, Appling, McNair, Lyons . . . . $200-$350
1939 Chicago (NL) - Hartnett, Herman, Leiber, Galan, Hartnett, Dean . . . . $275-$400
1939 Cincinnati - McKechnie, McCormick, Goodman, Lombardi, Simmons, Walters, Derringer . . . . $325-$500
1939 Cleveland - Trosky, Hale, Keltner, Boudreau, Feller . . . . $225-$350
1939 Detroit - Greenberg, Gehringer, McCosky, Averill, Bridges . . . . $300-$500
1939 New York (AL) - McCarthy, Rolfe, Keller, DiMaggio, Selkirk, Dickey, Ruffing, Gehring, Gomez . . . . $750-$1400
1939 New York (NL) - Terry, Bonura, Ott, Demaree, Danning, Lazzeri, Hubbell . . $325-$550
1939 Philadelphia (AL) - Mack, Moses, Johnson, Collins . . . . $300-$400
1939 Philadelphia (NL) - Suhr, Arnovich, Davis $175-$275
1939 Pittsburgh - Traynor, Fletcher, Vaughan, P. Waner, L. Waner, Manush . . . . $500-$1000
1939 St. Louis (AL) - McQuinn, Laabs . . . . $200-$300
1939 St. Louis (NL) - Mize, Slaughter, Medwick, P. Martin . . . . $375-$550
1939 Washington - Harris, Vernon, Lewis, Case, Wright, Ferrell, Leonard . . . . $200-$300
1940 Boston (AL) - Cronin, Foxx, Doerr, Williams, Wilson, Grove . . . . $600-$1000
1940 Boston (NL) - Stengel, Rowell, Cooney, Lopez . . . . $500-$750
1940 Brooklyn - Durocher, Reese, Medwick . . . . $450-$600
1940 Chicago (AL) - Appling, Wright, Solters, Lyons . . . . $200-$300
1940 Chicago (NL) - Hartnett, Herman, Dean . . . . $200-$300
1940 Cincinnati - McKechnie, F. McCormick, Lombardi . . . . $350-$550
1940 Cleveland - Boudreau, Weatherly, Feller, Smith . . . . $200-$300
1940 Detroit - York, Gehringer, McCosky, Greenberg, Averill, Newsom . . . . $500-$750
1940 New York (AL) - McCarthy, DiMaggio, Dickey, Ruffing, Gomez . . . . $450-$700
1940 New York (NL) - Terry, Ott, Demaree, Danning, Hubbell . . . . $400-$600
1940 Philadelphia (AL) - Mack, Moses, Hayes, Simmons . . . . $400-$750
1940 Philadelphia (NL) - . . . . $250-$400
1940 Pittsburgh - Frisch, Vaughan, P. Waner, L. Waner, Lopez . . . . $500-$1000
1940 St. Louis (AL) - Judnich, Radcliff . . . . $175-$275
1940 St. Louis (NL) - Mize, Slaughter, P. Martin, Medwick . . . . $325-$475
1940 Washington - Harris, Lewis, Ferrell, Vernon . . . . $200-$325
1941 Boston (AL) - Cronin, Foxx, Doerr, DiMaggio, Williams, Grove . . . . $500-$675
1941 Boston (NL) - Cooney, Waner, Stengel . . . . $300-$400
1941 Brooklyn - Durocher, Camilli, Herman, Reese, Medwick, Waner . . . . $750-$1250
1941 Chicago (AL) - Appling, Lyons $225-$350
1941 Chicago (NL) - Hack, Herman, Dean . . . . $175-$300
1941 Cincinnati - McKechnie, Lombardi, Waner . . . . $400-$600
1941 Cleveland - Boudreau, Heath, Lemon, Feller . . . . $200-$400
1941 Detroit - Gehringer, McCosky, Radcliff, Greenberg, Benton . . . . $450-$700

1941 Brooklyn Dodgers

1941 New York (AL) - McCarthy, Rizzuto, DiMaggio, Dickey, Gomez, Ruffing . . $800-$1200
1941 New York (NL) - Terry, Bartell, Ott, Hubbell . . . . $525-$600
1941 Philadelphia (AL) - Mack, Siebert, Moses, Chapman, Collins, Simmons . . . . $325-$500
1941 Philadelphia (NL) - Litwhiler, Etten . . . . $400-$500
1941 Pittsburgh - Frisch, Vaughan, Lopez, Waner . . . . $700-$800
1941 St. Louis (AL) - Ferrell . . . . . . $200-$325
1941 St. Louis (NL) - Mize, Brown, Slaughter, Hopp, Musial . . . . $300-$450
1941 Washington - Harris, Vernon, Travis, Ferrell, Wynn . . . . $225-$350
1942 Boston (AL) - Cronin, Doerr, Williams, Foxx . . . . $400-$575
1942 Boston (NL) - Stengel, Lombardi, Sain, Spahn . . . . $800-$1000
1942 Brooklyn - Durocher, Herman, Reese, Vaughan, Reiser, Medwick, Wyatt, French . . . . $400-$600
1942 Chicago (AL) - Appling, Lyons $250-$350
1942 Chicago (NL) - Cavarretta, Hack, Novikoff, Foxx . . . . $250-$400
1942 Cincinnati - McKechnie, Vander Meer . . . . $200-$325
1942 Cleveland - Boudreau . . . . $200-$300
1942 Detroit - Gehringer, Trucks, Newhouser . . . . $300-$400
1942 New York (AL) - McCarthy, Gordon, Rizzuto, DiMaggio, Dickey, Ruffing, Gomez . . . . $600-$900
1942 New York (NL) - Ott, Mize, Hubbell . . . . $500-$800
1942 Philadelphia (AL) - Mack, Collins . . . . $300-$450
1942 Philadelphia (NL) - Waner . . . . $500-$750
1942 Pittsburgh - Frisch, Lopez . . . . . $700-$900
1942 St. Louis (AL) - Ferrell . . . . $200-$375
1942 St. Louis (NL) - Slaughter, Musial, W. Cooper, M. Cooper, Beazley . . . . $750-$1000

1941 Cleveland Indians

1943 St. Louis Browns

1942 Washington - Harris, Vernon, Wynn ....$200-$300
1943 Boston (AL) - Cronin, Doerr ..$300-$550
1943 Boston (NL) - Stengel, McCarthy ....$250-$325
1943 Brooklyn - Durocher, Herman, Vaughan, Bordagaray, Walker, Olmo, Waner, Hodges, Medwick, Wyatt ....$350-$700
1943 Chicago (AL) - Appling, Grove $200-$350
1943 Chicago (NL) - Cavarretta, Nicholson, Goodman ....$250-$400
1943 Cincinnati - McKechnie, McCormick, Vander Meer ....$200-$350
1943 Cleveland - Boudreau, Smith ..$200-$275
1943 Detroit - Cramer, Wakefield, Trout, Trucks ....$200-$300
1943 New York (AL) - McCarthy, Dickey, Chandler ....$1200-$1500
1943 New York (NL) - Ott, Witek, Medwick, Lombardi, Adams ....$325-$500
1943 Philadelphia (AL) - Mack, Kell $200-$350
1943 Philadelphia (NL) - Rowe, Barrett ....$400-$600
1943 Pittsburgh - Frisch, Elliott, Lopez, Sewell . ...$225-$350
1943 St. Louis (AL) - Ferrell, Dean ..$200-$450
1943 St. Louis (NL) - Musial, W. Cooper ....$350-$475
1943 Washington - Vernon, Wynn, Gomez ... .$200-$300
1944 Boston (AL) - Cronin, Doerr, Fox, Johnson, Hughson ....$225-$350
1944 Boston (NL) - Holmes ....$200-$300
1944 Brooklyn - Durocher, Walker, Galan, P. Waner, L. Waner, Vaughan ....$250-$500
1944 Chicago (AL) - Schalk ....$200-$325
1944 Chicago (NL) - Grimm, Cavarretta, Dallessandro, Foxx ....$175-$325
1944 Cincinnati - McKechnie, McCormick, Tiptop, Walters ....$200-$325
1944 Cleveland - Boudreau ....$275-$450
1944 Detroit - Wakefield, Newhouser $225-$375

1944 New York (AL) - McCarthy, Lindell, Martin, Waner ....$250-$425
1944 New York (NL) - Ott, Weintraub, Medwick, Lombardi, Voiselle ....$400-$600
1944 Philadelphia (AL) - Mack, Simmons ....$250-$400
1944 Philadelphia (NL) ....$300-$500
1944 Pittsburgh - Russell, Lopez, Sewell, Frisch . ...$300-$400
1944 St. Louis (AL) - Kreevich, Potter ....$300-$500
1944 St. Louis (NL) - Marion, Musial, Hopp, W. Cooper, Martin, M. Cooper ....$400-$500
1944 Washington - Spence, Ferrell, Wynn ....$200-$300
1945 Boston (AL) - Cronin ....$200-$300
1945 Boston (NL) - Holmes ....$175-$250
1945 Brooklyn - Durocher, Galan, Walker, Rosen, Olmo ....$200-$350
1945 Chicago (AL) - Appling ......$175-$300
1945 Chicago (NL) - Grimm, Cavarretta, Johnson, Hack, Wyse ....$350-$500
1945 Cincinnati - McKechnie ......$225-$325
1945 Cleveland - Boudreau, Feller ..$275-$350
1945 Detroit (AL) - Greenberg, Newhouser ... .$325-$450
1945 New York (AL) - McCarthy, Waner, Ruffing ....$200-$325
1945 New York (NL) - Ott, Lombardi, Mungo . ...$300-$650
1945 Philadelphia (AL) - Mack, Kell $225-$350
1945 Philadelphia (NL) - Wasdell, Foxx ....$700-$900
1945 Pittsburgh - Frisch, Lopez, Waner ....$600-$800
1945 St. Louis (AL) - Muncrief ....$600-$800
1945 St. Louis (NL) - Kurowski, Schoendienst, Barrett, Burkhart, Brecheen ....$200-$350
1945 Washington - Lewis, Ferrell, Wolff ....$200-$300
1946 Boston (AL) - Cronin, Doerr, Pesky, DiMaggio, Williams, Ferriss ....$300-$450
1946 Boston (NL) - Holmes, Herman, Sain, Spahn ....$200-$350
1946 Brooklyn - Durocher, Reese, Medwick, Higbe ....$350-$500
1946 Chicago (AL) - Lyons, Appling, Caldwell . ...$250-$350
1946 Chicago (NL) - Grimm, Waitkus ....$175-$275
1946 Cincinnati - McKechnie, Walters ....$200-$300
1946 Cleveland - Boudreau, Edwards, Lemon, Feller ....$250-$350
1946 Detroit - Kell, Newhouser .....$225-$350
1946 New York (AL) - McCarthy, Rizzuto, DiMaggio, Dickey, Berra, Ruffing, Chandler ....$550-$1000

1946 New York Giants

1946 New York (NL) - Ott, Mize, Lombardi ... .$500-$650
1946 Philadelphia (AL) - Mack, Valo, McCosky, Kell ....$300-$400
1946 Philadelphia (NL) - Ennis, Rowe ....$200-$300
1946 Pittsburgh - Frisch, Kiner, Lopez $800-$950
1946 St. Louis (AL) - Stephens .....$200-$300
1946 St. Louis (NL) - Musial, Schoendienst, Kurowski, Slaughter, Walker, Garagiola, Pollet .. ..$400-$600
1946 Washington - Vernon, Grace, Leonard, Wynn ....$200-$300
1947 Boston (AL) - Cronin, Doerr, Pesky, Williams, Dobson ....$250-$400
1947 Boston (NL) - Elliott, Holmes, Spahn, Sain ....$200-$325
1947 Brooklyn - Robinson, Reese, Vaughan, Snider, Hodges, Branca, Hatten ....$900-$1100
1947 Chicago (AL) - Lyons, Appling, Wright .. ..$200-$300
1947 Chicago (NL) - Grimm, Pafko, Cavarretta ....$200-$300
1947 Cincinnati - Galan, Kluszewski, Blackwell . ...$200-$300
1947 Cleveland - Boudreau, Mitchell, Feller, Lemon ....$250-$350
1947 Detroit - Kell ....$250-$350
1947 New York (AL) - McQuinn, Rizzuto, DiMaggio, Berra, Reynolds, Shea ..$1000-$1250
1947 New York (NL) - Ott, Mize, Cooper, Jansen ....$350-$600
1947 Philadelphia (AL) - Mack, Valo, Fox, Marchildon ....$225-$350
1947 Philadelphia (NL) - Walker, Leonard, Rowe ....$250-$400
1947 Pittsburgh - Herman, Greenberg, Kiner .. ..$200-$300
1947 St. Louis (AL) - Dean ....$225-$350
1947 St. Louis (NL) - Musial, Schoendienst, Garagiola, Medwick, Munger ....$275-$400
1947 Washington - Vernon, Wynn ..$200-$300

1943 Boston Red Sox

1946 New York Yankees

1947 Chicago Cubs

Team Baseball Autographs — Chapter 5

1949 St. Louis Browns

1948 Boston (AL) - McCarthy, Doerr, Pesky, Williams ....$250-$375
1948 Boston (NL) - Dark, Sain, Spahn, Holmes, Southworth ....$500-$600
1948 Brooklyn - Durocher, Hodges, Robinson, Reese, Furillo, Campanella, Roe, Vaughan, Snider, Branca, Erskine ....$600-$900
1948 Chicago (AL) - Lyons, Appling $200-$300
1948 Chicago (NL) - Grimm ......$200-$300
1948 Cincinnati- Kluszewski ....$200-$300
1948 Cleveland - Boudreau, Mitchell, Bearden, Lemon, Feller, Paige ....$400-$575
1948 Detroit - Kell, Cramer, Newhouser, Trucks ....$250-$350
1948 New York (AL) - Rizzuto, DiMaggio, Berra, Raschi ....$400-$750
1948 New York (NL) - Ott, Durocher, Mize ....$400-$600
1948 Philadelphia (AL) - Mack, Fox $225-$350
1948 Philadelphia (NL) - Sisler, Ashburn, Leonard, Rowe, Roberts ....$300-$450
1948 Pittsburgh - Kiner ....$275-$375
1948 St. Louis (AL) - ....$200-$400
1948 St. Louis (NL) - Schoendienst, Slaughter, Musial, Garagiola, Medwick ....$275-$400
1948 Washington - Vernon, Wynn ..$225-$325
1949 Boston (AL) - McCarthy, Doerr, Williams, Parnell ....$200-$325
1949 Boston (NL) - Spahn, Sain ..$275-$350
1949 Brooklyn - Hodges, Robinson, Reese, Furillo, Roe, Newcombe, Campanella, Snider, Connors ....$700-$900
1949 Chicago (AL) - Appling ......$200-$300
1949 Chicago (NL) - Grimm, Frisch, Burgess ... .$250-$350
1949 Cincinnati - Kluszewski ....$200-$275
1949 Cleveland - Boudreau, Vernon, Mitchell, Lemon, Feller, Wynn ....$225-$300
1949 Detroit - Kell, Wertz, Evers, Trucks ....$200-$300
1949 New York (AL) - Stengel, Rizzuto, Berra, DiMaggio, Mize, Raschi, Reynolds .$1200-$1500

1949 Chicago Cubs

1949 New York (NL) - Durocher, Mize, Marshall, Thomson, Irvin ....$275-$550
1949 Philadelphia (AL) - Mack, Fox $225-$325
1949 Philadelphia (NL) - Sisler, Meyer, Roberts ....$300-$500
1949 Pittsburgh - Hopp, Kiner .....$300-$500
1949 St. Louis (AL) - Dillinger, Sievers ....$200-$300
1949 St. Louis (NL) - Schoendienst, Musial, Slaughter, Garagiola, Pollet ....$225-$350
1949 Washington ....$200-$300
1950 Boston (AL) - McCarthy, Dropo, Doerr, Pesky, Williams ....$250-$350
1950 Boston (NL) - Jethroe, Spahn, Sain ....$200-$300
1950 Brooklyn - Hodges, Robinson, Reese, Furillo, Roe, Campanella, Newcombe, Snider ... .$600-$900
1950 Chicago (AL) - Fox, Appling ..$200-$300
1950 Chicago (NL) - Frisch, Pafko ..$200-$300
1950 Cincinnati - Kluszewski, Adcock ....$200-$300
1950 Cleveland - Boudreau, Rosen, Doby, Mitchell, Lemon, Wynn, Feller ......$250-$350
1950 Detroit - Kell, Wertz, Groth, Evers ....$300-$400
1950 New York (AL) - Stengel, Martin, Rizzuto, Bauer, DiMaggio, Woodling, Berra, Mize, Ford .. ..$675-$1000
1950 New York (NL) - Dark, Irvin, Jansen, Maglie ....$300-$450
1950 Philadelphia (AL) - Mack, Dillinger, Lehner ....$300-$400
1950 Philadelphia (NL) - Ennis, Ashburn, Roberts, Simmons, Konstanty ....$300-$450
1950 Pittsburgh - Hopp, Kiner .....$200-$300
1950 St. Louis (AL) - ....$200-$275
1950 St. Louis (NL) - Musial, Schoendienst, Garagiola ....$225-$325
1950 Washington - Vernon ....$200-$275
1951 Boston (AL) - Doerr, Pesky, Boudreau ....$200-$300
1951 Boston (NL) - Spahn, Sain ....$200-$250
1951 Brooklyn - Hodges, Robinson, Reese, Snider, Campanella, Roe, Newcombe $575-$675
1951 Chicago (AL) - Fox, Minoso ...$200-$300
1951 Chicago (NL) - Frisch, Connors, Burgess . ...$225-$325
1951 Cincinnati - Kluszewski, Adcock ....$175-$275
1951 Cleveland - Lopez, Avila, Feller, Wynn, Lemon ....$225-$325
1951 Detroit - Kell, Trucks ....$250-$400
1951 New York (AL) - Stengel, Mize, Rizzuto, Brown, DiMaggio, Mantle, McDougald, Berra, Martin ....$2500-$4500
1951 New York (NL) - Durocher, Dark, Mays, Irvin, Maglie ....$1000-$1150
1951 Philadelphia (AL) - Fain, Shantz ....$200-$400
1951 Philadelphia (NL) - Ashburn, Roberts ... .$175-$275
1951 Pittsburgh - Kiner, Garagiola ..$275-$375
1951 St. Louis (AL) - Paige, Gaedel .$400-$600
1951 St. Louis (NL) - Schoendienst, Slaughter, Musial, Garagiola ....$225-$325
1951 Washington - Vernon ....$100-$225
1952 Boston (AL) - Boudreau, Goodman, Kell, Williams ....$175-$275
1952 Boston (NL) - Grimm, Mathews, Spahn .. ..$250-$325
1952 Brooklyn - Hodges, Robinson, Reese, Furillo, Snider, Campanella, Black, Erskine ....$500-$750

1952 New York Yankees

1952 Chicago (AL) - Fox, Minoso ...$200-$300
1952 Chicago (NL) - Fondy, Baumholtz, Sauer, Hacker ....$175-$275
1952 Cincinnati - Hornsby, Kluszewski, Adcock ....$275-$400
1952 Cleveland - Avila, Rosen, Mitchell, Wynn, Garcia, Lemon, Feller ....$300-$500
1952 Detroit - Kell, Kuenn ....$200-$300
1952 New York (AL) - Stengel, Martin, Reynolds, Mantle, Berra, Raschi, Woodling, Brown, Mize, Rizzuto ....$650-$800
1952 New York (NL) - Durocher, Dark, Irvin, Maglie, Wilhelm ....$300-$425
1952 Philadelphia (AL) - Fain, Shantz ....$200-$300
1952 Philadelphia (NL) - Ashburn, Roberts ... .$200-$300
1952 Pittsburgh - Groat, Kiner, Garagiola ....$200-$300
1952 St. Louis (AL) - Hornsby, Paige $350-$500
1952 St. Louis (NL) - Schoendienst, Slaughter, Musial ....$275-$400
1952 Washington - Vernon ....$175-$250
1953 Boston - Boudreau, Goodman, Kell, Williams, Parnell ....$400-$550
1953 Brooklyn - Hodges, Meyer, Reese, Furillo, Snider, Robinson, Campanella, Erskine, Gilliam . ...$700-$1000
1953 Chicago (AL) - Fox, Minoso, Trucks ....$225-$350
1953 Chicago (NL) - Fondy, Baumholtz, Kiner, Garagiola, Banks ....$200-$300
1953 Cincinnati - Hornsby, Kluszewski, Bell ....$275-$400
1953 Cleveland - Lopez, Rosen, Westlake, Mitchell, Lemon, Wynn, Feller ......$225-$300
1953 Detroit - Kuenn, Boone, Kaline $200-$275
1953 Milwaukee - Grimm, Adcock, Mathews, Spahn, Burdette ....$300-$375
1953 New York (AL) - Stengel, Martin, Rizzuto, Mantle, Berra, Mize, Ford ....$750-$1200
1953 New York (NL) - Durocher, Dark, Mueller, Thomson, Irvin ....$275-$450
1953 Philadelphia (AL) - Philley ....$200-$300
1953 Philadelphia (NL) - Ashburn, Roberts ... .$175-$275
1953 Pittsburgh - Kiner, Garagiola ..$200-$300
1953 St. Louis (AL) - ....$175-$250
1953 St. Louis (NL) - Schoendienst, Slaughter, Musial, Haddix, Staley ....$225-$275
1953 Washington - Vernon, Busby, Porterfield .. ..$175-$275
1954 Baltimore - ....$150-$225
1954 Boston - Boudreau, Jensen, Williams ....$400-$500
1954 Brooklyn- Alston, Hodges, Gilliam, Reese, Furillo, Lasorda, Robinson, Campanella, Erskine, Newcombe, Snider ....$1200-$1400

57

1954 Chicago (AL) - Fox, Kell, Trucks, Minoso . . . . $200-$325
1954 Chicago (NL) - Banks, Kiner, Garagiola . . . . $300-$500
1954 Cincinnati - Kluszewski, Temple $175-$275
1954 Cleveland - Lopez, Avila, Lemon, Wynn, Feller . . . . $300-$450
1954 Detroit - Kuenn, Kaline . . . . $350-$425
1954 Milwaukee - Grimm, Adcock, Mathews, Aaron, Spahn, Burdette . . . . $275-$400
1954 New York (AL) - Stengel, Rizzuto, Mantle, Berra, Slaughter, Grim, Ford . . . . . $500-$900
1954 New York (NL) - Durocher, Mays, Irvin, Antonelli, Maglie, Wilhelm . . . . . . $1200-$1500
1954 Philadelphia (NL) - Ashburn, Burgess, Roberts . . . . $250-$350
1954 Philadelphia (AL) - Finigan . . . $175-$250
1954 Pittsburgh - Gordon . . . . $150-$250
1954 St. Louis - Schoendienst, Musial, Moon . . . . $200-$300
1954 Washington - Vernon, Killebrew $150-$225
1955 Baltimore - Robinson . . . . $225-$325
1955 Boston - Goodman, Jensen, Piersall, Williams . . . . $175-$300
1955 Brooklyn - Hodges, Gilliam, Reese, Labine, Furillo, Snider, Campanella, Newcombe, Robinson, Erskine, Koufax . . . . $2500-$4000
1955 Chicago (AL) - Fox, Kell, Donovan, Trucks . . . . $200-$300
1955 Chicago (NL) - Banks . . . . $175-$250
1955 Cincinnati - Kluszewski, Burgess $200-$300
1955 Cleveland - Lopez, Smith, Kiner, Colavito, Lemon, Wynn, Score, Feller . . . . $375-$525
1955 Detroit - Kuenn, Kaline, Bunning . . . . $175-$275
1955 Kansas City - Boudreau, Slaughter . . . . $200-$275
1955 Milwaukee - Mathews, Aaron, Adcock, Spahn, Burdette . . . . $250-$400
1955 New York (AL) - Stengel, Mantle, Slaughter, Howard, Martin, Berra, Rizzuto, Ford, Larsen . . . . $500-$900
1955 New York (NL) - Durocher, Mays, Irvin, Antonelli . . . . $275-$475
1955 Philadelphia - Ashburn, Roberts . . . . $175-$250
1955 Pittsburgh - Groat, Clemente, Friend . . . . $500-$800
1955 St. Louis - Musial, Schoendienst, Boyer, Virdon, Haddix . . . . $200-$300
1955 Washington - Vernon, Killebrew . . . . $150-$225
1956 Baltimore - Kell, Gastall, Robinson . . . . $175-$250
1956 Boston - Vernon, Jensen, Williams . . . . $300-$400
1956 Brooklyn - Hodges, Gilliam, Reese, Furillo, Snider, Campanella, Koufax, Newcombe, Erskine,

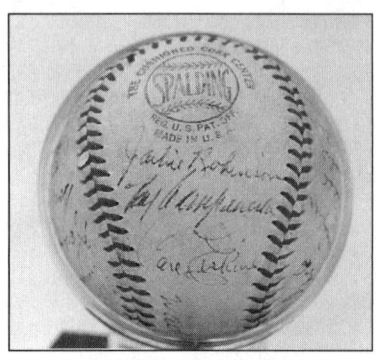

1955 Brooklyn Dodgers

1955 Boston Red Sox

Drysdale, Robinson . . . . $700-$900
1956 Chicago (AL) - Fox, Aparicio, Kell . . . . $200-$300
1956 Chicago (NL) - Banks, Irvin . . . $200-$275
1956 Cincinnati - Kluszewski, Robinson . . . . $225-$325
1956 Cleveland - Lopez, Colavito, Lemon, Wynn, Score, Feller . . . . $300-$400
1956 Detroit - Kuenn, Kaline, Bunning . . . . $200-$300
1956 Kansas City - Boudreau, Slaughter, Lasorda . . . . $200-$300
1956 Milwaukee - Grimm, Adcock, Mathews, Aaron, Spahn, Burdette . . . . $275-$425
1956 New York (AL) - Stengel, Martin, Mantle, Howard, Rizzuto, Slaughter, Berra, Bauer, Ford . . . . $650-$1000
1956 New York (NL) - White, Schoendienst, Mays, Antonelli . . . . $275-$475
1956 Philadelphia - Ashburn, Roberts . $150-$225
1956 Pittsburgh - Mazeroski, Groat, Clemente, Virdon . . . . $600-$850
1956 St. Louis - Musial, Boyer, Schoendienst, Peete . . . . $175-$300
1956 Washington - Killebrew . . . . $150-$225
1957 Baltimore - Kell, Robinson . . . . $200-$300
1957 Boston - Jensen, Williams, Vernon . . . . $200-$275
1957 Brooklyn - Hodges, Gilliam, Reese, Furillo, Snider, Campanella, Koufax, Drysdale . . . . $1000-$1300
1957 Chicago (AL) - Lopez, Fox, Aparicio . . . . $200-$300
1957 Chicago (NL) - Banks . . . . . . $175-$250
1957 Cincinnati - Robinson, Kluszewski . . . . $250-$375
1957 Cleveland - Colavito, Maris, Wynn, Wilhelm . . . . $450-$600
1957 Detroit - Kuenn, Kaline, Bunning . . . . $180-$270
1957 Kansas City - Martin . . . . $175-$275
1957 Milwaukee - Schoendienst, Mathews, Aaron, Adcock, Spahn . . . . $1000-$1500
1957 New York (AL) - Stengel, Slaughter, Berra, Howard, Sturdivant, Ford . . . . $700-$900
1957 New York (NL) - Mays, Schoendienst, McCormick, White . . . . $250-$350
1957 Philadelphia - Ashburn, Sanford, Roberts . . . . $275-$375
1957 Pittsburgh - Mazeroski, Groat, Clemente, Friend . . . . $900-$1000
1957 St. Louis - Musial, Boyer, Wilhelm . . . . $200-$300
1957 Washington - Killebrew . . . . $150-$225
1958 Baltimore - Robinson, Wilhelm $150-$225
1958 Boston - Runnels, Williams . . . $275-$500
1958 Chicago (AL) - Fox, Aparicio, Cash, Wynn . . . . $200-$300

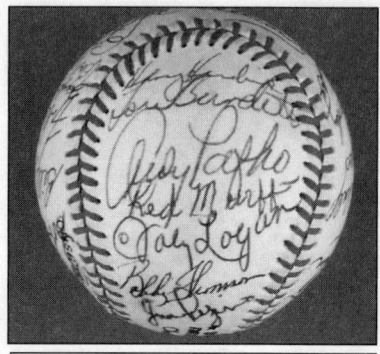

1957 Milwaukee Braves

1958 Chicago (NL) - Banks . . . . $175-$250
1958 Cincinnati - Robinson, Pinson . $150-$300
1958 Cleveland - Vernon, Colavito, Maris, Wilhelm, Lemon . . . . $200-$300
1958 Detroit - Martin, Kaline, Kuenn, Bunning . . . . $200-$300
1958 Kansas City - Maris . . . . $400-$550
1958 Los Angeles - Alston, Hodges, Furillo, Snider, Reese, Drysdale, Koufax, Howard . . . . $350-$600
1958 Milwaukee - Schoendienst, Mathews, Aaron, Spahn, Burdette . . . . $525-$800
1958 New York - Kubek, Mantle, Berra, Howard, Slaughter, Turley, Ford, Larsen . . . . $1100-$1350
1958 Philadelphia - Ashburn, Roberts $200-$350
1958 Pittsburgh - Kluszewski, Mazeroski, Groat, Clemente, Friend . . . . $575-$850
1958 San Francisco - Cepeda, Mays, White, McCormick . . . . $450-$600
1958 St. Louis - Musial, Boyer . . . . . . $175-$250
1958 Washington - Pearson, Killebrew . . . . $150-$225
1959 Baltimore - Robinson, Wilhelm $175-$250
1959 Boston - Runnels, Williams . . . $150-$250
1959 Chicago (AL) - Lopez, Fox, Aparicio, Cash, Kluszewski, Wynn . . . . $350-$525
1959 Chicago (NL) - Banks, Williams . . . . $175-$250
1959 Cincinnati - Robinson, Pinson . $300-$500
1959 Cleveland - Martin, Colavito, Perry, Score . . . . $175-$250
1959 Detroit - Kaline, Bunning $250
1959 Kansas City - Maris . . . . $200-$400
1959 Los Angeles - Alston, Hodges, Gilliam, Snider, Koufax, Furillo, Drysdale, Howard, Wills . . . . $800-$1000
1959 Milwaukee - Adcock, Mathews, Aaron, Vernon, Slaughter, Schoendienst, Spahn . . . . $350-$500
1959 New York - Stengel, Kubek, Mantle, Berra, Howard, Slaughter, Ford, Larsen . . . . $450-$600
1959 Philadelphia - Sparky Anderson, Ashburn,

1958 Baltimore Orioles

Team Baseball Autographs — Chapter 5

1958 Milwaukee Braves

1960 Chicago White Sox

1961 Detroit Tigers

Roberts . . . .$300-$400
1959 Pittsburgh - Stuart, Mazeroski, Groat, Clemente, Kluszewski, Friend . . . .$600-$800
1959 San Francisco - Cepeda, Mays, McCovey, McCormick . . . .$250-$375
1959 St. Louis - Musial, Boyer, White, McDaniel, Gibson . . . .$175-$250
1959 Washington - Killebrew, Allison, Kaat . . . .
. . . .$150-$225
1960 Baltimore - Hansen, Robinson, Wilhelm . .
. . . .$175-$250
1960 Boston - Runnels, Williams . . . .$375-$500
1960 Chicago (AL) - Lopez, Fox, Aparicio, Kluszewski, Wynn, Score . . . .$300-$500
1960 Chicago (NL) - Grimm, Boudreau, Banks, Santo, Ashburn, Williams . . . .$175-$250
1960 Cincinnati - Robinson, Martin, Pinson . . .
. . . .$250-$350
1960 Cleveland - Aspromonte, Kuenn, Piersall, Perry . . . .$150-$250
1960 Detroit - Cash, Colavito, Kaline, Bunning
. . . .$250-$350
1960 Kansas City - . . . .$150-$225
1960 Los Angeles - Alston, Wills, Howard, Davis, Snider, Hodges, Davis, Koufax, Drysdale, Gilliam
. . . .$425-$500
1960 Milwaukee - Adcock, Mathews, Aaron, Schoendienst, Spahn, Burdette, Torre $300-$400
1960 New York - Stengel, Kubek, Maris, Mantle, Howard, Berra, Ford . . . .$500-$750
1960 Philadelphia - Roberts . . . .$100-$150
1960 Pittsburgh - Stuart, Mazeroski, Clemente, Law, Vernon . . . .$800-$1200
1960 San Francisco - McCovey, Mays, Cepeda, McCormick, Marichal . . . .$250-$375
1960 St. Louis - White, Boyer, Musial, McCarver, Gibson . . . .$250-$350
1960 Washington - Killebrew, Versalles, Kaat . . .
. . . .$175-$275
1961 Baltimore - Robinson, Powell, Wilhelm . .
. . . .$150-$225
1961 Boston - Jensen, Yastrzemski . . .$175-$250

1961 Chicago (AL) - Lopez, Fox, Aparicio, Pierce, Wynn . . . .$175-$250
1961 Chicago (NL) - Banks, Santo, Ashburn, Hubbs, Brock, Williams . . . .$175-$275
1961 Cincinnati - Robinson, Pinson, Jay . . . . . .
. . . .$325-$500
1961 Cleveland - Piersall, McDowell .$125-$175
1961 Detroit - Cash, Kaline, Colavito, Bunning, Freehan . . . .$250-$350
1961 Kansas City - . . . .$75-$250
1961 Los Angeles (AL) - . . . .$200-$300
1961 Los Angeles (NL) - Alston, Wills, T. Davis, W. Davis, Howard, Snider, Drysdale, Koufax . . . .
. . . .$275-$400
1961 Milwaukee - Adcock, Mathews, Aaron, Torre, Spahn, Martin . . . .$175-$275
1961 Minnesota - Lavagetto, Killebrew, Martin, Versalles, Kaat . . . .$200-$300
1961 New York - Kubek, Maris, Mantle, Berra, Howard, Tresh, Ford . . . .$1400-$1800
1961 Philadelphia - . . . .$100-$150
1961 Pittsburgh - Stuart, Mazeroski, Clemente, Clendenon, Friend . . . .$550-$850
1961 San Francisco - McCovey, Mays, Cepeda, Marichal, McCormick . . . .$250-$350
1961 St. Louis - White, Boyer, Musial, Schoendienst, McCarver, Gibson . . . .$275-$350
1961 Washington - Vernon . . . .$150-$225
1962 Baltimore - Robinson, Powell, Roberts, Wilhelm . . . .$175-$250
1962 Boston - Yastrzemski . . . .$175-$250
1962 Chicago (AL) - Lopez, Fox, Wynn, Peters, DeBusschere . . . .$200-$400
1962 Chicago (NL) - Banks, Hubbs, Santo, Brock, Williams . . . .$172-$275
1962 Cincinnati - Robinson, Pinson .$250-$450
1962 Cleveland - McDowell . . . .$125-$200
1962 Detroit - Cash, Kaline, Colavito, Bunning
. . . .$125-$200
1962 Houston - Aspromonte . . . .$300-$425
1962 Kansas City - . . . .$100-$175
1962 Los Angeles (AL) - Lee Thomas, Fregosi .

. . . .$150-$225
1962 Los Angeles (NL) - Alston, Gilliam, Wills, Howard, W. Davis, T. Davis, Snider, Drysdale, Koufax . . . .$400-$800
1962 Milwaukee - Adcock, Mathews, Aaron, Uecker, Spahn . . . .$300-$400
1962 Minnesota - Versalles, Killebrew, Oliva, Kaat . . . .$175-$275
1962 New York (AL) - Tresh, Maris, Mantle, Howard, Berra, Kubek, Terry, Ford . . .$550-$800
1962 New York (NL) - Stengel, Hodges, Kranepool . . . .$300-$450
1962 Philadelphia - . . . .$100-$150
1962 Pittsburgh - Mazeroski, Groat, Clemente, Clendenon, Stargell . . . .$500-$750
1962 San Francisco - Cepeda, Mays, McCovey, Marichal, McCormick, Perry . . . .$400-$600
1962 St. Louis - White, Boyer, Musial, Schoendienst, Gibson . . . .$275-$350
1962 Washington - Vernon . . . .$150-$275
1963 Baltimore - Aparicio, Robinson, Powell, Roberts . . . .$200-$250
1963 Boston - Yastrzemski . . . .$150-$250
1963 Chicago (AL) - Lopez, Fox, Peters, Wilhelm, DeBusschere . . . .$175-$250
1963 Chicago (NL) - Banks, Hubbs, Santo, Brock, Williams . . . .$175-$250
1963 Cincinnati - Rose, Harper, Pinson, Robinson . . . .$200-$275
1963 Cleveland - Adcock, McDowell, John . . . .
. . . .$100-$150
1963 Detroit - Cash, Kaline, Colavito, Lolich, McLain . . . .$125-$200
1963 Houston - Staub, Aspromonte, Morgan, Umbricht . . . .$175-$250
1963 Kansas City - . . . .$150-$225
1963 Los Angeles (AL) - Fregosi, Chance . . . . .
. . . .$100-$150
1963 Los Angeles (NL) - Alston, Gilliam, Wills, Howard, W. Davis, T. Davis, Koufax, Drysdale . . .
. . . .$450-$650
1963 Milwaukee - Mathews, Aaron, Torre,

1958 New York Yankees

1961 Baltimore Orioles

1963 New York Yankees

1963 New York Mets

Uecker, Spahn ....$150-$225
1963 Minnesota - Versalles, Killebrew, Oliva, Kaat ....$175-$275
1963 New York (AL) - Maris, Howard, Mantle, Berra, Ford ....$450-$650
1963 New York (NL) - Stengel, Snider, Kranepool, Hodges ....$275-$400
1963 Philadelphia - Allen ....$100-$150
1963 Pittsburgh - Clendenon, Mazeroski, Clemente, Stargell, Mota ....$450-$800
1963 San Francisco - Cepeda, Mays, McCovey, Marichal, Larsen, Perry ....$225-$450
1963 St. Louis - Groat, Boyer, McCarver, Musial, Gibson ....$300-$550
1963 Washington - Vernon, Hodges ..$100-$150
1964 Baltimore - Aparicio, Robinson, Powell, Piniella, Roberts ....$200-$275
1964 Boston - Herman, Yastrzemski ..$200-$300
1964 Chicago (AL) - Lopez, Wilhelm ....$100-$150
1964 Chicago (NL) - Banks, Santo, Williams, Brock, Kessinger ....$150-$225
1964 Cincinnati - Rose, Robinson, Pinson, Perez ....$175-$250
1964 Cleveland - McDowell, Tiant, John ....$100-$150
1964 Detroit - Cash, Kaline, Freehan, Lolich, McLain ....$150-$200
1964 Houston - Fox, Aspromonte, Staub, Morgan ....$200-$300
1964 Kansas City - Colavito, Campaneris, Odom ....$150-$250
1964 Los Angeles (AL) - Adcock, Fregosi, Chance ....$75-$100
1964 Los Angeles (NL) - Alston, Wills, Howard, W. Davis, T. Davis, Koufax, Drysdale ..$250-$400
1964 Milwaukee - Mathews, Aaron, Carty, Torre, Spahn, Niekro ....$175-$250
1964 Minnesota - Versalles, Oliva, Killebrew, Kaat ....$200-$250
1964 New York (AL) - Berra, Maris, Mantle, Howard, Ford, Stottlemyre ....$350-$500

1964 New York (NL) - Stengel, Kranepool ....$350-$500
1964 Philadelphia - Allen, Bunning .$100-$135
1964 Pittsburgh - Clendenon, Mazeroski, Clemente, Mota ....$450-$650
1964 San Francisco - Cepeda, Mays, McCovey, Snider, Marichal, Perry, Larsen ......$200-$300
1964 St. Louis - White, Boyer, Brock, McCarver, Uecker, Gibson ....$375-$550
1964 Washington - Hodges ....$225-$350
1965 Baltimore - Powell, Aparicio, Robinson, Blefary, Palmer, Roberts ....$200-$300
1965 Boston - Herman, Yastrzemski .$200-$275
1965 California - Fregosi ....$115-$200
1965 Chicago (AL) - Lopez, John, Wilhelm ....$125-$175
1965 Chicago (NL) - Banks, Santo, Williams ....$100-$150
1965 Cincinnati - Rose, Robinson, Pinson, Perez ....$200-$400
1965 Cleveland - Colavito, McDowell, Tiant ....$125-$325
1965 Detroit - Cash, Kaline, Freehan, McLain, Lolich ....$150-$200
1965 Houston - Morgan, Staub, Fox, Roberts ....$150-$225
1965 Kansas City - Campaneris, Hunter, Paige, Odom ....$200-$400
1965 Los Angeles - Alston, Lefebvre, Wills, W. Davis, Koufax, Drysdale ....$350-$550
1965 Milwaukee - Mathews, Aaron, Torre, Niekro ....$250-$350
1965 Minnesota - Versalles, Oliva, Killebrew, Kaat ....$325-$575
1965 New York (AL) - Mantle, Howard, Maris, Murcer, Stottlemyre, Ford ....$400-$575
1965 New York (NL) - Stengel, Kranepool, Swoboda, Berra, Spahn ....$300-$375
1965 Philadelphia - Allen, Bunning, Jenkins ....$150-$250
1965 Pittsburgh - Mazeroski, Clemente, Stargell ....$1300-$1400
1965 San Francisco - McCovey, Mays, Cepeda, Marichal, Perry, Spahn ....$200-$350
1965 St. Louis - Schoendienst, White, Boyer, Brock, McCarver, Uecker, Gibson, Carlton $300-$350
1965 Washington - Hodges, Howard, McCormick ....$150-$225
1966 Atlanta - Mathews, Aaron, Torre, Niekro ....$325-$400
1966 Baltimore - Aparicio, B. Robinson, F. Robinson, Palmer ....$250-$450
1966 Boston - Herman, Yastrzemski, Lonborg ....$200-$300
1966 California - Fregosi ....$80-$120
1966 Chicago (AL) - Agee, John, Wilhelm ....$150-$250

1965 San Francisco Giants

1966 Chicago (NL) - Banks, Santo, Jenkins, Roberts ....$125-$200
1966 Cincinnati - Perez, Rose, Helms, Harper, Pinson ....$125-$175
1966 Cleveland - Colavito, Tiant, McDowell ....$100-$175
1966 Detroit - Cash, Kaline, Freehan, McLain, Lolich ....$125-$200
1966 Houston - Morgan, Staub, Roberts ....$100-$150
1966 Kansas City - Campaneris, Hunter, Odom ....$100-$150
1966 Los Angeles - Wills, W. Davis, T. Davis, Koufax, Drysdale, Sutton ....$175-$400
1966 Minnesota - Killebrew, Oliva, Kaat ....$150-$225
1966 New York (AL) - Maris, Mantle, Howard, Stottlemyre, Ford ....$400-$600
1966 New York (NL) - Kranepool, Boyer, Swoboda, Ryan ....$175-$250
1966 Philadelphia - White, Allen, Uecker, Bunning, Jenkins ....$100-$150
1966 Pittsburgh - Clendenon, Mazeroski, Clemente, Stargell, Mota ....$800-$1200
1966 San Francisco - McCovey, Mays, Cepeda, Marichal, Perry ....$175-$250
1966 St. Louis - Schoendienst, Cepeda, Brock, McCarver, Gibson, Carlton ....$250-$400
1966 Washington - Hodges, Howard .$125-$200
1967 Atlanta - Aaron, Carty, Uecker, Niekro ....$150-$225
1967 Baltimore (AL) - Powell, Aparicio, B. Robinson, F. Robinson, Palmer ......$200-$300
1967 Boston (AL) - Yastrzemski, Howard, Lonborg, Lyle ....$600-$1200
1967 California (AL) - Fregosi ......$75-$125
1967 Chicago (AL) - Colavito, Boyer, John, Wilhelm ....$100-$175
1967 Chicago (NL) - Durocher, Banks, Santo, Williams, Jenkins ....$125-$175
1967 Cincinnati - Pinson, Rose, Bench ....$150-$225

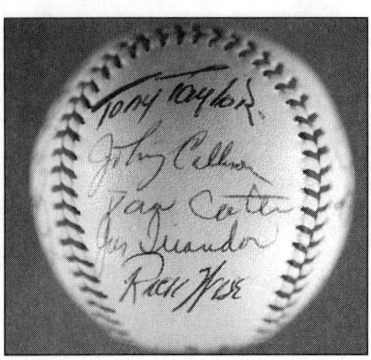

1964 Philadelphia Phillies

1965 Houston Astros

1966 California Angels

1967 Cleveland (AL) - Adcock, McDowell, Tiant .... $100-$150
1967 Detroit (AL) - Cash, Kaline, Freehan, Mathews, McLain, Lolich .... $150-$225
1967 Houston - Mathews, Morgan, Staub .... $100-$150
1967 Kansas City (AL) - Appling, Jackson, Hunter, Odom .... $150-$225
1967 Los Angeles - Alston, Davis, Drysdale, Sutton .... $200-$275
1967 Minnesota (AL) - Killebrew, Carew, Oliva, Kaat .... $275-$375
1967 New York (AL) - Mantle, Howard, Stottlemyre, Ford .... $350-$450
1967 New York (NL) - Kranepool, Harrelson, Swoboda, Seaver, Koosman ..... $325-$475
1967 Philadelphia - White, Allen, Uecker, Groat, Bunning .... $100-$150
1967 Pittsburgh - Mazeroski, Wills, Clemente, Stargell .... $400-$600
1967 San Francisco (NL) - McCovey, Mays, McCormick, Perry, Marichal ...... $175-$250
1967 St. Louis - Schoendienst, Cepeda, Maris, Brock, McCarver, Carlton, Gibson .. $550-$750
1967 Washington (AL) - Hodges, Howard .... $175-$250
1968 Atlanta - Aaron, Torre, Niekro .. $200-$300
1968 Baltimore - Weaver, Powell, B. Robinson, F. Robinson .... $150-$250
1968 Boston - Yastrzemski, Howard, Lyle .... $150-$200
1968 California - Fregosi .... $100-$125
1968 Chicago (AL) - Lopez, Aparicio, John .... $100-$150
1968 Chicago (NL) - Durocher, Banks, Santo, Williams, Jenkins .... $125-$200
1968 Cincinnati - Perez, Rose, Pinson, Bench .. .. $175-$250
1968 Cleveland - Tiant, McDowell .. $100-$150
1968 Detroit - Cash, Freehan, Kaline, McLain, Lolich, Mathews .... $375-$600
1968 Houston - Staub, Morgan ..... $100-$150
1968 Los Angeles - Alston, Davis, Drysdale, Sutton .... $125-$200
1968 Minnesota - Carew, Oliva, Killebrew, Kaat .... $175-$250
1968 New York (AL) - Mantle, Bahnsen .... $200-$300
1968 New York (NL) - Hodges, Kranepool, Harrelson, Swoboda, Koosman, Seaver, Ryan ... . $500-$800
1968 Oakland - Bando, Jackson, Odom, Hunter, Fingers .... $200-$300
1968 Philadelphia - White, Allen .... $75-$125
1968 Pittsburgh - Mazeroski, Wills, Clemente, Stargell, Oliver, Bunning ...... $450-$650
1968 San Francisco - McCovey, Bonds, Mays, Marichal, Perry, McCormick .... $175-$250

1968 St. Louis Cardinals

1969 New York Mets

1968 St. Louis - Schoendienst, Cepeda, Maris, Brock, Simmons, Gibson, Carlton, McCarver ... . $450-$600
1968 Washington - Howard .... $100-$150
1969 Atlanta - Cepeda, Aaron, Evans, Niekro, Wilhelm .... $200-$300
1969 Baltimore - Weaver, Powell, B. Robinson, F. Robinson, Cueller, Palmer .... $150-$275
1969 Boston - Yastrzemski, Lyle ..... $300-$400
1969 California - Fregosi, Wilhelm ... $75-$125
1969 Chicago (AL) - Lopez, Aparicio, John .... $150-$200
1969 Chicago (NL) - Durocher, Banks, Santo, Williams, Jenkins .... $125-$200
1969 Cincinnati - Perez, Rose, Bench $175-$250
1969 Cleveland - McDowell, Tiant ... $75-$125
1969 Detroit - Cash, Kaline, Freehan, McLain, Lolich .... $125-$175
1969 Houston - Morgan .... $75-$125
1969 Kansas City - Piniella .... $250-$375
1969 Los Angeles - Alston, Sizemore, Wills, Davis, Drysdale, Bunning, Buckner, Garvey .... $175-$250
1969 Minnesota - Carew, Killebrew, Oliva, Nettles, Kaat .... $275-$375
1969 Montreal - Staub .... $275-$450
1969 New York (AL) - Murcer, Munson, Stottlemyre .... $200-$275
1969 New York (NL) - Harrelson, Swoboda, Seaver, Koosman, Ryan .... $750-$2000
1969 Oakland - Bando, Jackson, Odom, Hunter, Fingers, Blue .... $250-$325
1969 Philadelphia - Allen .... $100-$150
1969 Pittsburgh - Oliver, Mazeroski, Clemente, Stargell, Bunning .... $325-$575
1969 San Diego - .... $200-$300
1969 San Francisco - McCovey, Bonds, Mays, Marichal, Perry .... $125-$250
1969 Seattle - Harper .... $400-$600
1969 St. Louis - Pinson, Torre, Simmons, Gibson, Carlton, Schoendienst, Brock, McCarver .... $125-$225

1969 Atlanta Braves

1969 Washington - Williams, Howard $150-$200
1970 Atlanta - Cepeda, Aaron, Evans, Niekro, Wilhelm .... $125-$200
1970 Baltimore - Weaver, Powell, B. Robinson, F. Robinson, Palmer .... $325-$400
1970 Boston - Yastrzemski, Lyle ..... $125-$175
1970 California - Fregosi .... $75-$125
1970 Chicago (AL) - Aparicio, John . $150-$200
1970 Chicago (NL) - Durocher, Banks, Santo, Williams, Jenkins, Wilhelm .... $150-$225
1970 Cincinnati - Anderson, Concepcion, Perez, Rose, Bench .... $225-$300
1970 Cleveland - Nettles, Pinson, McDowell ... . $75-$125
1970 Detroit - Cash, Kaline, Freehan, Lolich ... . $100-$150
1970 Houston - Morgan .... $75-$125
1970 Kansas City - Lemon, Piniella . $125-$175
1970 Los Angeles - Alston, Wills, Garvey, Buckner, Sutton .... $175-$250
1970 Milwaukee - Harper .... $100-$150
1970 Minnesota - Killebrew, Oliva, Carew, Perry, Kaat, Tiant .... $200-$400
1970 Montreal - Staub, Morton ..... $100-$150
1970 New York (AL) - Murcer, Munson, Stottlemyre .... $275-$375
1970 New York (NL) - Hodges, Koosman, Harrelson, Swoboda, Kranepool, Seaver, Ryan, Clendenon .... $275-$400
1970 Oakland - Bando, Jackson, Hunter, Fingers .... $150-$250
1970 Philadelphia - Bowa, McCarver, Bunning, Luzinski .... $100-$150
1970 Pittsburgh - Mazeroski, Clemente, Stargell, Oliver .... $600-$800
1970 San Diego - .... $100-$150
1970 San Francisco - McCovey, Bonds, Mays, Foster, Perry, Marichal .... $175-$275
1970 St. Louis - Allen, Torre, Brock, Simmons, Gibson, Carlton .... $150-$200
1970 Washington - Williams, Howard .... $150-$200
1971 Atlanta - Aaron, Evans, Williams, Cepeda, Niekro, Wilhelm .... $125-$200
1971 Baltimore - Weaver, Powell, B. Robinson, F. Robinson, Palmer .... $250-$300
1971 Boston - Aparicio, Fisk, Lyle, Tiant .... $125-$175
1971 California - Fregosi .... $100-$125
1971 Chicago (AL) - John .... $100-$125
1971 Chicago (NL) - Santo, Williams, Banks, Jenkins .... $100-$150
1971 Cincinnati - Concepcion, Perez, Rose, Foster, Bench .... $175-$250
1971 Cleveland - Chambliss, Nettles, Pinson, McDowell .... $100-$125
1971 Detroit - Martin, Cash, Kaline, Freehan, Lolich .... $150-$200
1971 Houston - Morgan .... $75-$125
1971 Kansas City - Lemon, Piniella .. $75-$125
1971 Los Angeles - Alston, Wills, Garvey, Buckner, Sutton, Wilhelm .... $175-$250
1971 Milwaukee - Harper .... $75-$100
1971 Minnesota - Killebrew, Carew, Oliva, Blyleven, Kaat .... $100-$150
1971 Montreal - Staub .... $75-$100
1971 New York (AL) - Murcer, Munson, Stottlemyre .... $250-$450
1971 New York (NL) - Hodges, Kranepool, Harrelson, Seaver, Ryan, Koosman ... $250-$375
1971 Oakland - Bando, Jackson, Hunter, Blue, Fingers .... $200-$275
1971 Philadelphia - Bowa, McCarver, Luzinski, Bunning .... $100-$150

Team Baseball Autographs — Chapter 5

1972 Oakland A's

1971 Pittsburgh - Clemente, Oliver, Stargell, Mazeroski ....$500-$700
1971 San Diego - ....$100-$150
1971 San Francisco - McCovey, Bonds, Mays, Kingman, Foster, Marichal, Perry ....$175-$300
1971 St. Louis - Schoendienst, Torre, Brock, Simmons, Carlton, Gibson ....$150-$250
1971 Washington - Williams, Harrah, Howard, McLain ....$200-$250
1972 Atlanta - Mathews, Aaron, Evans, Cepeda, Niekro ....$125-$200
1972 Baltimore - Weaver, Powell, Robinson ... .$150-$175
1972 Boston - Aparicio, Yastrzemski, Fisk, Tiant ....$150-$200
1972 California - Pinson, Ryan .....$100-$150
1972 Chicago (AL) - Allen, Gossage ..$50-$125
1972 Chicago (NL) - Durocher, Santo, Williams, Jenkins ....$100-$150
1972 Cincinnati - Anderson, Perez, Morgan, Concepcion, Rose, Bench, Foster ....$275-$375
1972 Cleveland - Nettles, Bell, Perry .$100-$125
1972 Detroit - Cash, Northrup, Freehan, Kaline, Lolich ....$150-$225
1972 Houston - Durocher ....$65-$85
1972 Kansas City - Piniella ....$85-$110
1972 Los Angeles - Alston, Garvey, Robinson, Davis, Sutton, John, Wilhelm .....$175-$250
1972 Milwaukee - Scott ....$75-$110
1972 Minnesota - Killebrew, Carew, Oliva, Blyleven, Kaat ....$125-$175
1972 Montreal - Singleton, McCarver ....$100-$150
1972 New York (AL) - Murcer, Munson, Stottlemyre ....$200-$275
1972 New York (NL) - Hodges, Berra, Staub, Kranepool, Harrelson, Mays, Seaver, Matlack, Koosman ....$200-$300
1972 Oakland - Bando, Jackson, Cepeda, Hunter, Fingers, Blue ....$350-$400
1972 Philadelphia - Bowa, Luzinski, McCarver, Boone, Schmidt, Carlton ....$125-$175

1972 Houston Astros

1972 Pittsburgh - Stargell, Clemente, Oliver, Mazeroski ....$500-$725
1972 San Diego - ....$75-$100
1972 San Francisco - McCovey, Bonds, Mays, Marichal ....$200-$300
1972 St. Louis - Schoendienst, Torre, Brock, Simmons, Gibson ....$150-$200
1972 Texas - Williams, Howard, Harrah ....$150-$210
1973 Atlanta - Mathews, Aaron, P. Niekro, J. Niekro ....$125-$200
1973 Baltimore - Weaver, Powell, Robinson, Bumbry, Palmer ....$175-$250
1973 Boston - Yastrzemski, Aparicio, Fisk, Cepeda, Evans, Tiant ....$100-$175
1973 California - Pinson, Robinson, Ryan ....$75-$150
1973 Chicago (AL) - Kaat, Gossage ..$75-$125
1973 Chicago (NL) - Kessinger, Williams, Jenkins ....$75-$100
1973 Cincinnati - Anderson, Perez, Concepcion, Rose, Bench, Foster ....$225-$350
1973 Cleveland - Perry ....$85-$125
1973 Detroit - Martin, Cash, Northrup, Freehan, Kaline, Lolich, Perry ....$150-$180
1973 Houston - Richard ....$75-$100
1973 Kansas City - Piniella, Brett ..$175-$300
1973 Los Angeles - Alston, Buckner, Cey, Davis, Garvey, Sutton, John ....$125-$200
1973 Milwaukee - Thomas ....$80-$120
1973 Minnesota - Carew, Oliva, Killebrew, Kaat-Blyleven ....$100-$150
1973 Montreal - Singleton ....$80-$100
1973 New York (AL) - Nettles, Murcer, Munson, Stottlemyre, McDowell, Lyle .....$200-$235
1973 New York (NL) - Berra, Harrelson, Staub, Jones, Kranepool, Seaver, Koosman ..$275-$425
1973 Oakland - Bando, Jackson, Hunter, Blue, Fingers ....$275-$425
1973 Philadelphia - Bowa, Schmidt, Luzinski, Boone, Carlton ....$125-$175
1973 Pittsburgh - Oliver, Stargell, Parker ....$125-$175
1973 San Diego - Winfield ....$100-$125
1973 San Francisco - McCovey, Bonds, Matthews, Marichal ....$100-$150
1973 St. Louis - Schoendienst, Torre, Brock, Simmons, McCarver, Gibson ....$100-$150
1973 Texas - Martin, Harrah, Burroughs, Madlock ....$65-$125
1974 Atlanta - Mathews, Evans, Aaron, P. Niekro ....$150-$200
1974 Baltimore - Weaver, Powell, Robinson, Palmer ....$200-$300
1974 Boston - Yastrzemski, Evans, Fisk, Cooper, Rice, Lynn, McCarver, Marichal ....$150-$225
1974 California - Robinson, Ryan ...$100-$150
1974 Chicago (AL) - Allen, Kaat, Gossage ....$75-$125
1974 Chicago (NL) - Kessinger, Madlock ....$75-$100
1974 Cincinnati - Anderson, Perez, Morgan, Concepcion, Foster, Rose, Bench ....$225-$350
1974 Cleveland - G. Perry, J. Perry ...$100-$150
1974 Detroit - Freehan, Horton, Kaline, Lolich . ...$150-$200
1974 Houston - Wilson, Richard .....$75-$100
1974 Kansas City - Brett, Pinson ....$100-$150
1974 Los Angeles - Alston, Garvey, Cey, Buckner, Sutton, Marshall, John ....$150-$225
1974 Milwaukee - Yount ....$150-$200
1974 Minnesota - Carew, Oliva, Killebrew, Blyleven ....$125-$150
1974 Montreal - Singleton, Davis, Carter ......

1973 Chicago White Sox

.................$75-$100
1974 New York (AL) - Nettles, Murcer, Munson, Lyle, McDowell ....$175-$250
1974 New York (NL) - Harrelson, Staub, Jones, Kranepool, Koosman, Seaver ....$135-$200
1974 Oakland - Bando, Jackson, Hunter, Blue, Fingers ....$250-$375
1974 Philadelphia - Bowa, Schmidt, Luzinski, Boone ....$100-$150
1974 Pittsburgh - Oliver, Stargell, Parker, Tekulve ....$150-$200
1974 San Diego - McCovey, Winfield .$75-$125
1974 San Francisco - Kingman, Bonds $50-$100
1974 St. Louis - Torre, McBride, Brock, Simmons, McCarver, Gibson ....$125-$175
1974 Texas - Martin, Hargrove, Harrah, Burroughs, Jenkins ....$100-$145
1975 Atlanta - Evans, Niekro ....$100-$150
1975 Baltimore - Weaver, Robinson, Palmer ... .$150-$250
1975 Boston - Yastrzemski, Evans, Lynn, Rice, Fisk, Cooper, Conigliaro, Tiant ......$375-$550
1975 California - Ryan ....$200-$275
1975 Chicago (AL) - Kaat, Gossage ..$75-$100
1975 Chicago (NL) - Madlock ....$75-$125
1975 Cincinnati - Anderson, Perez, Morgan, Concepcion, Rose, Foster, Bench ....$350-$400
1975 Cleveland - Robinson ....$150-$225
1975 Detroit - Freehan, Horton, Lolich ....$75-$115
1975 Houston - Richard ....$65-$95
1975 Kansas City - Brett, Killebrew .$150-$200
1975 Los Angeles - Alston, Garvey, Cey, Buckner, Sutton, John ....$125-$175
1975 Milwaukee - Yount, Aaron ....$200-$275
1975 Minnesota - Carew, Bostock, Oliva, Blyleven ....$200-$300
1975 Montreal - Carter ....$75-$125
1975 New York (AL) - Martin, Nettles, Bonds, Munson, Piniella, Hunter, Lyle, Guidry$250-$450
1975 New York (NL) - Kranepool, Staub, Kingman, Grote, Seaver, Koosman ....$115-$125

1975 Cincinnati Reds

62

1975 Oakland - Bando, Jackson, Williams, Blue, Fingers, Odom . . . .$250-$350
1975 Philadelphia - Allen, Schmidt, Luzinski, Boone, McCarver, Carlton . . . .$100-$150
1975 Pittsburgh - Stargell, Parker, Oliver, Candelaria, Tekulve . . . .$175-$225
1975 San Diego - McCovey, Winfield .$85-$125
1975 San Francisco - Murcer, Clark . .$45-$100
1975 St. Louis - Schoendienst, Brock, Simmons, Hernandez, Gibson . . . .$100-$150
1975 Texas - Martin, Harrah, Jenkins, Perry . . . .$100-$200
1976 Atlanta - Murphy, Niekro . . . . . .$75-$100
1976 Baltimore - Weaver, Jackson, Robinson, Palmer . . . .$150-$200
1976 Boston - Yastrzemski, Evans, Lynn, Rice, Fisk, Cooper, Tiant, Jenkins . . . .$175-$300
1976 California - Ryan . . . .$125-$175
1976 Chicago (AL) - Gossage . . . .$60-$90
1976 Chicago (NL) - Madlock . . . .$60-$90
1976 Cincinnati - Anderson, Perez, Morgan, Concepcion, Rose, Griffey, Foster, Bench, Zachry . . . .$400-$600
1976 Cleveland - Robinson, Powell, Bell . . . .$75-$125
1976 Detroit - Staub, Freehan, Horton, Fidrych . . . .$100-$125
1976 Houston - Richard . . . .$60-$90
1976 Kansas City - Brett . . . .$125-$200
1976 Los Angeles - Alston, Garvey, Cey, Buckner, Sutton, John . . . .$100-$150
1976 Milwaukee - Yount, Aaron, Frisella . . . .$100-$150
1976 Minnesota - Carew, Bostock, Oliva, Blyleven . . . .$75-$125
1976 Montreal - Carter, Dawson . . . . .$75-$125
1976 New York (AL) - Martin, Nettles, Munson, Hunter, Lyle . . . .$150-$300
1976 New York (NL) - Kranepool, Harrelson, Kingman, Torre, Koosman, Seaver, Lolich . . . .$150-$200
1976 Oakland - Williams, Blue, Fingers . . . .$100-$125
1976 Philadelphia - Allen, Bowa, Schmidt, Luzinski, Boone, McCarver, Carlton, Kaat .$125-$200
1976 Pittsburgh - Stargell, Parker, Oliver, Candelaria, Tekulve . . . .$150-$175
1976 San Diego - Winfield, McCovey, Jones, Metzger . . . .$100-$125
1976 San Francisco - Evans, Murcer, Clark . . . .$75-$100
1976 St. Louis - Schoendienst, Hernandez, Brock, Simmons . . . .$125-$200
1976 Texas - Harrah, Thompson, Perry, Blyleven . . . .$75-$100
1977 Atlanta - Niekro . . . .$60-$90
1977 Baltimore - Weaver, Murray, Robinson, Palmer . . . .$100-$150
1977 Boston - Evans, Lynn, Yastrzemski, Fisk, Rice, Tiant, Jenkins . . . .$125-$175
1977 California - Grich, Bonds, Ryan $100-$150
1977 Chicago (AL) - B. Lemon . . . .$60-$90
1977 Chicago (NL) - Buckner, Trillo, Murcer, R. Reuschel . . . .$60-$75
1977 Cincinnati - Anderson, Morgan, Concepcion, Rose, Griffey, Foster, Bench, Seaver . . . .$125-$175
1977 Cleveland - Robinson, Bell, Eckersley . . . .$125-$175
1977 Detroit - Staub, Trammell, Whitaker, Morris . . . .$100-$150
1977 Houston - Richard . . . .$60-$90
1977 Kansas City - Brett . . . .$150-$200
1977 Los Angeles - Lasorda, Garvey, Cey, Mota, John, Sutton . . . .$175-$250
1977 Milwaukee - Cooper, Yount . . . .$75-$125
1977 Minnesota - Carew, Bostock . . . .$85-$100
1977 Montreal - Perez, Dawson, Carter . . . .$80-$120
1977 New York (AL) - Martin, Nettles, Jackson, Munson, Piniella, Guidry, Lyle, Hunter . . . .$350-$450
1977 New York (NL) - Harrelson, Kranepool, Kingman, Grote, Koosman, Seaver . . .$100-$150
1977 Oakland - Allen, Armas, Blue . . . .$60-$90
1977 Philadelphia - Bowa, Schmidt, Luzinski, Boone, McCarver, Carlton, Kaat . . . .$125-$175
1977 Pittsburgh - Stargell, Parker, Oliver, Gossage, Tekulve . . . .$125-$200
1977 San Diego - Winfield, Kingman, Fingers . . . .$100-$150
1977 San Francisco - McCovey, Madlock, Clark . . . .$100-$150
1977 Seattle - . . . .$125-$175
1977 St. Louis - Hernandez, Brock, Simmons . . . .$80-$120
1977 Texas - Perry, Blyleven . . . .$50-$100
1977 Toronto . . . .$150-$200
1978 Atlanta - Murphy, Horner, Neikro . . . .$75-$100
1978 Baltimore - Weaver, Murray, Palmer . . . .$125-$175
1978 Boston - Evans, Lynn, Yastrzemski, Fisk, Rice, Eckersley . . . .$100-$150
1978 California - Bostock, Ryan . . . . .$80-$120
1978 Chicago (AL) - Bob Lemon . . . . .$60-$90
1978 Chicago (NL) - Murcer, Kingman $60-$90
1978 Cincinnati - Anderson, Morgan, Concepcion, Rose, Foster, Bench, Seaver . . . .$150-$200
1978 Cleveland - Bell . . . .$85-$100
1978 Detroit - Whitaker, Trammell, Staub, Morris . . . .$100-$150
1978 Houston - Richard . . . .$60-$90
1978 Kansas City - Brett . . . .$120-$180
1978 Los Angeles - Lasorda, Garvey, Cey, Guerrero, John, Sutton . . . .$150-$225
1978 Milwaukee - Molitor, Yount . . . .$80-$120
1978 Minnesota - Carew . . . .$70-$125
1978 Montreal - Perez, Dawson, Carter$80-$120
1978 New York (AL) - Martin, Jackson, Lyle, Munson, Guidry, Hunter, Gossage, Lemon, Piniella . . . .$275-$400
1978 New York (NL) - Kranepool, Koosman . . . .$75-$100
1978 Oakland - Armas . . . .$60-$90
1978 Philadephia - Schmidt, Luzinski, Boone, Carlton, Kaat . . . .$125-$175
1978 Pittsburgh - Stargell, Parker, Blyleven, Candelaria, Tekulve . . . .$125-$175
1978 San Diego - Smith, Winfield, Perry, Fingers . . . .$125-$175
1978 San Francisco - McCovey, Clark, Blue . . . .$100-$150
1978 Seattle - . . . .$60-$90
1978 St. Louis - Boyer, Hernandez, Brock, Simmons . . . .$130-$160
1978 Texas - Harrah, Oliver, Jenkins . .$75-$100
1978 Toronto - . . . .$65-$150
1979 Atlanta - Murphy, Horner, Niekro . . . .$75-$125
1979 Baltimore - Weaver, Murray, Flanagan, Palmer . . . .$175-$250
1979 Boston - Lynn, Rice, Fisk, Yastrzemski, Eckersley . . . .$125-$175
1979 California - Carew, Lansford, Baylor, Ryan . . . .$125-$175
1979 Chicago (AL) - . . . .$75-$100
1979 Chicago (NL) - Buckner, Kingman, Sutter . . . .$60-$90
1979 Cincinnati - Morgan, Concepcion, Griffey, Foster, Bench, Seaver . . . .$125-$175
1979 Cleveland - Harrah . . . .$60-$90
1979 Detroit - Anderson, Whitaker, Trammell, Staub, Morris . . . .$100-$150
1979 Houston - Richard . . . .$75-$100
1979 Kansas City - Brett, Quisenberry . . . .$100-$150
1979 Los Angeles - Lasorda, Garvey, Cey, Guerrero, Sutcliffe, Sutton . . . .$100-$150
1979 Milwaukee - Molitor, Yount . . .$150-$200
1979 Minnesota - Castino, Koosman . . .$75-$90
1979 Montreal - Perez, Dawson, Carter, Staub, Raines . . . .$100-$150
1979 New York (AL) - Martin, Nettles, Jackson, Munson, Murcer, John,Guidry, Tiant, Gossage, Kaat, Hunter . . . .$175-$250
1979 New York (NL) - Kranepool . . .$85-$100
1979 Oakland - Armas, Henderson . . . .$75-$90
1979 Philadelphia - Rose, Trillo, Bowa, Schmidt, Luzinski, Boone, Carlton, Kaat . . . . . .$150-$200
1979 Pittsburgh - Stargell, Madlock, Parker, Candelaria, Blyleven, Tekulve . . . .$275-$375
1979 San Diego - Smith, Winfield, Perry, Fingers, Lolich . . . .$125-$175
1979 San Francisco - McCovey, Clark, Madlock, Blue . . . .$125-$150
1979 Seattle - . . . .$60-$90
1979 St. Louis - Boyer, Hernandez, Brock, Simmons . . . .$125-$175
1979 Texas - Bell, Oliver, Jenkins, Lyle .$65-$95
1979 Toronto - Griffin, Stieb . . . .$60-$90
1980 Atlanta - Horner, Murphy, Niekro . . . .$90-$125
1980 Baltimore - Weaver, Murray, Stone, Palmer . . . .$150-$225
1980 Boston - Perez, Evans, Lynn, Rice, Fisk, Yastrzemski, Eckersley . . . .$125-$200
1980 California - Carew, Lansford . . . .$75-$100
1980 Chicago (AL) - Baines . . . .$60-$90
1980 Chicago (NL) - Buckner, Kingman . . . .$60-$90
1980 Cincinnati - Concepcion, Griffey, Foster, Bench, Seaver . . . .$75-$100
1980 Cleveland - Harrah, Charboneau .$45-$75
1980 Detroit - Anderson, Whitaker, Trammell, Gibson, Morris . . . .$100-$150
1980 Houston - Morgan, Ryan . . . . . .$125-$175
1980 Kansas City - Brett, Quisenberry . . . .$175-$250
1980 Los Angeles - Lasorda, Garvey, Guerrero, Welch, Sutton, Howe, Valenzuela . . . .$100-$150
1980 Milwaukee - Molitor, Yount . . . .$80-$120
1980 Minnesota - Koosman . . . .$60-$85
1980 Montreal - Dawson, Carter, Raines . . . .$100-$150
1980 New York (AL) - Nettles, Jackson, Piniella, Murcer, Guidry, Tiant, Gossage, John, Perry, Kaat . . . .$200-$250
1980 New York (NL) - Wilson . . . . . .$75-$100
1980 Oakland - Martin, Henderson . .$140-$210
1980 Philadelphia - Rose, Bowa, Schmidt, Luzinski, Boone, Carlton,Lyle . . . .$275-$350
1980 Pittsburgh - Stargell, Madlock, Parker, Candelaria, Tekulve, Blyleven . . . .$150-$175
1980 San Diego - Smith, Winfield, Fingers . . . .$80-$120
1980 San Francisco - Clark, McCovey, Blue . . . .$75-$120
1980 Seattle - . . . .$60-$90
1980 St. Louis - Schoendienst, Hernandez, Simmons, Kaat . . . .$80-$120
1980 Texas - Bell, Oliver, Staub, Jenkins, Perry,

Team Baseball Autographs — Chapter 5

1981 New York Yankees

Lyle ....$75-$100
1980 Toronto - Stieb ....$60-$90
1981 Atlanta - Murphy, Butler, Perry, Niekro ... .$100-$150
1981 Baltimore - Weaver, Murray, Ripken, Palmer ....$100-$150
1981 Boston - Lansford, Rice, Yastrzemski, Eckersley ....$100-$150
1981 California - Carew, Lynn ....$60-$90
1981 Chicago (AL) - Baines, Fisk, Luzinski, Hoyt ....$75-$100
1981 Chicago (NL) - Buckner ....$60-$90
1981 Cincinnati - Concepcion, Griffey, Foster, Bench, Seaver ....$80-$120
1981 Cleveland - Harrah, Blyleven ....$60-$90
1981 Detroit - Anderson, Whitaker, Trammell, Gibson, Morris ....$100-$125
1981 Houston - Ryan, Sutton ....$100-$125
1981 Kansas City - Brett, Quisenberry $75-$100
1981 Los Angeles - Garvey, Cey, Guerrero, Sax, Valenzuela, Stewart ......$275-$350
1981 Milwaukee - Yount, Molitor, Fingers ....$100-$150
1981 Minnesota - ....$60-$90
1981 Montreal - Dawson, Raines, Carter ....$150-$175
1981 New York - Kingman, Staub ..$100-$125
1981 New York (AL) - Nettles, Jackson, Winfield, Murcer, Piniella, Guidry, John, Gossage ....$200-$250
1981 Oakland - Martin, Henderson ..$125-$200
1981 Philadelphia - Rose, Bowa, Schmidt, Boone, Sandberg, Carlton, Lyle ....$100-$150
1981 Pittsburgh - Parker, Stargell, Madlock ....$75-$125
1981 San Diego - Smith, Kennedy .....$60-$95
1981 San Francisco - Morgan, Clark, Blue ....$65-$95
1981 Seattle - Henderson ....$50-$85
1981 St. Louis - Hernandez, Kaat ..$100-$135
1981 Texas - Bell, Oliver, Jenkins .....$65-$95
1981 Toronto - Bell, Barfield, Stieb ...$60-$100

1982 New York Yankees

1982 Atlanta - Murphy, Butler, Niekro $90-$150
1982 Baltimore - Weaver, Murray, Ripken, Palmer ....$100-$150
1982 Boston - Lansford, Rice, Yastrzemski, Boggs, Perez, Eckersley ....$150-$250
1982 California - Carew, Jackson, Lynn, Boone, John, Tiant ....$125-$200
1982 Chicago (AL) - Baines, Fisk, Luzinski, Hoyt, Lyle ....$75-$125
1982 Chicago (NL) - Buckner, Sandberg, Jenkins, Hernandez ....$80-$120
1982 Cincinnati - Concepcion, Bench, Seaver .. ..$75-$125
1982 Cleveland - Harrah, Blyleven ....$60-$90
1982 Detroit - Anderson, Whitaker, Trammell, Gibson, Johnson, Morris ....$100-$150
1982 Houston - Ryan, Sutton ......$75-$125
1982 Kansas City - Brett, Quisenberry $75-$100
1982 Los Angeles - Garvey, Sax, Guerrero, Valenzuela, Stewart ....$100-$150
1982 Milwaukee - Yount, Molitor, Vuckovich, Fingers, Sutton ....$250-$350
1982 Minnesota - Hrbek, Brunansky, Viola ....$60-$90
1982 Montreal - Oliver, Dawson, Raines, Carter, Reardon ....$75-$125
1982 New York(AL) - Lemon, Nettles, Winfield, Piniella, Murcer, Mattingly, John, Guidry, Gossage ....$125-$175
1982 New York (NL) - Kingman, Foster ....$80-$120
1982 Oakland - Martin, Henderson ..$150-$180
1982 Philadelphia - Rose, Schmidt, Carlton, Lyle ....$150-$175
1982 Pittsburgh - Madlock, Parker, Stargell, Candelaria, Tekulve ....$90-$135
1982 San Diego - Kennedy, Gwynn ...$80-$120
1982 San Francisco - Robinson, Morgan, Clark, Leonard ....$60-$90
1982 Seattle - Perry ....$60-$90
1982 St. Louis - Hernandez, Smith, McGee ....$275-$350
1982 Texas - Bell ....$60-$90
1982 Toronto - Barfield, Stieb ....$60-$90
1983 Atlanta - Murphy, Butler, Niekro .$60-$90
1983 Baltimore - Murray, Ripken, Palmer ....$300-$450
1983 Boston - Boggs, Rice, Yastrzemski, Eckersley ....$150-$200
1983 California - Carew, Lynn, Boone, Jackson, John ....$80-$120
1983 Chicago (AL) - Baines, Kittle, Fisk, Hoyt . ...$150-$180
1983 Chicago (NL) - Buckner, Sandberg, Jenkins, Hernandez ....$100-$150
1983 Cincinnati - Concepcion, Bench $75-$100
1983 Cleveland - Franco, Harrah, Blyleven ....$60-$90

1983 Milwaukee Brewers

1983 Detroit - Anderson, Whitaker, Trammell, Johnson, Morris ....$125-$150
1983 Houston - Ryan ....$100-$150
1983 Kansas City - Brett, Quisenberry, Perry ... .$80-$120
1983 Los Angeles - Sax, Guerrero, Valenzuela, Welch, Stewart, Hershiser ......$125-$175
1983 Milwaukee - Yount, Molitor, Simmons, Fingers, Kuenn ....$100-$200
1983 Minnesota - Hrbek, Brunansky, Viola ....$60-$90
1983 Montreal - Oliver, Dawson, Raines, Carter ....$75-$100
1983 New York (AL) - Martin, Nettles, Winfield, Piniella, Murcer, Guidry, Gossage ....$200-$300
1983 New York (NL) - Strawberry, Foster, Staub, Kingman, Seaver ....$100-$150
1983 Oakland - Lansford, Henderson ..$75-$85
1983 Philadelphia - Rose, Morgan, Schmidt, Perez, Denny, Hernandez ....$175-$250
1983 Pittsburgh - Madlock, Parker, Candelaria, Tekulve ....$60-$90
1983 San Diego - Garvey, Gwynn ..$100-$150
1983 San Francisco - Robinson .....$60-$90
1983 Seattle - Perry ....$60-$90
1983 St. Louis - Smith, McGee, Hernandez ....$100-$125.
1983 Texas - Bell, Stewart ....$60-$90
1983 Toronto - Bell, Fernandez, Stieb ..$60-$90.
1984 Atlanta - Murphy ....$60-$90.
1984 Baltimore - Murray, Ripken, Palmer ....$175-$225.
1984 Boston - Buckner, Boggs, Rice, Clemens .. ..$85-$110
1984 California - Carew, Lynn, Boone, Jackson, John ....$80-$120
1984 Chicago (AL) - Baines, Fisk, Seaver ....$75-$90.
1984 Chicago (NL) - Sandberg, Sutcliffe, Eckersley ....$175-$275
1984 Cincinnati - Rose, Concepcion, Parker, Perez, Davis ....$75-$125
1984 Cleveland - Franco, Blyleven. ....$75-$90
1984 Detroit - Anderson, Whitaker, Trammell, Johnson, Gibson, Morris, Hernandez ..$350-$500
1984 Houston - Davis, Ryan ....$65-$100
1984 Kansas City - Brett, Saberhagen$100-$150
1984 Los Angeles - Sax, Guerrero, Valenzuela, Hershiser ....$125-$150
1984 Milwaukee - Yount, Sutton ....$100-$125
1984 Minnesota - Hrbek, Puckett, Viola ....$85-$150
1984 Montreal - Dawson, Raines, Carter, Rose . ...$100-$150
1984 New York (AL) - Berra, Mattingly, Winfield, Piniella, Niekro, Guidry. ....$125-$175
1984 New York (NL) - Hernandez, Strawberry, Foster, Gooden ....$125-$150
1984 Oakland - Morgan, Lansford, Henderson .. ..$85-$100
1984 Philadelphia - Schmidt, Carlton ....$100-$150
1984 Pittsburgh - Madlock, Candelaria, Tekulve ....$65-$90
1984 San Diego - Garvey, Nettles, Gwynn, Gossage ....$175-$250
1984 San Francisco - Oliver, Leonard, Clark ... .$75-$90
1984 Seattle - Davis, Tartabull, Langston ....$60-$90
1984 St. Louis - O. Smith, McGee ..$125-$150
1984 Texas - Stewart ....$60-$90
1984 Toronto - Bell, Fernandez, Stieb $100-$125

1985 Atlanta - Murphy ....$60-$90
1985 Baltimore - Weaver, Murray, Ripken, Lynn ....$50-$85
1985 Boston - Boggs, Rice, Clemens ...$60-$90
1985 California - Carew, Jackson, Boone, Sutton, John ....$80-$120
1985 Chicago (AL) - Guillen, Baines, Fisk, Seaver ....$75-$100
1985 Chicago (NL) - Sandberg, Eckersley ....$60-$90
1985 Cincinnati - Rose, Concepcion, Parker, Perez, Davis ....$75-$125
1985 Cleveland - Franco, Carter, Blyleven ....$50-$85
1985 Detroit - Anderson, Whitaker, Trammell, Gibson, Morris ....$75-$125
1985 Houston - Davis, Ryan ....$75-$100
1985 Kansas City - Brett, Saberhagen $300-$400
1985 Los Angeles - Sax, Oliver, Hershiser, Valenzuela................................$60-$150
1985 Milwaukee - Yount, Fingers ......$60-$90
1985 Minnesota - Hrbek, Puckett, Viola, Blyleven ....$75-$100
1985 Montreal - Dawson, Raines ......$45-$75
1985 New York (AL) - Berra, Martin, Mattingly, Winfield, Henderson, Guidry, Niekro .$125-$175
1985 New York (NL) - Hernandez, Johnson, Strawberry, Foster, Carter, Gooden ...$200-$300
1985 Oakland - Lansford, Kingman, Sutton ....$60-$90
1985 Philadelphia - Schmidt, Carlton .$75-$100
1985 Pittsburgh - Madlock ....$60-$90
1985 San Diego - Garvey, Nettles, Gwynn, Gossage ....$75-$100
1985 San Francisco - Leonard ....$60-$90
1985 Seattle - Tartabull, Langston .....$60-$90
1985 St. Louis - Clark, McGee, Coleman ....$175-$250
1985 Texas - Harrah ....$70-$95
1985 Toronto - Fernandez, Bell, Fielder, Stieb ....$100-$150
1986 Atlanta - Murphy ....$50-$80
1986 Baltimore - Weaver, Murray, Ripken, Lynn ....$75-$100
1986 Boston - Boggs, Rice, Clemens, Seaver ....$200-$400
1986 California - Joyner, Boone, Jackson, Sutton ....$60-$90
1986 Chicago (AL) - Baines, Fisk, Carlton, Seaver ....$75-$100
1986 Chicago (NL) - Sandberg, Palmeiro, Eckersley ....$75-$100
1986 Cincinnati - Parker, Davis, Concepcion, Perez, Rose ....$60-$90
1986 Cleveland - Franco, Carter, Niekro $60-$75
1986 Detroit - Anderson, Whitaker, Trammell, Gibson, Morris ....$100-$125
1986 Houston - Davis, Scott, Ryan ....
.................................$75-$100
1986 Kansas City - Howser, Brett, Jackson, Saberhagen ....$60-$90
1986 Los Angeles - Guerrero, Valenzuela, Hershiser ....$75-$100
1986 Milwaukee - Yount, Molitor .....$50-$75
1986 Minnesota - Hrbek, Puckett, Blyleven, Viola ....$80-$120
1986 Montreal - Dawson, Raines ......$50-$75
1986 New York (AL) - Mattingly, Winfield, Henderson, Guidry, John ....$125-$200
1986 New York (NL) - Hernandez, Strawberry, Carter, Mitchell, Foster, Gooden .....$350-$525
1986 Oakland - Canseco, McGwire, Stewart ....$100-$125
1986 Philadelphia - Schmidt, Carlton .$75-$100
1986 Pittsburgh - Bonds, Bonilla ......$50-$75
1986 San Diego - Garvey, Gwynn, Gossage ....$60-$75
1986 San Francisco - Clark, Carlton ....
.................................$50-$75
1986 Seattle - Tartabull, Langston .....$60-$75
1986 St. Louis - Smith, McGee ......$75-$100
1986 Texas - Sierra ....$60-$75
1986 Toronto - Fernandez, Bell, Stieb ..$60-$75
1987 Atlanta - Murphy, Niekro ....$50-$75
1987 Baltimore - Murray, Ripken, Lynn $60-$85
1987 Boston - Boggs, Rice, Clemens ..$75-$100
1987 California - Joyner, Boone, Buckner, Sutton $65-$80
1987 Chicago (AL) - Fisk, Baines ....$75-$115
1987 Chicago (NL) - Sandberg, Dawson, Palmeiro ....$50-$75
1987 Cincinnati - Rose, Parker, Davis, Concepcion ....$75-$100
1987 Cleveland - Carter, Franco, Niekro, Carlton ....$75-$100
1987 Detroit - Anderson, Whitaker, Trammell, Gibson, Morris ....$175-$200
1987 Houston - Davis, Ryan ....$100-$165
1987 Kansas City - Brett, Tartabull, Jackson, Saberhagen ....$85-$100
1987 Los Angeles - Lasorda, Sax, Guerrero, Hershiser, Valenzuela ....$80-$120
1987 Milwaukee - Molitor, Yount ....$45-$90
1987 Minnesota - Hrbek, Puckett, Viola, Blyleven, Carlton ....$300-$400
1987 Montreal - Raines ....$75-$100
1987 New York (AL) - Mattingly, Henderson, Winfield, John, Guidry ....$100-$150
1987 New York (NL) - Hernandez, Johnson, Strawberry, Carter, Gooden ....$150-$175
1987 Oakland - McGwire, Canseco, Jackson, Stewart, Eckersley ....$100-$150
1987 Philadelphia - Schmidt ....$50-$75
1987 Pittsburgh - Bonilla, Van Slyke, Bonds ...
.................................$75-$100
1987 San Diego - Gwynn, Garvey, Gossage ....$50-$75
1987 San Francisco - Clark, Mitchell, Williams .
.................................$100-$150
1987 Seattle - Langston ....$50-$75
1987 St. Louis - Smith, McGee .....$175-$225
1987 Texas - Sierra ....$60-$90
1987 Toronto - Fernandez, Bell, McGriff, Stieb, Niekro ....$75-$100
1988 Atlanta - Murphy ....$50-$80
1988 Baltimore - Robinson, Murray, Ripken, Lynn ....$75-$100
1988 Boston - Boggs, Rice, Clemens .$75-$125
1988 California - Joyner, Boone, Buckner .....
.................................$60-$75
1988 Chicago (AL) - Fisk, Baines ....$65-$75
1988 Chicago (NL) - Grace, Sandberg, Dawson, Palmeiro, Gossage ....$50-$80
1988 Cincinnati - Sabo ....$75-$100
1988 Cleveland - Franco, Carter ......$50-$75
1988 Detroit - Whitaker, Trammell, Lynn, Morris ....$85-$100
1988 Houston - Davis, Ryan ....$75-$125
1988 Kansas City - Brett, Tartabull, Jackson, Buckner, Saberhagen ....$100-$125
1988 Los Angeles - Sax, Gibson, Hershiser, Valenzuela ....$200-$300
1988 Milwaukee - Yount, Molitor ....$50-$75
1988 Minnesota - Hrbek, Puckett, Viola, Blyleven, Carlton ....$60-$85
1988 Montreal - Raines ....$50-$75
1988 New York (AL) - Martin, Mattingly, Winfield, Henderson, John, Guidry ..$150-$200
1988 New York (NL) - Hernandez, Johnson, Strawberry, Carter, Gooden ....$75-$150
1988 Oakland - McGwire, Lansford, Canseco, Parker, Stewart, Welch, Eckersley ....$200-$250
1988 Philadelphia - Schmidt ....$75-$100
1988 Pittsburgh - Bonilla, Van Slyke, Bonds, Drabek ....$50-$75
1988 San Diego - Gwynn ....$60-$80
1988 San Francisco - Clark, Mitchell, Williams .
.................................$60-$85
1988 Seattle - Langston ....$50-$75
1988 St. Louis - Smith, McGee, Guerrero .....
.................................$45-$70
1988 Texas - Sierra ....$50-$75
1988 Toronto - McGriff, Fernandez, Bell, Stieb .
.................................$60-$85
1989 Atlanta - Murphy ....$100-$150
1989 Baltimore - Robinson, Ripken ..$75-$125
1989 Boston - Boggs, Clemens ......$75-$100
1989 California - Joyner, Blyleven .....$50-$75
1989 Chicago (AL) - Fisk, Baines .....$50-$75
1989 Chicago (NL) - Grace, Sandberg, Dawson ....$150-$225
1989 Cincinnati - Davis ....$50-$85
1989 Cleveland - Carter ....$50-$75
1989 Detroit - Anderson, Trammell, Lynn, Morris ....$50-$75
1989 Houston - Davis ....$40-$60
1989 Kansas City - Brett, Jackson, Boone, Tartabull, Saberhagen ....$100-$150
1989 Los Angeles - Lasorda, Murray, Randolph, Gibson, Hershiser, Valenzuela ....$125-$175
1989 Milwaukee - Yount, Molitor ....$90-$125
1989 Minnesota - Hrbek, Puckett, Viola $50-$85
1989 Montreal - Raines ....$75-$100
1989 New York (AL) - Mattingly, Sax, Winfield, Gossage ....$125-$150
1989 New York (NL) - Johnson, Strawberry, Hernandez, Carter, Gooden ....$75-$145
1989 Oakland - LaRussa, McGwire, Canseco, D. Henderson, R. Henderson, Parker, Stewart, Eckersley ....$225-$300
1989 Philadelphia - Dykstra, Schmidt .$60-$100
1989 Pittsburgh - Bonilla, Van Slyke, Bonds ...
.................................$75-$100
1989 San Diego - Clark, Gwynn ......$50-$85
1989 San Francisco - Clark, Williams, Mitchell, Gossage ....$150-$200
1989 Seattle - Griffey Jr ....$175-$250
1989 St. Louis - Guerrero, Smith, McGee .....
.................................$85-$125
1989 Texas - Palmeiro, Franco, Sierra, Baines, Ryan ....$75-$100
1989 Toronto - McGriff, Fernandez, Stieb .....
.................................$100-$150
1990 Atlanta - Justice, Murphy .....$100-$175
1990 Baltimore - F. Robinson, C. Ripken Jr. ....
.................................$75-$100

1986 New York Mets

1990 Boston - Boggs, Clemens . . . .$100-$150
1990 California - Joyner, Winfield, Blyleven . . . .$75-$100
1990 Chicago (AL) - Fisk . . . .$50-$85
1990 Chicago (NL) - Dawson, Grace, Sandberg . . . .$100-$135
1990 Cincinnati - Larkin, Davis, Piniella . . . .$225-$300
1990 Cleveland - Hernandez . . . .$40-$60
1990 Detroit - Anderson, Fielder, Morris, Trammell, Whitaker . . . .$75-$100
1990 Houston - Davis . . . .$40-$60
1990 Kansas City - Brett, Tartabull, Jackson, Saberhagen . . . .$75-$125
1990 Los Angeles - Lasorda, Murray, Gibson, Valenzuela . . . .$85-$125
1990 Milwaukee - Yount, Molitor, Parker . . . .$50-$75
1990 Minnesota - Hrbek, Puckett . . . . .$50-$85
1990 Montreal - Raines . . . .$50-$85
1990 New York (AL) - Mattingly . . .$125-$175
1990 New York (NL) - Strawberry, Johnson, Viola, Gooden . . . .$100-$125
1990 Oakland - McGwire, Randolph, Canseco, R. Henderson, D Henderson, Baines, McGee, Welch, Stewart, Eckersley . . . .$150-$200
1990 Philadelphia - Dykstra, Murphy . .$40-$60
1990 Pittsburgh - Bonds, Bonilla, Van Slyke, Drabek . . . .$100-$135
1990 San Diego - Gwynn, Carter, Clark $50-$75
1990 San Francisco - Clark, Mitchell, Williams . . . .$75-$100
1990 Seattle - Ken Griffey Jr., Ken Griffey Sr . . . .$75-$100
1990 St. Louis - Guerrero, Smith, McGee . . . .$50-$85
1990 Texas - Palmeiro, Franco, Sierra, Ryan . . . .$85-$100
1990 Toronto - McGriff, Stieb, Fernandez . . . .$60-$85
1991 Atlanta - Glavine, Pendleton . .$150-$200
1991 Baltimore - F. Robinson, C Ripken . . . .$65-$100
1991 Boston - Boggs, Clemens . . . . . .$80-$100
1991 California - Joyner, Winfield . . . . .$45-$65
1991 Chicago (AL) - Fisk, Thomas . . .$85-$150
1991 Chicago (NL) - Sandberg, Dawson . . . .$75-$100
1991 Cincinnati - Larkin, Davis, Piniella . . . .$65-$85
1991 Cleveland - Swindell . . . .$45-$75
1991 Detroit - Anderson, Whitaker, Trammell, Fielder . . . .$75-$100
1991 Houston - Bagwell, Hamisch . . . .$50-$75
1991 Kansas City - Brett, Saberhagen, Tartabull . . . .$85-$100
1991 Los Angeles - Lasorda, Murray, Strawberry . . . .$65-$90

1991 Milwaukee - Yount, Molitor . . .$85-$100
1991 Minnesota - Knoblauch, Morris, Puckett, Hrbek . . . .$150-$225
1991 Montreal - Calderon . . . .$30-$50
1991 New York (AL) - Mattingly . .$75-$125
1991 New York (NL) - Johnson, Gooden, Viola . . . .$60-$90
1991 Oakland - R Henderson, Stewart, Eckersley, Canseco . . . .$80-$120
1991 Philadelphia - Dykstra, Murphy . .$50-$85
1991 Pittsburgh - Bonds, Bonilla . .$100-$150
1991 San Diego - Gwynn, McGriff, Fernandez . . . .$50-$80
1991 San Francisco - Mitchell, Clark . .$40-$60
1991 Seattle - Griffey Jr., Griffey Sr. . . .$75-$100
1991 St. Louis - O. Smith, L. Smith . . . .$45-$60
1991 Texas - Franco, Ryan, Sierra, Palmeiro . . . .$60-$85
1991 Toronto - Carter, Alomar, Stieb .$80-$125
1992 Atlanta - Pendleton, Justice, Glavine $325
1992 Baltimore - Devereaux, Ripken, Mussina $115
1992 Boston - Boggs, Clemens $100
1992 California - Langston $75
1992 Chicago (AL) - Thomas, McDowell . .$85
1992 Chicago (NL) - Maddux, Grace, Dawson, Sandberg $125
1992 Cincinnati - Larkin, Rijo $85
1992 Cleveland - Baerga, Belle, Nagy $100
1992 Detroit - Fryman, Whitaker, Trammell, Fielder $85
1992 Houston - Biggio, Bagwell $40
1992 Kansas City - Brett, Jefferies, Joyner . .$85
1992 Los Angeles - Karros, Butler $80
1992 Milwaukee - Listach, Yount, Eldred, Molitor $60
1992 Minnesota - Puckett, Knoblauch $85
1992 Montreal - Grissom, Walker, Martinez .$50
1992 New York (AL) - Mattingly $90
1992 New York (NL) - Murray, Bonilla, Cone $85
1992 Oakland - Eckersley, McGwire, Henderson, Canseco $150
1992 Philadelphia - Hollins, Dykstra, Kruk, Schilling, Daulton $100
1992 Pittsburgh - Bonds, Van Slyke, Drabek $125
1992 San Diego - Gwynn, Sheffield, McGriff $85
1992 San Francisco - Clark, Williams $110
1992 Seattle - Griffey Jr., Martinez $115
1992 St. Louis - O Smith, L Smith, Lankford $60
1992 Texas - Sierra, Gonzalez $125
1992 Toronto - Alomar, Carter, Winfield, Morris $200
1993 Atlanta - Maddux, McGriff $250
1993 Baltimore - Ripken, Mussina $115
1993 Boston - Dawson, Clemens, Vaughn . .$80
1993 California - Salmon, Langston $75
1993 Chicago (AL) - Thomas, McDowell .$175
1993 Chicago (NL) - Sandberg, Grace $85
1993 Cincinnati - Larkin, Rijo $45
1993 Cleveland - Baerga, Belle, Nagy $125
1993 Colorado - Galarraga, Hayes $150
1993 Detroit - Whitaker, Trammell, Fielder .$90
1993 Florida - Harvey, Weiss, Destrade . . .$150
1993 Houston - Swindell, Drabek, Bagwell .$40
1993 Kansas City - Brett, Cone $125
1993 Los Angeles - Piazza, Karros $150
1993 Milwaukee - Listach, Hamilton, Vaughn, Yount $50
1993 Minnesota - Puckett, Winfield $100

1993 Montreal - D. Martinez, Grissom, Walker $50
1993 New York (AL) - Boggs, Mattingly . .$115
1993 New York (NL) - Bonilla, Murray, Gooden $75
1993 Oakland - Sierra, McGwire, Eckersley .$75
1993 Philadelphia - Schilling, Dykstra, Kruk, Daulton $300
1993 Pittsburgh - Van Slyke, Bell $95
1993 San Diego - Gwynn, Sheffield $80
1993 San Francisco - Bonds, Clark $150
1993 Seattle - Griffey Jr., R Johnson $85
1993 St. Louis - O Smith, Lankford $50
1993 Texas - Ryan, Gonzalez, Canseco . .$125
1993 Toronto - Alomar, Molitor, Carter, Olerud, Stewart $200
1994 Atlanta - Maddux, McGriff $275
1994 Baltimore - Ripken, Mussina $125
1994 Boston - Greenwell, Clemens, Vaughn $125
1994 California - Salmon, Langston, Edmonds$95
1994 Chicago (AL) - Thomas, McDowell, Ventura $125
1994 Chicago (NL) - Sandberg, Grace $95
1994 Cincinnati - Larkin $65
1994 Cleveland - Baerga, Belle, Lofton, Martinez, Nagy $175
1994 Colorado - Galarraga, Hayes $150
1994 Detroit - Whitaker, Trammell, Fielder, Anderson $95
1994 Florida - Sheffield, Harvey $75
1994 Houston - Drabek, Bagwell $50
1994 Kansas City - Appier, Cone $95
1994 Los Angeles - Piazza, Karros $150
1994 Milwaukee - Eldred, Vaughn $85
1994 Minnesota - Puckett, Winfield, Knoblauch $110
1994 Montreal - D. Martinez, Grissom, Walker $60
1994 New York (AL) - Boggs, Mattingly, Key, Abbott $125
1994 New York (NL) - Bonilla $75
1994 Oakland - Sierra, McGwire, Eckersley $110
1994 Philadelphia - Dykstra, Kruk, Daulton $250
1994 Pittsburgh - Van Slyke, Bell $85
1994 San Diego - Gwynn $80
1994 San Francisco - Bonds, Clark $150
1994 Seattle - Griffey Jr., R.Johnson, Piniella $85
1994 St. Louis - O. Smith, Lankford $65
1994 Texas - Ryan, Gonzalez, Canseco . .$125
1994 Toronto - Alomar, Molitor, Carter, Olerud, Stewart $125
1995 Atlanta - Smoltz, Glavine $250
1995 Baltimore - Ripken, Mussina $125
1995 Boston - Canseco $110
1995 California - D. Easley, C. Davis $125
1995 Chicago (AL) - Thomas, Ventura, Guillen $110
1995 Chicago (NL) - Sosa, Sandberg $145
1995 Cincinnati - Larkin $150
1995 Cleveland - Thome, A. Belle $250
1995 Colorado - Bichette, Castilla, Galarraga, Walker, Burks $135
1995 Detroit - Fielder, Fryman, Trammell .$100
1995 Florida - Sheffield, W. Fraser $175
1995 Houston- Bagwell, D. Bell $125
1995 Kansas City- Hamelin, Gaetti, Cone, Gagne $90
1995 Los Angeles - Piazza, Nomo $125

1991 Cincinnati Reds

1995 Cleveland Indians

1995 Milwaukee - Garner, Seitzer, Cirillo ..$75
1995 Minnesota - Knoblauch, Puckett $90
1995 Montreal - P. Martinez, M. Alou, Grissom .
.................................$110
1995 New York (AL) O'Neill, Boggs $125
1995 New York (NL) Saberhagen $95
1995 Oakland - McGwire $75
1995 Philadelphia - Dykstra, Daulton, Morandini, Schilling $95
1995 Pittsburgh - King $100
1995 San Diego - Gwynn, Caminiti, Finley .$90
1995 San Francisco - Bonds $140
1995 Seattle - Griffey, Buhner $150
1995 St. Louis - O. Smith, Gilkey $125
1995 Texas - Gonzalez, Rodriguez $125
1995 Toronto - R. Alomar, Molitor, J. Carter ...
..................................$100
1996 Atlanta - Maddux, Glavine, Justice, Grissom $175
1996 Baltimore - Ripken, R. Alomar, Mussina ..
..................................$100
1996 Boston - Vaughn, Clemens $110
1996 California - Salmon $90
1996 Chicago (AL) - Thomas, Ventura, Guillen
..................................$100
1996 Chicago (NL) - Sosa, Grace $110
1996 Cincinnati - Larkin, Boone $90
1996 Cleveland - Thome, Lofton, Nagy ...$175
1996 Colorado - Bichette, Castilla, Walker Galarraga, Burks $145
1996 Detroit - Clark $80
1996 Florida - Sheffield, K. Brown, C. Johnson, A. Leiter $100
1996 Houston - Bagwell, Biggio $100
1996 Kansas City - $80
1996 Los Angeles - Piazza, Mondesi, Nomo, Karros $110
1996 Milwaukee -G. Vaughn $90
1996 Minnesota - Molitor, Knoblauch $90
1996 Montreal - P. Martinez, M. Alou, Grudzielanek $75
1996 New York (AL) - Jeter, T. Martinez, Torre, Williams, O'Neill $325
1996 New York (NL) - Hundley, Gilkey, J. Kent
..................................$175
1996 Oakland - McGwire $120
1996 Philadelphia- Dykstra, Schilling $90
1996 Pittsburgh- Kendall $80
1996 San Diego - Gwynn, R. Henderson ..$100
1996 San Francisco - Bonds, Baker $90
1996 Seattle - Griffey, Buhner, Rodriguez ..$120
1996 St. Louis - O. Smith, Gaetti $100
1996 Texas - Gonzalez, Clark $90

1996 New York Yankees

1996 Toronto - J. Guzman, Olerud, Hentgen $80
1997 Anaheim - Edmonds, Salmon $100
1997 Atlanta - C. Jones, Maddux, Glavine, Lofton, Smoltz $150
1997 Baltimore - C. Ripken, Mussina $110
1997 Boston - Vaughn, Garciaparra $100
1997 Chicago (AL) - Thomas, Belle $110
1997 Chicago (NL) - Sosa, Grace $120
1997 Cincinnati- Larkin, Tomko, Stynes ..$100
1997 Cleveland - Thome, Justice, M. Williams .
..................................$175
1997 Colorado - Bichette, Castilla, Galarraga, Walker $140
1997 Detroit - Easley, Clark, Higginson $75
1997 Florida - M. Alou, K. Brown, Sheffield, Bonilla, Leyland $155
1997 Houston - Bagwell, Biggio, Kile $145
1997 Kansas City - Damon, Bell $125
1997 Los Angeles - Piazza, Mondesi, Nomo $110
1997 Milwaukee - Garner, Cirillo $90
1997 Minnesota - Molitor, Knoblauch $90
1997 Montreal - Guerrero, P. Martinez, F. Alou .
..................................$80
1997 New York (AL) - Jeter, Williams, Torre, O'Neill $395
1997 New York (NL) Hundley, Franco ...$150
1997 Oakland - Canseco $100
1997 Philadelphia - Rolen, Jefferies $135
1997 Pittsburgh - Kendall $125
1997 San Diego - Gwynn, Caminiti $175
1997 San Francisco - Bonds, Baker $100
1997 Seattle - A. Rodriguez, Griffey $125
1997 St. Louis - McGwire, Gant $150
1997 Texas - Gonzalez, Rodriguez $100
1997 Toronto - Clemens, Delgado $100
1998 Anaheim - Edmonds, Salmon $110
1998 Arizona - Lee, Bell, M. Williams, Showalter $245
1998 Atlanta - Glavine, Maddux, C. Jones, Galarraga $295
1998 Baltimore - C. Ripken, Mussina $120
1998 Boston - Vaughn, Garciaparra, P. Martinez
..................................$110
1998 Chicago (AL) - Thomas, Belle $100
1998 Chicago (NL) - Sosa, Wood $200
1998 Cincinnati - Larkin, Tomko, Greene ..$125
1998 Cleveland - Thome, Justice, Lofton ..$210
1998 Colorado - Bichette, Castilla, Walker $190
1998 Detroit - Clark, Higginson, Easley, Cruz ..
..................................$130
1998 Florida - Renteria, Hernandez, Leyland $80
1998 Houston - Bagwell, Biggio, R. Johnson, M. Alou $180

Team Baseball Autographs — Chapter 5

1998 Kansas City - Palmer $90
1998 Los Angeles - Sheffield, Mondesi $110
1998 Milwaukee - Cirillo, Vina, Jenkins $90
1998 Minnesota - Molitor $100
1998 Montreal - Guerrero, F. Alou $90
1998 New York (AL) Jeter, Wells, Williams, Brosius, Torre $320
1998 New York (NL) - Piazza, Nomo, Franco ..
..................................$225
1998 Oakland - Grieve, Henderson $120
1998 Philadelphia - Rolen, Schilling $110
1998 Pittsburgh - Kendall, Guillen $125
1998 San Diego - K. Brown, Gwynn, Caminiti, Hoffman, Vaughn $225
1998 San Francisco - Bonds, Baker $100
1998 Seattle - Griffey, A. Rodriguez $160
1998 St. Louis - McGwire, Drew, LaRussa .$250
1998 Tampa Bay - McGriff, Boggs $275
1998 Texas - Gonzalez, Rodriguez $100
1998 Toronto - Clemens, Canseco $140
1999 Anaheim - Edmonds, Salmon, Vaughn $110
1999 Arizona -M. Williams, Showalter, R. Johnson $245
1999 Atlanta - Glavine, Maddux, C. Jones, Smoltz $295
1999 Baltimore - C. Ripken, Mussina, Belle $120
1999 Boston - Garciaparra, P. Martinez $110
1999 Chicago (AL) - Thomas, Durham ...$100
1999 Chicago (NL) - Sosa, Grace $200
1999 Cincinnati - Larkin,Tomko, Greene,Vaughn $125
1999 Cleveland - Thome, Justice, Lofton ..$190
1999 Colorado - Bichette, Castilla, Walker $180
1999 Detroit - Clark, Higginson, Easley, Cruz ..
..................................$135
1999 Florida - Hernandez, Floyd $80
1999 Houston - Bagwell, Biggio, M. Alou .$180
1999 Kansas City - Beltran, Dye $90
1999 Los Angeles - K. Brown, Sheffield, Mondesi $110
1999 Milwaukee - Cirillo, Vina, Nomo, Jenkins
..................................$90
1999 Minnesota - Radke, Walker $100
1999 Montreal - Guerrero, F. Alou $90
1999 New York (AL) Jeter, Clemens, Williams, Brosius, Torre $320
1999 New York (NL) - Piazza, Franco $140
1999 Oakland - Grieve, Giambi $110
1999 Philadelphia - Rolen, Schilling $110
1999 Pittsburgh - Kendall, Guillen $125
1999 San Diego - Gwynn, Caminiti, Hoffman, .
..................................$225
1999 San Francisco - Bonds, Baker, Kent ..$120
1999 Seattle - Griffey, A. Rodriguez, Buhner $130
1999 St. Louis - McGwire, Drew, Tatis, Renteria,
..................................$240
1999 Tampa Bay - McGriff, Boggs, Canseco $275
1999 Texas - Gonzalez, Rodriguez $110
1999 Toronto - Wells, Delgado $90

Autographed All-Star Baseballs

Key signatures follow each team name

1933 American League All-Star Team - Mack, Collins, Gehrig, Ruth $6500-$9750
1933 National League All-Star Team - McGraw, Traynor, Waner, Frisch ....$2500-$3500
1934 American League All-Star Team - Gehrig, Ruth, Foxx ....$5750-$8500
1934 National League All-Star Team - Ott, Traynor, Vaughan, Waner $2000-$3000
1935 American League All-Star Team - Foxx, Gehrig, Hornsby .....$4000-$6000
1935 National League All-Star Team - Frisch, Ott, Vaughan ....$1400-$2100
1936 American League All-Star Team - Foxx, Gehrig, DiMaggio ....$5000-$7500
1936 National League All-Star Team - Ott, Vaughan, Traynor .....$1200-$1800
1937 American League All-Star Team - Foxx, DiMaggio, Gehrig ....$4500-$6750
1937 National League All-Star Team - Frisch, Ott, Vaughan ....$1500-$2350
1938 American League All-Star Team - Foxx, DiMaggio, Gehrig ....$4500-$6800
1938 National League All-Star Team - Ott, Vaughan, Frisch ....$1200-$1800
1939 American League All-Star Team - Foxx, DiMaggio, Gehrig ....$4000-$6000
1939 National League All-Star Team - Ott, Vaughan ....$800-$1200
1940 American League All-Star Team - Foxx, Williams, DiMaggio ....$600-$850
1940 National League All-Star Team - Ott, Vaughan ....$750-$1200
1941 American League All-Star Team - Foxx, Williams, DiMaggio ....$600-$900
1941 National League All-Star Team - **Ott,** Vaughan ....$650-$1000
1942 American League All-Star Team - Williams, Joe DiMaggio ......$500-$750
1942 National League All-Star Team - McKechnie, Frisch, Ott, Vaughan ....$700-$1200
1943 American League All-Star Team - McCarthy ....$400-$600

1943 A.L. All-Star Team

1940 N.L. All-Star Team

1943 National League All-Star Team - Frisch, Ott, Musial ....$500-$750
1944 American League All-Star Team - McCarthy, Cronin ....$400-$600
1944 National League All-Star Team - Wagner, Ott, Musial ....$500-$750
1945 (There was no All-Star Game)
1946 American League All-Star Team - Williams, DiMaggio ....$450-$675
1946 National League All-Star Team - Musial ....$500-$750
1947 American League All-Star Team - Williams, DiMaggio ....$500-$725
1947 National League All-Star Team - Ott, Musial ....$525-$800
1948 American League All-Star Team - Williams, DiMaggio ....$475-$750
1948 National League All-Star Team - Ott, Musial ....$525-$800
1949 American League All-Star Team - Williams, DiMaggio ....$475-$750
1949 National League All-Star Team - Campanella, Robinson, Musial .$550-$850
1950 American League All-Star Team - Williams, DiMaggio ....$500-$750
1950 National League All-Star Team - Campanella, Robinson, Musial .$550-$850
1951 American League All-Star Team - Williams, J. DiMaggio ....$500-$725
1951 National League All-Star Team - Campanella, Robinson, Musial .$575-$875
1952 American League All-Star Team - Mantle, Paige ....$800-$1300
1952 National League All-Star Team - Campanella, Robinson, Musial .$575-$825
1953 American League All-Star Team - Mantle, Williams, Paige ......$500-$725
1953 National League All-Star Team - Campanella, Robinson, Musial .$550-$850
1954 American League All-Star Team - Williams, Mantle ....$450-$675
1954 National League All-Star Team - Campanella, Robinson, Musial .$550-$825
1955 American League All-Star Team - Williams, Mantle ....$400-$600
1955 National League All-Star Team - Musial ....$400-$600
1956 American League All-Star Team - Williams, Mantle, Berra, Martin, Ford ... .$450-$675
1956 National League All-Star Team - Campanella, Musial ....$500-$750
1957 American League All-Star Team - Williams, Mantle ....$400-$600
1957 National League All-Star Team - Musial ....$400-$600
1958 American League All-Star Team - Williams, Mantle, Martin, Berra, Ford ... .$500-$800
1958 National League All-Star Team - Musial ....$700-$900
1959 American League All-Star Team - Williams, Mantle ....$400-$600
1959 American League 2nd Game All-Stars - Mantle, Maris, Williams $475-$725
1959 National League All-Star Team - Musial, Drysdale ....$400-$575
1959 National League 2nd Game All-Stars - Musial, Drysdale ......$400-$575
1960 American League All-Star Team, both teams - Mantle, Maris ....$475-$700
1960 National League All-Star Team, both teams - Clemente ....$425-$650
1961 American League All-Star Team - Mantle, Maris ....$500-$750
1961 American League 2nd Game All-Stars - Mantle, Maris ....$500-$725
1961 National League All-Star Team - Clemente, Koufax ....$450-$650
1961 National League 2nd Game All-Stars - Clemente, Koufax .....$450-$650
1962 American League All-Star Team - Mantle, Maris ....$400-$600
1962 American League 2nd Game All-Stars - Mantle, Maris ....$400-$600
1962 National League All-Star Team - Clemente ....$420-$630
1962 National League 2nd Game All-Stars - Clemente ....$425-$625
1963 American League All-Star Team - Fox, Yastrzemski ....$325-$425
1963 National League All-Star Team - Musial, Clemente ....$375-$550
1964 American League All-Star Team - Mantle, E. Howard ....$325-$500
1964 National League All-Star Team - Clemente ....$400-$600
1965 American League All-Star Team - Kaline, Killebrew ....$325-$450
1965 National League All-Star Team - Clemente ....$450-$675
1966 American League All-Star Team - Killebrew, Kaline, B. Robinson, F. Robinson ....$375-$550
1966 National League All-Star Team - Clemente ....$400-$600
1967 American League All-Star Team - Mantle ....$375-$550
1967 National League All-Star Team - Clemente ....$400-$600
1968 American League All-Star Team - Mantle ....$350-$525

1968 National League All-Star Team - Aaron, Drysdale, Mays, Seaver .$350-$525
1969 American League All-Star Team - Williams ....$350-$525
1969 National League All-Star Team - Aaron, Clemente ....$400-$600
1970 American League All-Star Team - Aparicio, Killebrew, B. Robinson, F. Robinson, Yastrzemski ....$325-$500
1970 National League All-Star Team - Hodges, Clemente, Aaron, Bench, Mays, Rose, Seaver ....$400-$600
1971 American League All-Star Team - Munson, Martin, Killebrew, B. Robinson, F. Robinson, Yastrzemski ....$375-$550
1971 National League All-Star Team - Clemente, Aaron, Mays, Rose, Seaver, McCovey ....$400-$600
1972 American League All-Star Team - R. Jackson, B. Robinson, Yastrzemski ....
..........................$300-$450
1972 National League All-Star Team - Clemente, Aaron, Bench, Carlton, Stargell
..........................$400-$600
1973 American League All-Star Team - Munson, R. Jackson, B. Robinson, Ryan ..
..........................$325-$500
1973 National League All-Star Team - Aaron, Bench, Mays, Rose, Seaver, Stargell
..........................$300-$450
1974 American League All-Star Team - R. Jackson, B. Robinson, F. Robinson, Kaline, Yastrzemski ....$325-$500
1974 National League All-Star Team - Aaron, Rose, Schmidt ....$325-$500
1975 American League All-Star Team - Munson, Martin, Aaron, Yastrzemski ....
..........................$325-$500
1975 National League All-Star Team - Bench, Brock, Rose, Seaver ...$300-$425
1976 American League All-Star Team - Munson, Brett, Carew, Yastrzemski ......
..........................$325-$500
1976 National League All-Star Team - Bench, Rose, Schmidt, Seaver .$300-$425
1977 American League All-Star Team - Munson, Martin, Brett, Carew, R. Jackson, Yastrzemski ....$350-$550

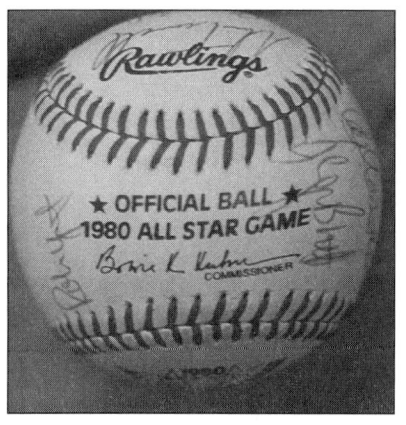

1980 A.L. All-Star Team

1983 A.L. All-Star Team

1977 National League All-Star Team - Bench, Rose, Schmidt, Seaver .$275-$425
1978 American League All-Star Team - Martin, Brett, Carew, Palmer ..$300-$450
1978 National League All-Star Team - Rose, Seaver, Stargell, Winfield $275-$425
1979 American League All-Star Team - Brett, Carew, R. Jackson, Ryan, Yastrzemski
..........................$300-$450
1979 National League All-Star Team - Brock, Carlton, Rose, Schmidt .$300-$450
1980 American League All-Star Team - Carew, Yount ....$300-$425
1980 National League All-Star Team - Bench, Rose, Schmidt, Winfield$250-$375
1981 American League All-Star Team - Brett, Carew, R. Jackson, Winfield ...$300-$425
1981 National League All-Star Team - Rose, Ryan, Schmidt. Seaver ..$300-$425
1982 American League All-Star Team - Brett, Carew, R. Jackson, Winfield, Yastrzemski, Yount ....$300-$450
1982 National League All-Star Team - Carlton, Rose, Schmidt ....$275-$400
1983 American League All-Star Team - Brett, Carew, R. Jackson, Ripken, Winfield, Yastrzemski, Yount ....$250-$375
1983 National League All-Star Team - Bench, Schmidt ....$250-$375
1984 American League All-Star Team - Brett, Carew, R. Jackson, Ripken, Winfield

1984 N.L. All-Star Team

..........................$250-$375
1984 National League All-Star Team - Sandberg, Schmidt ....$250-$375
1985 American League All-Star Team - Brett, Mattingly ....$250-$375
1985 National League All-Star Team - Rose, Ryan ....$275-$425
1986 American League All-Star Team - Clemens, Mattingly, Ripken ...$250-$375
1986 National League All-Star Team - Sandberg, Schmidt ....$250-$375
1987 American League All-Star Team - Mattingly, McGwire, Ripken ..$250-$375
1987 National League All-Star Team - Gwynn, Sandberg, Schmidt ...$250-$375
1988 American League All-Star Team - Mattingly. McGwire, Ripken ..$225-$350
1988 National League All-Star Team - Sandberg ....$225-$350
1989 American League All-Star Team - Mattingly, Ripken, Ryan .....$225-$350
1989 National League All-Star Team - Gwynn, Sandberg ....$225-$350
1990 American League All-Star Team - Clemens, Griffey Jr., Ripken ...$225-$350
1990 National League All-Star Team - Bonds, Gwynn ....$225-$350
1991 American League All-Star Team - Clemens, Griffey Jr., Ripken ...$150-$200
1991 National League All-Star Team - E. Murray, Sandberg ....$150-$200
1992 American League All-Star Team - Griffey Jr., McGwire, Ripken ..$150-$225
1992 National League All-Star Team - Bonds, Maddux, Sandberg ....$125-$200
1993 American League All-Star Team - Griffey Jr., Puckett, F. Thomas, Ripken, R. Johnson, J. Gonzalez ....$100-$150
1993 National League All-Star Team - Bonds, Gwynn, Piazza, Sandberg $100-$150
1994 American League All-Star Team - Griffey Jr., Puckett, C. Ripken $250
1994 National League All-Star Team - . Bonds, Maddux, Piazza $250
1995 American League All-Star Team -. F. Thomas, Griffey Jr. $300
1995 National League All-Star Team - Sosa $275
1996 American League All-Star Team - McGwire, F. Thomas ....$250-$375
1996 National League All-Star Team - Bonds ....$250-$375
1997 American League All-Star Team - Griffey Jr., F. Thomas ....$250-$375
1997 National League All-Star Team - Piazza, Sosa ....$250-$375
1998 American League All-Star Team - Griffey Jr. ....$225-$350
1998 National League All-Star Team - McGwire, Bonds, Sosa ....$225-$350
1999 American League All-Star Team - Griffey Jr., Ripken, Garciaparra $225-$350
1999 National League All-Star Team - McGwire, Piazza, Sosa ....$225-$350

Multiple-signed Milestone Baseball Items

500 Home Run Club Poster
(Ron Lewis, 1989)

500 Home Run Club

Only 16 players in major league history have reached the benchmark 500 Home Run Club. Babe Ruth, Jimmie Foxx and Mel Ott were the first to enter the club. Since they died before autograph collecting became enormously popular, obtaining their signatures can be a difficult challenge.

It is unlikely there are but a few (if any) items bearing the signatures of all 16 members. Most collectors consider a 500 Home Run item complete if it includes signatures of all members except the original three (or all players portrayed on an item).

500 Home Run Club Photo

The most common items signed by club members are baseballs, lithographs, bats and photos.

Official Baseball
Signed (w/o Ruth, Foxx, Ott) $750
Signed (w/o Mantle) $500
Signed (w/o Murray, McGwire) $700

Baseball Bat
Signed (w/o Ruth, Foxx, Ott) $3,500
Signed (w/o Mantle) $1,500
Signed (w/o Williams) $1,800
Signed (w/o Murray, McGwire) . . . $3,300

8x10 Photo
Signed (w/o Ruth, Foxx, Ott, Murray, McGwire) $750

**Limited Edition 1989
Ron Lewis Litho of 100**
Signed (w/o Ruth, Foxx, Ott) $3,200
*Murray and McGwire are not featured on artwork

**Limited Edition 1989
Ron Lewis Litho of 5,000**

500 Home Run Club Poster (By Ron Lewis for Hit King Marketing/Capital Cards)

500 Home Run Club

Hank Aaron (755)
Babe Ruth (714)
Willie Mays (660)
Frank Robinson (586)
Harmon Killebrew (573)
Reggie Jackson (563)
Mark McGwire (552)*
Mike Schmidt (548)
Mickey Mantle (536)
Jimmie Foxx (534)
Willie McCovey (521)
Ted Williams (521)
Ernie Banks (512)
Eddie Mathews (512)
Mel Ott (511)
Eddie Murray (504)

* Still active through July 2000

Signed (w/o Ruth, Foxx, Ott) $2,000
Unsigned $75

1996 Doo S. Oh Poster
Limited Edition of 5,000
Signed (w/o Ruth, Foxx, Ott) $1,500

Craig Pursley Painting 40x28
Signed (w/o Ruth, Foxx, Ott) $3,000

1999 Bob Allen/Bill Gilbert Book
The 500 Home Run Club
Signed by Hank Aaron $75

Mitchell & Ness Replica Hank Aaron
1957 Braves Tomahawk Jersey
Signed (w/o Ruth, Foxx, Ott) $3,500

500 Home Run Club Book
by Bob Allen and Bill Gilbert

500 Home Run Club Original Painting
(Craig Pursley)

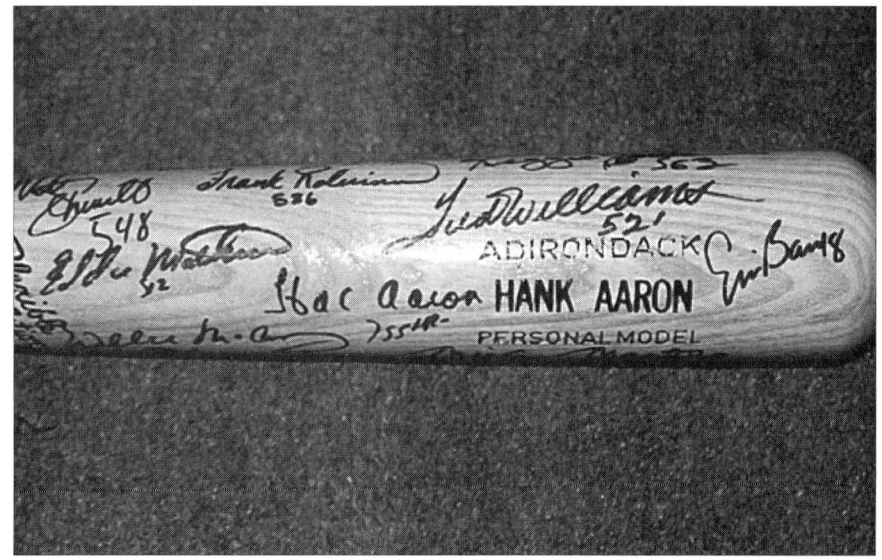

500 Home Run Club Bat

500 Home Run Club Ball

500 Home Run Club Poster
(Doo S. Oh, 1996)

3000 Hit Club

Pete Rose (4,256)
Ty Cobb (4,189)
Hank Aaron (3,771)
Stan Musial (3,630)
Tris Speaker (3,514)
Carl Yastrzemski (3,419)
Honus Wagner (3,415)
Paul Molitor (3,319)
Eddie Collins (3,312)
Willie Mays (3,283)
Eddie Murray (3,255)
Nap Lajoie (3,242)
George Brett (3,154)
Paul Waner (3,152)
Robin Yount (3,142)
Dave Winfield (3,110)
Tony Gwynn (3,108) *
Rod Carew (3,053)
Cal Ripken Jr. (3,047)
Lou Brock (3,023)
Wade Boggs (3,010)
Al Kaline (3,007)
Roberto Clemente (3,000)

* Still active through July, 2000

3000 Hit Club Poster (Ron Lewis)

3000 Hit Club

Just 23 players in major league history have reached the exclusive 3,000 career hit plateau. Collectors consider 3,000 hit items complete without the signatures of Ty Cobb, Honus Wagner, Tris Speaker, Eddie Collins, Nap Lajoie, Paul Waner and Roberto Clemente. You can expect to pay top dollar for signatures of the deceased members.

Official Baseball
Signed (w/o Cobb, Wagner, Speaker, Collins, Lajoie, Waner or Clemente) $550

Bat
Signed (w/o Cobb, Wagner, Speaker, Collins, Lajoie, Waner or Clemente)$1,250

1995 Ron Lewis Limited Edition Poster
Signed (w/o Cobb, Wagner, Speaker, Collins, Lajoie, Waner or Clemente) $800
Unsigned $25
*Murray, Molitor, Ripken, Gwynn and Boggs are not featured on poster

1997 Doo S. Oh Limited Edition (4,000) Poster
Signed (w/o Cobb, Wagner, Speaker, Collins, Lajoie, Waner or Clemente) $900
Unsigned $25
*Ripken, Gwynn, Boggs are not featured on poster

3000 Hit Club Ball

3,000 Hit Club Poster 1997 (Doo S. Oh)

300 Game Winners

Cy Young (511)
Walter Johnson (417)
Grover Cleveland Alexander (373)
Christy Mathewson (373)
Warren Spahn (363)
Kid Nichols (361)
Pud Galvin (360)
Tim Keefe (342)
Steve Carlton (329)
John Clarkson (328)
Eddie Plank (326)
Nolan Ryan (324)
Don Sutton (324)
Phil Niekro (318)
Gaylord Perry (311)
Ol' Hoss Radbourn (309)
Mickey Welch (307)
Lefty Grove (300)
Early Wynn (300)

300 Game Winners Litho (Anthony Brunelli 1994)

300 Game Winner Ball

300 Game Winners Poster (1991, by Ron Lewis)

300 Win Club

Only 20 pitchers in baseball history have achieved 300 career victories. Thirteen of the pitchers who accomplished this feat are now deceased. Most 300 Win Club items are considered complete with the signatures of Warren Spahn, Steve Carlton, Nolan Ryan, Don Sutton, Phil Niekro, Gaylord Perry, Tom Seaver and the late Early Wynn.

Official Baseball
Signed (by Spahn, Carlton, Ryan, Sutton, Niekro, Perry, Seaver and Wynn) $25

Bat
Signed (by Spahn, Carlton, Ryan, Sutton, Niekro, Perry, Seaver and Wynn) . . . $750

Pitching Rubber
Signed (by Spahn, Carlton, Ryan, Sutton, Niekro, Perry, Seaver and Wynn) . . . $500

1994 Anthony Brunelli Litho
Signed (by Spahn, Carlton, Ryan, Sutton, Niekro, Perry, Seaver and Wynn) . . $1,000

1991 Ron Lewis Poster
Signed (by Spahn, Carlton, Ryan, Sutton, Niekro, Perry, Seaver and Wynn) . . . $800
Unsigned $45

Other Popular Items

In 1998, artist Ron Lewis created artwork for a limited edition (5,000) posters of major league baseball career leaders in four major statistical categories: Pete Rose (hits), Hank Aaron (home runs), Nolan Ryan (strikeouts) and Rickey Henderson (stolen bases).

Baseball Kings (1998, by Ron Lewis) Featuring Pete Rose, Hank Aaron, Nolan Ryan and Rickey Henderson.

1998 Baseball Kings
Limited Edition of 150
Signed $575
Unsigned $25

Official Baseball
Signed $200

Bat
Signed $325

Negro League Autographs
(Non-Hall of Fame)

Newt Allen *
Photo $100
Ball $250
Cut signature or 3x5 index card . .$50-$75

Tom Alston *
Photo . . . .$30-$35
Ball $50
Cut signature or 3x5 index card . .$10-$12

George Altman
Photo . . . .$20-$25
Ball $30
Cut signature or 3x5 index card . . .$6-$8

Russell Awkard
Photo . . . .$20-$25
Ball $30
Cut signature or 3x5 index card $6

Gene Baker *
Photo $25
Ball $30
Cut signature or 3x5 index card . . . .$7-$8

Dan Bankhead *
Photo $30
Ball $60
Cut signature or 3x5 index card . .$15-$20

[signature: Sam Bankhead]

Sam Bankhead *
Photo . . . .$50-$75
Ball $100
Cut signature or 3x5 index card . .$20-$25

David Barnhill *
Photo . . . .$60-$75
Ball $100
Cut signature or 3x5 index card . .$20-$25

Frank Barnes
Photo . . . .$20-$25
Ball . . . .$25-$30
Cut signature or 3x5 index card . . .$6-$8

Gene Benson
Photo . . . .$20-$25
Ball $30
Cut signature or 3x5 index card . . .$5-$6

Bill "Fireball" Beverly *
Photo . . . .$25-$30
Ball $35
Cut signature or 3x5 index card . .$8-$10

Dennis Biddle
Photo $20
Ball $25
Cut signature or 3x5 index card $5

Charlie Biot
Photo . . . .$20-$25
Ball . . . .$25-$30
Cut signature or 3x5 index card . . .$6-$8

Joe Black
Photo . . . .$20-$25
Ball . . . .$25-$30
Cut signature or 3x5 index card . . .$6-$8

Lyman Bostock Sr.
Photo . . . .$20-$25
Ball $30
Cut signature or 3x5 index card $6

Chet Brewer *
Photo $25
Ball $50
Cut signature or 3x5 index card $10

Bill Byrd *
Photo . . . .$25-$30
Ball $50
Cut signature or 3x5 index card . .$10-$12

Bill "Ready" Cash
Photo . . . .$25-$30
Ball . . . .$30-$35
Cut signature or 3x5 index card . . .$6-$8

Bus Clarkson *
Photo . . . .$40-$50
Ball . . . .$50-$60
Cut signature or 3x5 index card $15

Sam Crawford *
Photo . . . .$100-$125
Ball $150
Cut signature or 3x5 index card $25

George Crowe
Photo . . . .$20-$25
Ball . . . .$25-$30
Cut signature or 3x5 index card . . .$6-$7

Jimmie Crutchfield *
Photo $40
Ball $50
Cut signature or 3x5 index card . .$12-$15

Piper Davis *
Photo . . . .$35-$40
Ball . . . .$40-$50
Cut signature or 3x5 index card . . .$9-$10

Lou Dials *
Photo . . . .$20-$25
Ball . . . .$25-$30
Cut signature or 3x5 index card . . .$7-$9

Mahlon Duckett
Photo . . . .$25-$30
Ball $30
Cut signature or 3x5 index card . . .$7-$9

Luke Easter *
Photo $50
Ball . . . .$60-$75
Cut signature or 3x5 index card $12

Wilmer Fields
Photo . . . .$25-$30
Ball $35
Cut signature or 3x5 index card $8

Josh Gibson Jr.
Photo . . . .$25-$30
Ball $35
Cut signature or 3x5 index card $8

George Giles *
Photo . . . .$30-$35
Ball $40
Cut signature or 3x5 index card $10

Willie Grace
Photo . . . .$25-$30
Ball . . . .$30-$35
Cut signature or 3x5 index card . . .$8-$10

Nap Gulley *
Photo $20
Ball $25
Cut signature or 3x5 index card . . .$5-$7

Sam Hairston
Photo $20
Ball $25
Cut signature or 3x5 index card . . .$5-$7

Jehosie Heard
Photo $25
Ball $30
Cut signature or 3x5 index card . . .$6-$8

[signature: Rats Henderson]

Rats Henderson *
Photo . . . .$75-$100
Ball . . . .$100-$150
Cut signature or 3x5 index card . .$15-$20

[signature: Bill Holland]

Bill Holland *
Photo . . . .$35-$40
Ball . . . .$40-$50
Cut signature or 3x5 index card . .$10-$12

Cowan "Bubba" Hyde

Photo . . . . $20-$25
Ball . . . . $25-$30
Cut signature or 3x5 index card . . . .$5-$7

Connie Johnson
Photo . . . . $20-$25
Ball $30
Cut signature or 3x5 index card . . . .$7-$8

Don Johnson
Photo $25
Ball $30
Cut signature or 3x5 index card . . . .$6-$8

Josh Johnson
Photo $25
Ball $30
Cut signature or 3x5 index card . . . .$6-$8

Clinton "Casey" Jones
Photo . . . . $25-$30
Ball . . . . $30-$35
Cut signature or 3x5 index card . . .$9-$12

Brooks Lawrence *
Photo $25
Ball $30
Cut signature or 3x5 index card . . . .$7-$9

Rufus Lewis *
Photo . . . . $20-$25
Ball $30
Cut signature or 3x5 index card $7

Lester Lockett
Photo . . . . $25-$30
Ball . . . . $30-$35
Cut signature or 3x5 index card . . . .$7-$9

Biz Mackey *
Photo . . . . $125-$150
Ball . . . . $200-$250
Cut signature or 3x5 index card . . $50-$75

Dave Malarcher *
Photo . . . . $150-$175
Ball $200
Cut signature or 3x5 index card .$75-$100

Max Manning
Photo $20
Ball $25
Cut signature or 3x5 index card $5

Luis Marquez *
Photo . . . . $50-$75
Ball . . . . $75-$100
Cut signature or 3x5 index card . .$15-$20

Verdell "Lefty" Mathis *

Photo $20
Ball $25
Cut signature or 3x5 index card . . . .$7-$8

Charlie Neal *
Photo . . . . $25-$30
Ball $40
Cut signature or 3x5 index card . . .$8-$10

Ray Noble *
Photo . . . . $25-$30
Ball . . . . $35-$40
Cut signature or 3x5 index card . . .$8-$10

Buck O'Neil
Photo . . . . $25-$30
Ball $35
Cut signature or 3x5 index card . . . .$6-$8

William Warren Peace
Photo . . . . $20-$25
Ball . . . . $25-$30
Cut signature or 3x5 index card . . . .$7-$8

Jim Pendleton *
Photo . . . . $25-$30
Ball . . . . $30-$35
Cut signature or 3x5 index card . . . .$6-$8

Art "Superman" Pennington
Photo $25
Ball $30
Cut signature or 3x5 index card . . . .$6-$8

Willie Pope
Photo . . . . $20-$25
Ball . . . . $25-$30
Cut signature or 3x5 index card . . . .$5-$7

Dave Pope *
Photo $25
Ball $30
Cut signature or 3x5 index card . . . .$7-$8

Ted "Double Duty" Radcliffe
Photo . . . . $20-$25
Ball $30
Cut signature or 3x5 index card . . . .$6-$8

Bobby Robinson
Photo $20
Ball $25
Cut signature or 3x5 index card . . . .$5-$7

Hilton Smith *
Photo . . . . $75-$100
Ball . . . . $100-$150
Cut signature or 3x5 index card . .$25-$30

Toni Stone *

Photo . . . . $50-$75
Ball $100
Cut signature or 3x5 index card $20

Alfred "Slick" Surratt
Photo $20
Ball $25
Cut signature or 3x5 index card . . . .$5-$7

Mule Suttles *
Photo $150
Ball $200
Cut signature or 3x5 index card . .$50-$75

Hank Thompson *
Photo . . . . $75-$90
Ball $100
Cut signature or 3x5 index card . .$15-$20

Bob Thurman *
Photo $25
Ball $30
Cut signature or 3x5 index card . . . .$6-$8

Luis Tiant Sr. *
Photo . . . . $30-$35
Ball $40
Cut signature or 3x5 index card . .$10-$12

Quincy Trouppe *
Photo $35
Ball $40
Cut signature or 3x5 index card . . .$8-$10

Armado Vasquez *
Photo . . . . $30-$35
Ball . . . . $35-$40
Cut signature or 3x5 index card $12

Artie Wilson
Photo $25
Ball $30
Cut signature or 3x5 index card . . . .$6-$8

Earl Wilson Sr. *
Photo $25
Ball $30
Cut signature or 3x5 index card . . . .$7-$8

Wild Bill Wright *
Photo . . . . $25-$30
Ball $35
Cut signature or 3x5 index card . . .$8-$10

Basketball Hall of Fame Autographs — Chapter 9

Basketball Autographs Hall of Famers

Kareem Abdul-Jabbar (Lew Alcindor) (1947-) 1995
Basketball $150
Cut signature $15
3x5 index card $25
8x10 photograph .... $30-$40

Nate Archibald (1948-) 1991
Basketball .... $90-$110
Cut signature $6
3x5 index card $10
8x10 photograph .... $15-$20

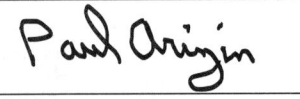

Paul Arizin (1928-) 1977
Basketball $100
Cut signature $5
3x5 index card $10
8x10 photograph $30

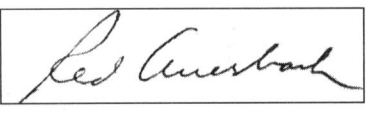

Red Auerbach (1917-) 1968
Basketball .... $150-$175
Cut signature .... $8-$10
3x5 index card $12
8x10 photograph .... $25-$30

Thomas Barlow (1896-1983) 1980
Basketball $100
Cut signature $5
3x5 index card $8
8x10 photograph $35

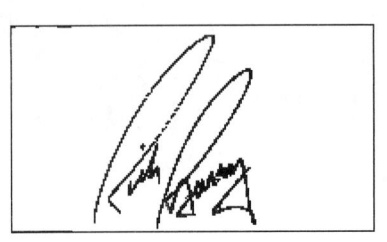

Rick Barry (1944-) 1987
Basketball $125
Cut signature .... $7-$10
3x5 index card $12
8x10 photograph $20

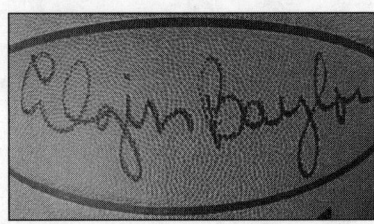

Elgin Baylor (1934-) 1976
Basketball $150
Cut signature .... $7-$10
3x5 index card .... $12-$15
8x10 photograph $20

John Beckman (1895-1968) 1972
Basketball $100
Cut signature $4
3x5 index card $10
8x10 photograph $40

Clair Bee (1896-1983) 1967
Basketball $100
Cut signature $5
3x5 index card $10
8x10 photograph $40

Walt Bellamy (1939-) 1992
Basketball .... $75-$100
Cut signature $5
3x5 index card $10
8x10 photograph .... $15-$20

Danny Biasone (19??-1992) 2000
Basketball $100
Cut signature $6
3x5 index card $8
8x10 photograph .... $20-$25

Sergei Belov (1944-) 1992
Basketball .... $75-$100
Cut signature $5
3x5 index card .... $6-$8
8x10 photograph .... $15-$17

Dave Bing (1943-) 1990
Basketball .... $100-$110
Cut signature .... $4-$5
3x5 index card $10
8x10 photograph .... $15-$18

Larry Bird (1956-) 1998
Basketball $200
Cut Signature .... $15-$20

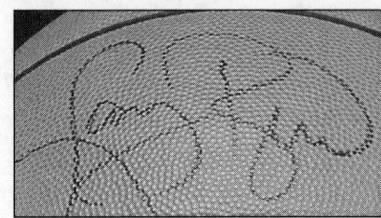

3x5 index card $20
8x10 photograph $50

Carol Blazejowski (1956-) 1994
Basketball .... $75-$100
Cut signature $5
3x5 index card .... $6-$7
8x10 photograph .... $15-$17

Ernest Blood (1872-1955) 1960
Basketball $110
Cut signature $8
3x5 index card $10
8x10 photograph .... $25-$30

Bennie Borgmann (1899-1978) 1961
Basketball $100
Cut signature $4
3x5 index card $8
8x10 photograph $40

Bill Bradley (1943-) 1982
Basketball .... $125-$150
Cut signature .... $8-$12
3x5 index card $15
8x10 photograph .... $30-$35

Joseph Brennan (1900-1989) 1974
Basketball $100
Cut signature $5
3x5 index card $10
8x10 photograph $35

Lou Carnesseca (1925-) 1991
Basketball $100
Cut signature $7
3x5 index card $10
8x10 photograph .... $12-$16

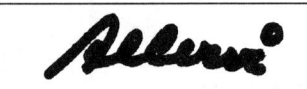

Alfred Cervi (1917-) 1984
Basketball $100
Cut signature .... $4-$6
3x5 index card $10

8x10 photograph . . . .$12-$14

Wilt Chamberlain (1936-1999) 1978
Basketball . . . .$250-$300
Cut signature $20
3x5 index card $40
8x10 photograph . . . .$75-$100

Jody Conradt (1941-) 1998
Basketball . . . .$75-$100
Cut signature $5
3x5 index card $7
8x10 photograph . . . .$12-$15

Charles Cooper (1926-1984) 1976
Basketball $100
Cut signature $15
3x5 index card $17
8x10 photograph $35

Bob Cousy (1928-) 1970
Basketball $150
Cut signature . . . .$9-$10
3x5 index card $25
8x10 photograph . . . .$25-$30

Dave Cowens (1948-) 1991
Basketball . . . .$100-$125
Cut signature . . . .$6-$7
3x5 index card $7
8x10 photograph $30

Billy Cunningham (1943-) 1986
Basketball $110
Cut signature . . . .$6-$7
3x5 index card $9
8x10 photograph . . . .$15-$17

Chuck Daly (1930-) 1994
Basketball $100
Cut signature $5
3x5 index card $7

8x10 photograph . . . .$15-$18

Robert Davies (1920-1990) 1969
Basketball $100
Cut signature $20
3x5 index card $25
8x10 photograph $45

Forrest DeBernardi (1899-1970) 1961
Basketball $100
Cut signature $15
3x5 index card $18
8x10 photograph $35

Dave DeBusschere (1940-) 1982
Basketball . . . .$125-$150
Cut signature . . . .$5-$6
3x5 index card $8
8x10 photograph . . . .$15-$20

Henry Dehnert (1898-1979) 1968
Basketball $100
Cut signature $7
3x5 index card $9
8x10 photograph . . . .$12-$17

Antonio Diaz-Miguel (1933-2000) 1997
Basketball $100
Cut signature . . . .$5-$6
3x5 index card $8
8x10 photograph . . . .$15-$20

Anne Donovan (1961-) 1995
Basketball $75-100
Cut signature . . . .$5-$6
3x5 index card $8
8x10 photograph . . . .$15-$20

Wayne Embry (1937-) 1999
Basketball . . . .$80-$100
Cut signature $6
3x5 index card $10
8x10 photograph . . . .$15-$18

Paul Endacott (1902-1977) 1971
Basketball $100
Cut signature $6
3x5 index card $10
8x10 photograph . . . .$12-$17

Alex English (1954-) 1997
Basketball $125
Cut signature . . . .$8-$10
3x5 index card $20

8x10 photo $35

Julius Erving (1950-) 1992
Basketball . . . .$175-$225
Cut signature $15
3x5 index card $25
8x10 photograph $30

Bud Foster (1906-1996) 1964
Basketball $125
Cut signature $30
3x5 index card $35
8x10 photograph $50

Walt Frazier (1945-) 1987
Basketball . . . .$100-$125
Cut signature $15
3x5 index card $20
8x10 photograph $20

Marty Friedman (1889-1986) 1971
Basketball $100
Cut signature $15
3x5 index card $20
8x10 photograph $40

Joe Fulks (1921-1976) 1977
Basketball $125
Cut signature $20
3x5 index card $25
8x10 photograph $50

Clarence Gaines (1923-) 1981
Basketball $100
Cut signature . . . .$7-$9
3x5 index card $15
8x10 photograph $20

Laddie Gale (1917-1996) 1976
Basketball $100
Cut signature $7
3x5 index card $12
8x10 photograph $15

Harry Gallatin (1927-) 1990
Basketball $110

Cut signature . . . . $6-$8
3x5 index card $15
8x10 photograph . . . . $15-$18

William Gates (1917-1999) 1988
Basketball $125
Cut signature . . . . $8-$10
3x5 index card $12
8x10 photograph . . . . $20-$25

George Gervin (1952-) 1996
Basketball . . . . $110-$120
Cut signature $6
3x5 index card $10
8x10 photograph . . . . $20-$25

Tom Gola (1933-) 1975
Basketball . . . . $90-$100
Cut signature $5
3x5 index card $8
8x10 photograph . . . . $15-$18

Alexsandr Gomelsky (1928-) 1995
Basketball . . . . $75-$100
Cut signature $5
3x5 index card $7
8x10 photograph . . . . $15-$17

Gail Goodrich (1943-) 1996
Basketball . . . . $100-$110
Cut signature . . . . $6-$8
3x5 index card $10
8x10 photograph . . . . $15-$20

Edward Gottlieb (1898-1979) 1972
Basketball $110
Cut signature $8
3x5 index card $10
8x10 photograph . . . . $25-$30

Hal Greer (1936-) 1981
Basketball $120
Cut signature $4
3x5 index card . . . . $3-$6

8x10 photograph . . . . $17-$22

Robert Gruenig (1913-1958) 1963
Basketball $125
Cut signature . . . . $10-$15
3x5 index card $12
8x10 photograph . . . . $25-$35

Cliff Hagan (1931-) 1977
Basketball $125
Cut signature . . . . $4-$7
3x5 index card $6
8x10 photograph $20

Alex Hannum (1923-) 1998
Basketball . . . . $75-$100
Cut signature $5
3x5 index card $6
8x10 photograph . . . . $15-$17

Victor Hanson (1903-1982) 1960
Basketball $125
Cut signature . . . . $10-$14
3x5 index card $15
8x10 photograph $40

Lusia Harris-Stewart (1955-) 1992
Basketball . . . . $75-$100
Cut signature $5
3x5 index card . . . . $6-$7
8x10 photograph . . . . $15-$17

Marv Harshman (1917-) 1985
Basketball . . . . $75-$100
Cut signature . . . . $5-$6
3x5 index card . . . . $7-$8
8x10 photograph . . . . $15-$17

Don Haskins (1930-) 1997
Basketball . . . . $75-$100
Cut signature $5
3x5 index card . . . . $6-$7
8x10 photograph . . . . $15-$17

John Havlicek (1940-) 1983
Basketball . . . . $150-$160
Cut signature $10
3x5 index card $15
8x10 photograph $25

Connie Hawkins (1942-) 1991
Basketball $125
Cut signature $8
3x5 index card $10
8x10 photograph $22

Elvin Hayes (1945-) 1990
Basketball $125
Cut signature $8
3x5 index card $12
8x10 photograph $17

Marques Haynes (1926-) 1998
Basketball $120
Cut signature $7
3x5 index card $10
8x10 photograph $20

Tommy Heinsohn (1934-) 1985
Basketball $125
Cut signature $6
3x5 index card $8
8x10 photograph $17

Nat Holman (1896-1995) 1964
Basketball $150
Cut signature $15
3x5 index card $20
8x10 photograph $100

Red Holzman (1920-1998) 1985
Basketball $125
Cut signature . . . . $8-$10
3x5 index card $15
8x10 photograph . . . . $22-$27

Robert Houbregs (1932-) 1986
Basketball $110
Cut signature . . . . $5-$7
3x5 index card $10
8x10 photograph $15

Bailey Howell (1937-) 1997
Basketball $100
Cut signature` . . . . $6-$8
3x5 index card $10
8x10 photo . . . . $15-$20

Chuck Hyatt (1908-1978) 1959
Basketball $100
Cut signature $5
3x5 index card $10
8x10 photograph $25

Henry Iba (1904-1993) 1968
Basketball $150
Cut signature $10
3x5 index card $15
8x10 photograph $30

Edward "Ned" Irish (1905-1982) 1964
Basketball . . . .$100-$110
Cut signature $8
3x5 index card $10
8x10 photograph . . . .$25-$30

Dan Issel (1948-) 1992
Basketball $115
Cut signature $7
3x5 index card $12
8x10 photograph $15

Buddy Jeannette (1917-1998) 1994
Basketball $110
Cut signature . . . .$4-$7
3x5 index card $9
8x10 photograph . . . .$15-$17

William Johnson (1911-1980) 1976
Basketball $125
Cut signature $5
3x5 index card $10
8x10 photograph $30

Neil Johnston (1929-1978) 1989
Basketball $110
Cut signature $10
3x5 index card $15
8x10 photograph $35

K.C. Jones (1932-) 1988
Basketball $100
Cut signature $6
3x5 index card $8
8x10 photograph $15

Sam Jones (1933-) 1983
Basketball $120
Cut signature . . . .$6-$7
3x5 index card $8
8x10 photograph $20

Bobby Knight (1931-) 1990
Basketball $100
Cut signature $10
3x5 index card $12
8x10 photograph $15

Edward Krause (1913-1942) 1975
Basketball $110
Cut signature $5
3x5 index card $10
8x10 photograph $20

John Kundla (1916-) 1995
Basketball . . . .$75-$100
Cut signature $5
3x5 index card . . . .$6-$7
8x10 photograph . . . .$15-$17

Bob Kurland (1924-) 1961
Basketball $110
Cut signature $5
3x5 index card $10
8x10 photograph . . . .$15-$20

Bob Lanier (1948-) 1992
Basketball $100
Cut signature $7
3x5 index card $10
8x10 photograph $15

Joe Lapchick (1900-1970) 1966
Basketball $150
Cut signature $10
3x5 index card $15
8x10 photograph $35

Nancy Lieberman-Cline (1958-) 1996
Basketball . . . .$75-$100
Cut signature $5
3x5 index card . . . .$7-$8

8x10 photograph . . . .$15-$17

Clyde Lovellette (1929-) 1987
Basketball $110
Cut signature . . . .$4-$7
3x5 index card $9
8x10 photograph . . . .$15-$17

Jerry Lucas (1940-) 1979
Basketball $125
Cut signature $5
3x5 index card $10
8x10 photograph . . . .$15-$20

Hank Luisetti (1916-) 1959
Basketball $125
Cut signature $7
3x5 index card $12
8x10 photograph . . . .$15-$25

Ed Macauley (1928-) 1960
Basketball $150
Cut signature $15
3x5 index card $20
8x10 photograph $30

Pete Maravich (1947-1988) 1987
Basketball . . . .$500-$600
Cut signature $10
3x5 index card $15
8x10 photograph . . . .$225-$250

Slater Martin (1925-) 1981
Basketball $130
Cut signature . . . .$4-$6
3x5 index card $9
8x10 photograph $17

Bob McAdoo (1961-) 2000
Basketball ....$100-$110
Cut signature ....$6-$8
3x5 index card $9
8x10 photograph ....$20-$25

John McLendon (1915-1999) 1979
Basketball $100
Cut signature $7
3x5 index card $10
8x10 photograph $20

Branch McCracken (1908-1970) 1960
Basketball $100
Cut signature $7
3x5 index card $10
8x10 photograph $20

Jack McCracken (1911-1958) 1962
Basketball $100
Cut signature $7
3x5 index card $10
8x10 photograph $20

Bobby McDermott (1914-) 1987
Basketball $110
Cut signature ....$6-$7
3x5 index card $14
8x10 photograph ....$15-$20

Al McGuire (1928-) 1991
Basketball ....$75-$100
Cut signature $5
3x5 index card $10
8x10 photograph $15

Dick McGuire (1926-) 1992
Basketball ....$75-$100
Cut signature $5
3x5 index card $10
8x10 photograph $20

Frank McGuire (1916-1994) 1976
Basketball $110
Cut signature $7
3x5 index card $9
8x10 photograph ....$16-$18

Kevin McHale (1957-) 1999
Basketball $110
Cut signature $8
3x5 index card $10
8x10 photograph ....$18-$20

John McLendon (1915-1999) 1979
Basketball $100
Cut signature ....$6-$7
3x5 index card ....$8-$9
8x10 photograph ....$17-$20

Walter Meanwell (1884-1953) 1959
Basketball $110
Cut signature $8
3x5 index card $10
8x10 photograph ....$20-$25

Ray Meyer (1913-) 1978
Basketball $125
Cut signature $15
3x5 index card $20
8x10 photograph $30

Ann Meyers (1955-) 1993
Basketball ....$90-$100
Cut signature $5
3x5 index card $6
8x10 photograph ....$15-$20

George Mikan (1924-) 1959
Basketball $125
Cut signature $7
3x5 index card $10
8x10 photograph ....$20-$25

Vern Mikkelsen (1928-) 1995
Basketball $110
Cut signature $6
3x5 index card $9
8x10 photograph $20

Cheryl Miller (1964-) 1995
Basketball $100
Cut signature $6
3x5 index card $8
8x10 photograph ....$20-$25

William Mokray (1907-1974) 1965
Basketball $100
Cut signature $10
3x5 index card $15
8x10 photograph $35

Billie Moore (1943-) 1999
Basketball ....$75-$100
Cut signature $5
3x5 index card ....$6-$7
8x10 photograph ....$15-$17

Earl Monroe (1944-) 1989
Basketball $125
Cut signature ....$8-$10
3x5 index card $12
8x10 photograph ....$20-$25

Calvin Murphy (1948-) 1992
Basketball $100
Cut signature $6
3x5 index card $8
8x10 photograph $15

Charles Murphy (1907-1992) 1960
Basketball $100
Cut signature ....$7-$10
3x5 index card $12
8x10 photograph ....$15-$20

James Naismith (1861-1939) 1959
Basketball $1,000
Cut signature $200
3x5 index card $300
8x10 photograph $500

C. M. Newton (1931-) 2000
Basketball $100
Cut signature $6
3x5 index card $8
8x10 photograph ....$15-$17

Aleksandar Nikolic (1924-2000) 1998
Basketball $100
Cut signature $8
3x5 index card $10
8x10 photograph ....$20-$25

Larry O'Brien (1917-1990) 1990
Basketball $125
Cut signature $25
3x5 index card $15
8x10 photograph $65

Harlan Page (1887-1965) 1962
Basketball $100
Cut signature $5
3x5 index card $10
8x10 photograph $20

Bob Pettit (1932-) 1970
Basketball $150

Basketball Hall of Fame Autographs — Chapter 9

[Bob Pettit signature]

Cut signature $10
3x5 index card $15
8x10 photograph ....$20-$25

[Andy Phillip signature]

Andy Phillip (1922-) 1961
Basketball $100
Cut signature ....$5-$7
3x5 index card $7
8x10 photograph ....$15-$16

Maurice Podoloff (1890-1985) 1973
Basketball $100
Cut signature $5
3x5 index card $7
8x10 photograph $20

[Jim Pollard signature]

Jim Pollard (1922-1993) 1977
Basketball $100
Cut signature $5
3x5 index card $10
8x10 photograph $15

[Frank Ramsey signature]

Frank Ramsey (1931-) 1981
Basketball $100
Cut signature ....$6-$7
3x5 index card $10
8x10 photograph $15

Jack Ramsey (1925-) 1991
Basketball $125
Cut signature $7
3x5 index card $10
8x10 photograph $20

[Willis Reed signature]

Willis Reed (1942-) 1981
Basketball $100
Cut signature $9
3x5 index card $12
8x10 photograph $20

Arnie Risen (1924-) 1998
Basketball $110
Cut Signature $10
3x5 index card $12
8 x10 photograph ....$20-$25

Oscar Robertson (1938-) 1979
Basketball $125
Cut signature $8
3x5 index card $10
8x10 photograph ....$25-$35

John Roosma (1900-1983) 1961
Basketball $100
Cut signature $5
3x5 index card $10
8x10 photograph $15

Adolph Rupp (1901-1977) 1968
Basketball $120
Cut signature $10
3x5 index card $15
8x10 photograph $50

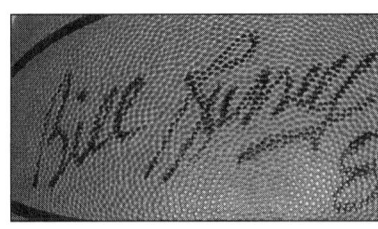

Bill Russell (1934-) 1974
Basketball $350
Cut signature $25
3x5 index card $30
8x10 photograph $160

John Russell (1902-1973) 1974
Basketball $150
Cut signature $20
3x5 index card $25
8x10 photograph $45

Abe Saperstein (1901-1966) 1970
Basketball $150
Cut signature $10
3x5 index card $20
8x10 photograph $75

Dolph Schayes (1928-) 1972
Basketball $125

[Dolph Schayes signature]

Cut signature $10
3x5 index card $15
8x10 photograph ....$15-$20

Ernest Schmidt (1911-1986) 1973
Basketball $110
Cut signature $7
3x5 index card $12
8x10 photograph ....$20-$30

John Schommer (1884-1960) 1959
Basketball $100
Cut signature $5
3x5 index card $10
8x10 photograph $15

Barney Sedran (1891-1964) 1962
Basketball $100
Cut signature $5
3x5 index card $7
8x10 photograph $15

Bill Sharman (1926-) 1975
Basketball $100
Cut signature $5
3x5 index card $7
8x10 photograph $20

Dean Smith (1931-) 1982
Basketball $100
Cut signature ....$15-$18
3x5 index card $20
8x10 photograph ....$25-$35

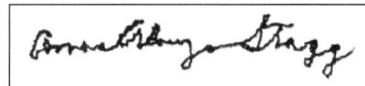

Amos Alonzo Stagg (1862-1965) 1959
Basketball ....$150-$175
Cut signature ....$8-$10
3x5 index card $20
8x10 photograph $30

Christian Steinmetz (1887-1963) 1961
Basketball $110
Cut signature $8
3x5 index card $12
8x10 photograph ....$20-$30

Basketball Hall of Fame Autographs — Chapter 9

Earl Strom (1927-1994) 1995
Basketball ....$75-$100
Cut signature ....$6-$7
3x5 index card ....$8-$10
8x10 photograph ....$17-$20

Pat Summitt (1952-) 2000
Basketball ....$75-$100
Cut signature ....$5-$6
3x5 index card ....$7-$8
8x10 photograph ....$15-$17

Isiah Thomas (1961-) 2000
Basketball $125
Cut signature $10
3x5 index card $12
8x10 photograph ....$25-$30

David Thompson (1954-) 1996
Basketball $110
Cut signature ....$5-$8
3x5 index card $7
8x10 photograph ....$20-$25

John Thompson (1906-1990) 1962
Basketball $100
Cut signature $8
3x5 index card $10
8x10 photograph $30

John R. Thompson (1941-) 1999
Basketball $100
Cut signature $7
3x5 index card $9
8x10 photograph $25

Nate Thurmond (1941-) 1984
Basketball $115
Cut signature ....$6-$8
3x5 index card $12
8x10 photograph ....$15-$20

Arthur Trester (1878-1944) 1995
Basketball $125
Cut signature ....$12-$14
3x5 index card ....$15-$20
8x10 photograph $40

Jack Twyman (1934-) 1982
Basketball $125
Cut signature ....$6-$9
3x5 index card ....$9-$10
8x10 photograph ....$15-$18

Wes Unseld (1946-) 1987
Basketball $110
Cut signature ....$6-$10
3x5 index card $9
8x10 photograph ....$15-$20

Robert Vandivier (1903-1993) 1974
Basketball $100
Cut signature $5
3x5 index card $7
8x10 photograph $25

Edward Wachter (1883-1966) 1961
Basketball $100
Cut signature $6
3x5 index card $8
8x10 photograph $35

Margaret Wade (1912-1995) 1985
Basketball ....$75-$100
Cut signature $5
3x5 index card $7
8x10 photograph ....$15-$17

Bill Walton (1952-) 1992
Basketball $125
Cut signature $6
3x5 index card $10
8x10 photograph ....$20-$25

David Walsh (1889-1975) 1961
Basketball $125
Cut signature $10
3x5 index card $15
8x10 photograph ....$30-$40

Robert Wanzer (1921-) 1986
Basketball $125
Cut signature ....$5-$6
3x5 index card $10
8x10 photograph ....$16-$17

Stanley Watts (1911-2000) 1986
Basketball ....$75-$100
Cut signature ....$5-$6
3x5 index card ....$7-$8
8x10 photograph ....$15-$20

Clifford Wells (1896-1977) 1972
Basketball $100
Cut signature $8
3x5 index card $10
8x10 photograph ....$20-$25

Jerry West (1938-) 1979
Basketball $150
Cut signature $7
3x5 index card $10
8x10 photograph ....$25-$30

Lenny Wilkens (1937-) 1988 and 1998
Basketball $100
Cut signature ....$6-$10
3x5 index card $20
8x10 photograph ....$12-$15

John Wooden (1910-) 1972
Basketball $115
Cut signature ....$8-$10
3x5 index card $15
8x10 photograph ....$15-$20

Morgan Wootten (1931-) 2000
Basketball $100
Cut signature $6
3x5 index card ....$7-$8
8x10 photograph ....$15-$17

George Yardley (1928-) 1996
Basketball $110
Cut signature $10
3x5 signature $15
8x10 photograph ....$20-$25

Fred Zollner (1901-1982) 1999
Basketball $250
Cut signature $45
3x5 signature $50
8x10 photograph $100

Basketball Autographs
Inactive Players

Zaid Abdul-Aziz
Photo $6
Ball $30

Alvan Adams
Photo ....$10-$12
Ball $70

Michael Adams
Photo $10
Ball $60

Rick Adelman
Photo ....$8-$10
Ball $60

Mark Aguirre
Photo ....$10-$11
Ball $65

Danny Ainge
Photo $15
Ball $100

Lucius Allen
Photo $10
Ball $50

B.J. Armstrong
Photo $10
Ball $95

Curly Armstrong
Photo $25
Ball $75

Al Attles
Photo ....$12-$14
Ball $90

Dennis Awtrey
Photo $7
Ball $30

Thurl Bailey
Photo $11
Ball $70

Greg Ballard
Photo ....$9-$10
Ball $50

Mike Bantom
Photo $8
Ball $30

Charles Barkley

Photo $30
Ball $150

Marvin Barnes
Photo $12
Ball $50

Jim Barnett
Photo $7
Ball $30

Dick Barnett
Photo $20
Ball $75

Butch Beard
Photo $7
Ball $30

Zelmo Beatty
Photo ....$15-$16
Ball $90

Byron Beck
Photo $7
Ball $30

Ron Behagen
Photo $7
Ball $30

Benoit Benjamin
Photo ....$6-$8
Ball $60

Kent Benson
Photo ....$7-$8
Ball $30

Walter Berry
Photo $6
Ball $30

Henry Bibby
Photo $10
Ball $70

Otis Birdsong
Photo ....$10-$12
Ball $70

Rolando Blackman
Photo $10
Ball $60

John Block
Photo $7
Ball $30

Manute Bol
Photo ....$10-$15
Ball $65

Tom Boerwinkle
Photo ....$10-$11
Ball $65

Ron Boone
Photo $20
Ball $100

Bob Boozer
Photo $20
Ball $100

Sam Bowie
Photo ....$7-$10
Ball $75

Dudley Bradley
Photo $6
Ball $30

Carl Braun
Photo ....$20-$22
Ball $90

Jim Brewer
Photo $7
Ball $30

Ron Brewer
Photo $7
Ball $30

Frank Brickowski
Photo $6
Ball $30

Junior Bridgeman
Photo $12
Ball $85

Bill Bridges
Photo $7
Ball $30

Allan Bristow
Photo $8
Ball $35

Michael Brooks
Photo $7
Ball $30

Fred Brown
Photo ....$12-$14
Ball $75

Quinn Buckner
Photo $7
Ball $30

Tom Burleson
Photo ....$8-$9
Ball $65

Joe Caldwell
Photo $15
Ball $50

Corky Calhoun

Photo $8
Ball $40

Mack Calvin
Photo $9
Ball $65

Austin Carr
Photo ....$12-$13
Ball $100

Kenny Carr
Photo $8
Ball $30

M.L. Carr
Photo $15
Ball $100

Joe Barry Carroll
Photo ....$6-$10
Ball $55

Bill Cartwright
Photo ....$12-$13
Ball $95

Harvey Catchings
Photo ....$7-$10
Ball $50

Tom Chambers
Photo $11
Ball $75

Maurice Cheeks
Photo ....$8-$13
Ball $95

Phil Chenier
Photo ....$8-$10
Ball $80

Jim Chones
Photo ....$10-$12
Ball $85

Archie Clark
Photo ....$15-$18
Ball $90

Jim Cleamons
Photo $6
Ball $30

John Clemens
Photo $6
Ball $30

Sweetwater Clifton
Photo $35
Ball $100

Doug Collins
Photo $18
Ball $100

Lester Conner
Photo $6
Ball $35

Darwin Cook
Photo $7
Ball $30

Michael Cooper
Photo ....$8-$12
Ball $85

Larry Costello
Photo $18
Ball $100

Charlie Criss
Photo $6
Ball $30

Dick Cunningham
Photo ....$6-$8
Ball ....$30-$50

Adrian Dantley
Photo ....$14-$17
Ball $100

Louie Dampier
Photo $15
Ball $95

Bob Dandridge
Photo ....$15-$16
Ball $95

Mel Daniels
Photo $14
Ball $75

Adrian Dantley
Photo ....$14-$16
Ball $100

Brad Daugherty
Photo $13
Ball $90

Brad Davis
Photo ....$7-$8
Ball $50

Mickey Davis
Photo ....$6-$7
Ball $40

Walter Davis
Photo ....$12-$14
Ball $95

Darryl Dawkins
Photo ....$12-$13
Ball $90

Johnny Dawkins

Photo ....$6-$10
Ball $70

Connie Dierking
Photo ....$15-$18
Ball $70

Coby Dietrick
Photo $7
Ball $30

Ernie DiGregorio
Photo $12
Ball $85

James Donaldson
Photo ....$8-$10
Ball $60

John Drew
Photo $6
Ball $35

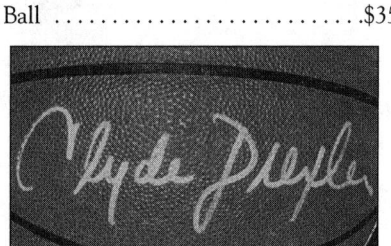

Clyde Drexler
Photo ....$17-$20
Ball $100

Kevin Duckworth
Photo ....$6-$10
Ball $70

Charles Dudley
Photo $6
Ball $30

Walter Dukes
Photo $35
Ball $100

Joe Dumars
Photo $14
Ball $85

Mike Dunleavy
Photo $12
Ball $75

T.R. Dunn
Photo $8
Ball $50

James Eakins
Photo $6
Ball $30

Mark Eaton
Photo $10

Ball $65

Dike Eddleman
Photo $15
Ball $70

LeRoy Ellis
Photo $14
Ball $70

Len Elmore
Photo $6
Ball $30

Gene Englund
Photo $22
Ball $100

Keith Erickson
Photo $9
Ball $60

Mike Evans
Photo $6
Ball $30

Joseph Fabel
Photo $25
Ball $100

Mike Farmer
Photo $8
Ball $45

Bob Ferry
Photo $9
Ball $60

Ken Fields
Photo $6
Ball $30

Hank Finkel
Photo $7
Ball $30

Jerry Fleishman
Photo $10
Ball $80

Eric Floyd
Photo ....$9-$10
Ball $70

Chris Ford
Photo $7
Ball $30

Phil Ford
Photo $14
Ball $85

Fred Foster
Photo $6
Ball $30

James Fox
Photo $7
Ball $30

Nat Frankel
Photo $25
Ball $75

World B. (Lloyd) Free
Photo $16
Ball $100

Donnie Freeman
Photo $14
Ball $60

Bill Gabor
Photo $20
Ball $75

Elmer Gainer
Photo $20
Ball $75

Mike Gale
Photo $6
Ball $30

Dave Gambee
Photo $9
Ball $50

Jack George
Photo $15
Ball $75

Gus Gerard
Photo $7
Ball $35

John Gianelli
Photo $9
Ball $40

Herm Gilliam
Photo $9
Ball $40

Artis Gilmore
Photo ....$15-$25
Ball $90

George Glamack
Photo $20
Ball $75

Mike Glenn
Photo $6
Ball $30

Mike Gminski
Photo $8
Ball $55

Gerald Govan
Photo $6

Ball $30

Joseph Graboski
Photo $20
Ball $100

Michael Green
Photo $6
Ball $30

Sihugo Green
Photo $18
Ball $75

David Greenwood
Photo $8
Ball $40

Kevin Grevey
Photo $9
Ball $45

Paul Griffin
Photo $7
Ball $30

Darrell Griffith
Photo $10
Ball $70

Bob Gross
Photo $9
Ball $35

Ernie Grunfeld
Photo $12
Ball $70

Richie Guerin
Photo $22
Ball $100

Matt Guokas
Photo $9
Ball $50

Happy Hairston
Photo ....$12-$14
Ball $100

Dale Hamilton
Photo $22
Ball $75

Alex Hannum
Photo $18
Ball $75

Bill Hanzlik
Photo $6
Ball $30

Derek Harper
Photo ....$9-$12
Ball $90

Clem Haskins
Photo $10
Ball $50

Steve Hawes
Photo $6
Ball $30

Tom Hawkins
Photo $14
Ball $60

Spencer Haywood
Photo $22
Ball $100

Garfield Heard
Photo $8
Ball $40

Clarence Hermsen
Photo $14
Ball $70

Fred Hetzel
Photo $6
Ball $30

William Hewitt
Photo $6
Ball $30

Arthur Heyman
Photo $10
Ball $45

Wayne Hightower
Photo $10
Ball $45

Armond Hill
Photo $7
Ball $40

Darnell Hillman
Photo $9
Ball $50

Craig Hodges
Photo ....$8-$12
Ball $70

Lionel Hollins
Photo ....$9-$14
Ball $75

Phil Hubbard
Photo $7
Ball $50

Lou Hudson
Photo $18
Ball $80

Rod Hundley
Photo $12

Ball $60

Marc Iavaroni
Photo $8
Ball $60

Warren Jabali
Photo $6
Ball $35

Phil Jackson
Photo $15
Ball $75

Charles Johnson
Photo $6
Ball $30

Clem Johnson
Photo $6
Ball $30

Dennis Johnson
Photo ....$12-$15
Ball $100

Eddie Johnson
Photo $9
Ball $75

George L. Johnson
Photo $6
Ball $30

George T. Johnson
Photo $6
Ball $30

Gus Johnson
Photo $35
Ball $150

Magic Johnson
Photo $45
Ball $225

Marques Johnson
Photo $12
Ball $50

Mickey Johnson
Photo $8
Ball $35

Ollie Johnson
Photo $8
Ball $45

Bobby Jones
Photo $15
Ball $90

Caldwell Jones
Photo $12
Ball $70

Steve Jones
Photo ....$12-$16
Ball $90

Wali Jones
Photo ....$6-$8
Ball $45

Michael Jordan
Photo $160
Ball $1,200

George Karl
Photo ....$8-$10
Ball $55

Richard Kelley
Photo $7
Ball $35

Clark Kellogg
Photo $7
Ball $40

Greg Kelser
Photo $6
Ball $30

Larry Kenon
Photo $12
Ball $80

Toby Kimball
Photo $7
Ball $35

Bernard King
Photo ....$15-$16
Ball $85

James King
Photo $6
Ball $30

Robert Kinney
Photo $25
Ball $100

Walter Kirk
Photo $10
Ball $65

Billy Knight
Photo ....$10-$13
Ball $70

Inactive Basketball Player Autographs — Chapter 10

Don Kojis
Photo $12
Ball $50

Jon Koncak
Photo $10
Ball $65

Jim Krebs
Photo $35
Ball $125

Steve Kuberski
Photo $7
Ball $35

Kevin Kunnert
Photo $7
Ball $35

Mitch Kupchak
Photo . . . . $8-$13
Ball $80

Sam Lacey
Photo . . . . $10-$13
Ball $75

Tom Lagarde
Photo $6
Ball $30

Bill Laimbeer
Photo . . . . $12-$14
Ball $90

Jeff Lamp
Photo $6
Ball $30

Mark Landsberger
Photo $6
Ball $30

Allen Leavell
Photo $8
Ball $40

Clyde Lee
Photo $8
Ball $40

George Lee
Photo $8
Ball $40

Keith Lee
Photo $7
Ball $35

Ronnie Lee
Photo $7
Ball $35

Bob Leonard
Photo $18
Ball $100

Fred Lewis
Photo $8
Ball $40

Michael Lewis
Photo $8
Ball $40

Reggie Lewis *
Photo $50
Ball $200

Alton Lister
Photo $8
Ball $30

Scott Lloyd
Photo $6
Ball $30

Don Lofgran
Photo $28
Ball $125

John Logan
Photo $25
Ball $125

Brad Lohaus
Photo $6
Ball $30

Jim Loscutoff
Photo $15
Ball $100

Kevin Loughery
Photo $12
Ball $70

Bob Love
Photo . . . . $15-$16
Ball $65

John Lucas
Photo $16
Ball $75

Maurice Lucas
Photo . . . . $12-$14
Ball $75

Raymond Lumpp
Photo $10
Ball $60

Kyle Macy
Photo $8
Ball $45

John Mahnken
Photo $12
Ball $65

Rick Mahorn
Photo . . . . $9-$13
Ball $70

Jeff Malone
Photo $12
Ball $75

Moses Malone
Photo $20
Ball $115

Ed Manning
Photo $6
Ball $30

Press Maravich
Photo $35
Ball $125

Jack Marin
Photo $14
Ball $90

Wes Mathews
Photo $6
Ball $30

Cedric Maxwell
Photo $14
Ball $90

Don May
Photo $6
Ball $30

Scott May
Photo $6
Ball $30

John McCarthy
Photo $8
Ball $40

Xavier McDaniel
Photo . . . . $10-$15
Ball $60

Bill McGill
Photo $7
Ball $30

George McGinnis
Photo $15
Ball $80

Jon McGlocklin
Photo . . . . $10-$12
Ball $60

Kevin McKenna
Photo $6
Ball $30

Stan McKenzie

Photo $8
Ball $40

Horace McKinnney
Photo $14
Ball $75

William McKinney
Photo $6
Ball $30

McCoy McLemore
Photo $7
Ball $35

Jack McMahon
Photo $25
Ball $125

Tom McMillen
Photo $15
Ball $85

James McMillian
Photo $7
Ball $35

Mark McNamara
Photo $6
Ball $30

Larry McNeill
Photo $6
Ball $30

Bill Melchionni
Photo $9
Ball $50

Dean Meminger
Photo $7
Ball $40

John Mengelt
Photo $8
Ball $40

Joe Meriweather
Photo $7
Ball $35

David Meyers
Photo $10
Ball $60

Eddie Miles
Photo $8
Ball $40

Walter Miller
Photo $25
Ball $100

Harold Miner
Photo $11
Ball $70

Steve Mix
Photo $9
Ball $40

Paul Mokeski
Photo $6
Ball $30

Sidney Moncrief
Photo ....$12-$15
Ball $80

Eric Money
Photo $6
Ball $30

Eugene Moore
Photo $6
Ball $30

John Moore
Photo $6
Ball $30

Jack Moreland
Photo $35
Ball $125

Rick Mount
Photo $12
Ball $85

Edwin Mueller
Photo $6
Ball $30

Jeff Mullins
Photo $15
Ball $85

Larry Nance
Photo $13
Ball $80

Swen Nater
Photo ....$9-$11
Ball $65

Lloyd Neal
Photo $8
Ball $40

Don Nelson
Photo ....$12-$14
Ball $75

Bob Netolicky
Photo $8
Ball $40

Mike Newlin
Photo $9
Ball $45

Kurt Nimphius
Photo $6
Ball $30

Norm Nixon
Photo ....$9-$12
Ball $70

Ken Norman
Photo $10
Ball $60

Willie Norwood
Photo $7
Ball $35

Mike O'Koren
Photo $6
Ball $30

Mark Olberding
Photo $8
Ball $40

Jawann Oldham
Photo $6
Ball $30

Louis Orr
Photo $7
Ball $35

Tom Owens
Photo $9
Ball $45

Togo Palazzi
Photo $9
Ball $45

Robert Parish
Photo $15
Ball $120

Billy Paultz
Photo ....$10-$13
Ball $65

John Paxson
Photo $14
Ball $75

John Pelkington
Photo $12
Ball $70

Curtis Perry
Photo $9
Ball $45

Geoff Petrie
Photo $12
Ball $80

Drazen Petrovic *
Photo $45
Ball $130

Inactive Basketball Player Autographs — Chapter 10

Bobby Phills *
Photo $14
Ball $85

Ed Pinckney
Photo $10
Ball $60

Ben Poquette
Photo $6
Ball $30

Howard Porter
Photo $6
Ball $30

Kevin Porter
Photo $7
Ball $35

Paul Pressey
Photo . . . . $7-$8
Ball $55

Mark Price
Photo $14
Ball $85

Kurt Rambis
Photo . . . . $8-$14
Ball $75

Clifford Ray
Photo $7
Ball $40

Kevin Restani
Photo $6
Ball $30

Michael Ray Richardson
Photo $7
Ball $35

Pat Riley
Photo $12
Ball $100

Mike Riordan
Photo $7
Ball $35

Doc Rivers
Photo . . . . $9-$13
Ball $90

Fred Roberts
Photo . . . . $6-$8
Ball $50

Alvin Robertson
Photo $8
Ball $45

Bill Robinzine
Photo $7
Ball $35

Dave Robisch
Photo $7
Ball $35

Red Rocha
Photo $18
Ball $100

Tree Rollins
Photo $7
Ball $40

Dan Roundfield
Photo $10
Ball $70

Curtis Rowe
Photo $7
Ball $40

Jeff Ruland
Photo $9
Ball $65

Cazzie Russell
Photo . . . . $16-$18
Ball $100

John Salley
Photo . . . . $8-$10
Ball $65

Ralph Sampson
Photo $12
Ball $75

Herman Schaefer
Photo $25
Ball $100

Fred Schaus
Photo $25
Ball $100

Dale Schlueter
Photo $6
Ball $30

Alvin Scott
Photo $6
Ball $30

Byron Scott
Photo $13
Ball $70

Charlie Scott
Photo $14
Ball $70

Malik Sealy *
Photo . . . . $15-$20
Ball $75

Charles Shipp
Photo $35
Ball $125

Purvis Short
Photo $9
Ball $60

Gene Shue
Photo . . . . $12-$18
Ball $55

John Shumate
Photo $8
Ball $40

Jack Sikma
Photo . . . . $10-$14
Ball $75

James Silas
Photo $15
Ball $75

Paul Silas
Photo $15
Ball $75

Ralph Simpson
Photo $8
Ball $40

Lionel Simmons
Photo $10
Ball $65

Scott Skiles
Photo $10
Ball $65

Jerry Sloan
Photo $10
Ball $80

Bobby Smith
Photo $8
Ball $45

Elmore Smith
Photo $12
Ball $60

Greg Smith
Photo $7
Ball $35

Kenny Smith
Photo $15
Ball $80

Phil Smith
Photo $7
Ball $35

Randy Smith

Photo $12
Ball $70

Dick Snyder
Photo $8
Ball $45

Rory Sparrow
Photo ....$7-$11
Ball $60

Kevin Stacom
Photo $6
Ball $30

Dave Stallworth
Photo $8
Ball $40

Larry Steele
Photo $7
Ball $35

Steve Stipanovich
Photo $7
Ball $35

Brian Taylor
Photo $7
Ball $40

Roy Tarpley
Photo $10
Ball $65

Thomas Thacker
Photo $7
Ball $35

Reggie Theus
Photo ....$10-$13
Ball $70

George Thompson
Photo $14
Ball $70

Mychal Thompson
Photo $8
Ball $40

Sedale Threatt
Photo $13
Ball $75

Wayman Tisdale
Photo ....$10-$12
Ball $80

Rudy Tomjanovich
Photo ....$12-$16
Ball $75

Dick Van Arsdale
Photo ....$12-$15
Ball $80

Tom Van Arsdale
Photo ....$12-$15
Ball $80

Jan Van Breda Kolff
Photo $10
Ball $65

Butch Van Breda Kolff
Photo $15
Ball $80

Norm Van Lier
Photo $12
Ball $90

Kiki Vandeweghe
Photo $12
Ball $70

Neal Walk
Photo $12
Ball $60

Chet Walker
Photo $20
Ball $80

Foots Walker
Photo ....$7-$10
Ball $65

Kermit Washington
Photo $9
Ball $60

Richard Washington
Photo $6
Ball $30

Slick Watts
Photo $15
Ball $75

Spud Webb
Photo $13
Ball $75

Marvin Webster
Photo $8
Ball $45

Scott Wedman
Photo $9
Ball $60

Robert Weiss
Photo $7
Ball $35

Walter Wesley
Photo $7
Ball $35

Mark West
Photo $10
Ball $50

Paul Westphal
Photo ....$9-$11
Ball $70

JoJo White
Photo ....$9-$12
Ball $75

Sidney Wicks
Photo ....$12-$14
Ball $80

Dominique Wilkins
Photo ....$18-$20
Ball $115

Jamaal Wilkes
Photo ....$15-$18
Ball $80

Chuck Williams
Photo $6
Ball $30

Freeman Williams
Photo $8
Ball $40

Ron Williams
Photo $6
Ball $30

Sly Williams
Photo $6
Ball $30

Brian Winters
Photo $16
Ball $75

Willie Wise
Photo $9
Ball $50

David Wohl
Photo $6
Ball $30

Orlando Woolridge
Photo $9
Ball $60

James Worthy
Photo $14
Ball $100

Basketball Autographs
Active Players

Shareef Abdur-Rahim
Photo $20
Ball $125

Ray Allen
Photo $19
Ball $120

Rafer Alston
Photo $15
Ball $80

Kenny Anderson
Photo $18
Ball $95

Greg Anthony
Photo $15
Ball $80

Ron Artest
Photo $20
Ball $100

William Avery
Photo $15
Ball $80

Stacey Augmon
Photo $15
Ball $90

Isaac Austin
Photo $15
Ball $90

Vin Baker
Photo $20
Ball $110

Dana Barros
Photo $15
Ball $90

Tony Battie
Photo $15
Ball $90

Jonathan Bender
Photo $15
Ball $80

Mike Bibby
Photo $25
Ball $110

Chauncy Billups
Photo $15
Ball $85

Mookie Blaylock
Photo $18
Ball $90

Muggsy Bogues
Photo $15
Ball $85

Elton Brand
Photo $30
Ball $125

Terrell Brandon
Photo $14
Ball $80

Kobe Bryant
Photo $30
Ball $150

Michael Cage
Photo $12
Ball $65

Marcus Camby
Photo $20
Ball $100

Antoine Carr
Photo $15
Ball $95

Vince Carter
Photo $50
Ball $175

Sam Cassell
Photo $15
Ball $90

Cedric Ceballos
Photo $14
Ball $80

Rex Chapman
Photo $14
Ball $85

Calbert Cheaney
Photo $18
Ball $95

Derrick Coleman
Photo $15
Ball $85

Austin Croshere
Photo $25
Ball $110

Terry Cummings
Photo $18
Ball $95

Vonteego Cummings
Photo $15
Ball $85

Del Curry
Photo $14
Ball $75

Antonio Daniels
Photo $15
Ball $90

Vlade Divac
Photo $14
Ball $75

Tim Duncan
Photo $35
Ball $140

Sean Elliott
Photo $13
Ball $75

Dale Ellis
Photo $13
Ball $75

Laphonso Ellis
Photo $25
Ball $120

Evan Eschmeyer
Photo $16
Ball $90

Patrick Ewing

Active Basketball Player Autographs — Chapter 11

Photo $50
Ball $175

Danny Ferry
Photo $14
Ball $80

Michael Finley
Photo $17
Ball $100

Steve Francis
Photo $14
Ball $80

Rick Fox
Photo $15
Ball $90

Kevin Garnett
Photo $25
Ball $120

Kendall Gill
Photo $18
Ball $90

Armen Gilliam
Photo $13
Ball $75

Dion Glover
Photo $20
Ball $100

Harvey Grant
Photo $12
Ball $70

Horace Grant
Photo $15
Ball $100

Paul Grant
Photo $12
Ball $75

A.C. Green
Photo $14
Ball $85

Anfernee Hardaway
Photo $30
Ball $125

Tim Hardaway
Photo $20

Ball $95

Derek Harper
Photo $15
Ball $90

Ron Harper
Photo $10
Ball $70

Hersey Hawkins
Photo $12
Ball $90

Alan Henderson
Photo $25
Ball $110

Grant Hill
Photo $50
Ball $175

Tyrone Hill
Photo $15
Ball $90

Jeff Hornacek
Photo $14
Ball $75

Robert Horry
Photo $23
Ball $115

Juwan Howard
Photo $16
Ball $90

Larry Hughes
Photo $14
Ball $75

Lindsey Hunter
Photo $18
Ball $90

Bobby Hurley
Photo $16
Ball $80

Allen Iverson
Photo $40
Ball $150

Jimmy Jackson
Photo $13
Ball $90

Mark Jackson
Photo $18
Ball $95

Tim James
Photo $16
Ball $90

Antawn Jamison
Photo $19
Ball $100

Kevin Johnson
Photo $15
Ball $95

Larry Johnson
Photo $25
Ball $115

Eddie Jones
Photo $17
Ball $100

Shawn Kemp
Photo $30
Ball $125

Steve Kerr
Photo $16
Ball $80

Jerome Kersey
Photo $16
Ball $80

Jason Kidd
Photo $30
Ball $125

Active Basketball Player Autographs — Chapter 11

Toni Kukoc
Photo $18
Ball $90

Christian Laettner
Photo $20
Ball $100

Raef LaFrentz
Photo $18
Ball $95

Quincy Lewis
Photo $14
Ball $90

Grant Long
Photo $13
Ball $85

Felipe Lopez
Photo $20
Ball $100

Dan Majerle
Photo $20
Ball $100

Karl Malone
Photo $25
Ball $125

Danny Manning
Photo $16
Ball $100

Stephon Marbury
Photo $16
Ball $95

Shawn Marion
Photo $20
Ball $100

Donyell Marshall
Photo $14
Ball $70

Jamal Mashburn
Photo $17
Ball $95

Don MacLean
Photo $14
Ball $75

Antonio McDyess
Photo $18
Ball $95

Tracy McGrady
Photo $17
Ball $90

Ron Mercer
Photo $20

Ball $100

Reggie Miller
Photo $40
Ball $130

Eric Montross
Photo $12
Ball $70

Alonzo Mourning
Photo $25
Ball $125

Chris Mullin
Photo $20
Ball $115

Dikembe Mutombo
Photo $17
Ball $100

Johnny Newman
Photo $14
Ball $70

Charles Oakley
Photo $15
Ball $85

Lamar Odom
Photo $30
Ball $135

Hakeem Olajuwon
Photo $30
Ball $150

Michael Olowokandi
Photo $25

Ball $110

Shaquille O'Neal
Photo $35
Ball $200

Billy Owens
Photo $12
Ball $65

Gary Payton
Photo ....$12-$15
Ball $85

Anthony Peeler
Photo $10
Ball $65

Paul Pierce
Photo ....$12-$15
Ball $85

Will Perdue
Photo $13
Ball $70

Sam Perkins
Photo $14
Ball $75

Paul Pierce
Photo $30
Ball $120

Scottie Pippen
Photo $25
Ball $125

Olden Polynice
Photo $13
Ball $70

Terry Porter
Photo $17
Ball $95

Mark Price
Photo $20
Ball $100

Laron Profit
Photo $18
Ball $95

Bryant Reeves
Photo $16
Ball $95

Active Basketball Player Autographs — Chapter 11

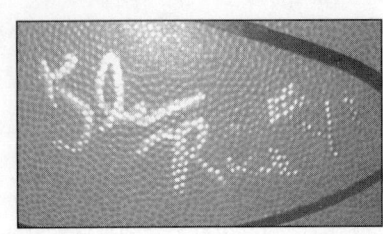

Glen Rice
Photo $20
Ball $120

Isaiah Rider
Photo $18
Ball $95

Mitch Richmond
Photo $15
Ball $90

Cliff Robinson
Photo $12
Ball $80

David Robinson
Photo $30
Ball $125

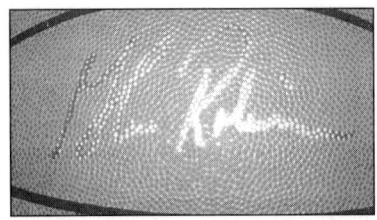

Glenn Robinson
Photo $25
Ball $115

Dennis Rodman
Photo $25
Ball $120

Rodney Rodgers
Photo $10
Ball $70

Jalen Rose
Photo $16
Ball $80

Arvydas Sabonis
Photo $20
Ball $90

Detlef Schrempf
Photo $16
Ball $80

Rony Seikaly
Photo $16
Ball $80

Joe Smith
Photo $18
Ball $95

Steve Smith
Photo $13
Ball $70

Rik Smits
Photo $12
Ball $65

Latrell Sprewell
Photo $10
Ball $90

Jerry Stackhouse
Photo $13
Ball $80

John Starks
Photo $12
Ball $70

John Stockton
Photo $15
Ball $95

Damon Stoudamire
Photo $16
Ball $90

Rod Strickland
Photo $12
Ball $75

Wally Szczerbiak
Photo $30
Ball $125

Maurice Taylor
Photo $15
Ball $90

Kenny Thomas
Photo $14
Ball $75

Tim Thomas
Photo $18
Ball $90

Otis Thorpe
Photo $13
Ball $75

Robert Traylor
Photo $15
Ball $85

Loy Vaught
Photo $15
Ball $90

Nick Van Exel
Photo $18
Ball $95

Keith Van Horn
Photo $24
Ball $120

Antoine Walker
Photo $17
Ball $90

John Wallace
Photo $15
Ball $85

Rasheed Wallace
Photo $30
Ball $125

C. Weatherspoon
Photo $13
Ball $75

Chris Webber
Photo $16
Ball $80

Jason Williams
Photo $18
Ball $110

Walt Williams
Photo $16
Ball $80

Kevin Willis
Photo $14
Ball $70

Football Autographs
Pro Football Hall of Famers

Herb Adderley (1939-) 1980
Football . . . .$75-$85
Cut signature . . . .$3-$7
Goal Line art $15
3x5 index card . . . .$5-$9
8x10 photograph . . . .$15-$20
Mini helmet $40

Lance Alworth (1940-) 1978
Football . . . .$75-$100
Cut signature . . . .$8-$10
Goal Line art $25
3x5 index card . . . .$7-$10
8x10 photograph $20
Mini helmet $50

Doug Atkins (1930-) 1982
Football . . . .$75-$85
Cut signature . . . .$2-$6
Goal Line art $15
3x5 index card . . . .$5-$9
8x10 photograph . . . .$15-$20
Mini helmet $40

Morris "Red" Badgro (1902-1998) 1981
Football . . . .$75-$100
Cut signature . . . .$3-$5
Goal Line art $30
3x5 index card . . . .$5-$8
8x10 photograph . . . .$18-$20
Mini helmet $45

Lem Barney (1945-) 1992
Football . . . .$85-$100
Cut signature . . . .$4-$5
Goal Line art $15
3x5 index card $7
8x10 photograph . . . .$12-$18
Mini helmet $40

Cliff Battles (1910-1981) 1968
Football . . . . .Unknown
Cut signature . . . .$40-$65
Goal Line art . . . . .Impossible
3x5 index card . . . .$40-$50
8x10 photograph . . . .$100-$200
Mini helmet . . . . .Impossible

Sammy Baugh (1914-) 1963
Football . . . .$250-$300
Cut signature . . . .$10-$15
Goal Line art $60
3x5 index card . . . .$20-$25
8x10 photograph $35-50
Mini helmet $75

Chuck Bednarik (1925-) 1967
Football . . . .$75-$100
Cut signature . . . .$3-$5
Goal Line art $20
3x5 index card . . . .$5-$8
8x10 photograph . . . .$12-$20
Mini helmet $40

Bert Bell (1895-1959) 1963
Football . . . . .Unknown
Cut signature $100
Goal Line art . . . . .Impossible
3x5 index card $150
8x10 photograph $400
Mini helmet . . . . .Impossible

Bobby Bell (1940-) 1983
Football . . . .$75-$100
Cut signature . . . .$4-$6
Goal Line art $20
3x5 index card . . . .$7-$12
8x10 photograph . . . .$15-$20
Mini helmet $40

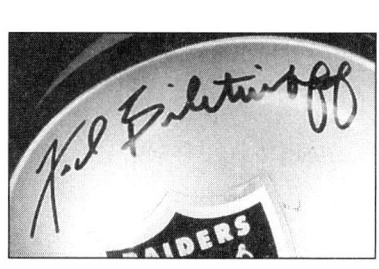

Raymond Berry (1933-) 1973
Football . . . .$75-$100
Cut signature $10
Goal Line art $20
3x5 index card . . . .$5-$7
8x10 photograph . . . .$15-$18
Mini helmet $40

Charles Bidwill (1895-1947) 1967
Football . . . . .Unknown
Cut signature $150
Goal Line art . . . . .Impossible
3x5 index card $450
8x10 photograph $750
Mini helmet . . . . .Impossible

Fred Biletnikoff (1943-) 1988
Football . . . .$80-$100
Cut signature . . . .$6-$10
Goal Line art $20
3x5 index card . . . .$6-$9
8x10 photograph . . . .$20-$25
Mini helmet $40

George Blanda (1927-) 1981
Football . . . .$100-$125
Cut signature . . . .$5-$10
Goal Line art $50
3x5 index card . . . .$8-$11
8x10 photograph $25
Mini helmet $40

Mel Blount (1948-) 1989
Football $75
Cut signature . . . .$3-$6
Goal Line art $15
3x5 index card . . . .$5-$9
8x10 photograph $20
Mini helmet $50

Terry Bradshaw (1948-) 1989
Football $150
Cut signature . . . .$7-$10
Goal Line art $25
3x5 index card $10
8x10 photograph $30
Mini helmet $125

Jim Brown (1936-) 1971
Football $150
Cut signature . . . .$7-$10
Goal Line art $25
3x5 index card $12
8x10 photograph . . . .$25-$35
Mini helmet $100

Paul Brown (1908-1991) 1967
Football . . . .$150-$250
Cut signature . . . .$10-$15
Goal Line art $50
3x5 index card . . . .$18-$25
8x10 photograph $75

Pro Football Hall of Fame Autographs — Chapter 12

Mini helmet . . . . Impossible

Roosevelt Brown (1932-) 1975
Football $75
Cut signature . . . . $5-$10
Goal Line art $15
3x5 index card $7
8x10 photograph $20
Mini helmet $40

Willie Brown (1940-) 1984
Football $75
Cut signature . . . . $3-$6
Goal Line art $20
3x5 index card . . . . $5-$6
8x10 photograph . . . . $15-$20
Mini helmet $40

Buck Buchanan (1940-1992) 1990
Football . . . . $150-$200
Cut signature . . . . $7-$8
Goal Line art $50
3x5 index card $15
8x10 photograph . . . . $40-$60
Mini helmet . . . . Impossible

Dick Butkus (1942-) 1979
Football . . . . $125-$150
Cut signature $10
Goal Line art $25
3x5 index card . . . . $8-$12
8x10 photograph $25
Mini helmet $50

Earl Campbell (1955-) 1991
Football . . . . $100-$125
Cut signature . . . . $10-$12
Goal Line art $15
3x5 index card . . . . $5-$10
8x10 photograph $20
Mini helmet $50

Tony Canadeo (1919-) 1974
Football $75
Cut signature . . . . $3-$4
Goal Line art $20
3x5 index card $5
8x10 photograph $20
Mini helmet $40

Joe Carr (1880-1939) 1963
Football . . . . Unknown
Cut signature $500
Goal Line art . . . . Impossible
3x5 index card $700
8x10 photograph $1,000
Mini helmet . . . . Impossible

Guy Chamberlin (1894-1967) 1965
Football . . . . Unknown
Cut signature $60
Goal Line art . . . . Impossible
3x5 index card $75
8x10 photograph $150
Mini helmet . . . . Impossible

Jack Christiansen (1928-1986) 1970
Football . . . . Unknown
Cut signature $15
Goal Line art . . . . Impossible
3x5 index card $40
8x10 photograph . . . . $100-$150
Mini helmet . . . . Impossible

Dutch Clark (1906-1978) 1963
Football . . . . Unknown
Cut signature $15
Goal Line art . . . . Impossible
3x5 index card $40
8x10 photograph $100
Mini helmet . . . . Impossible

George Connor (1925-) 1975
Football $75
Cut signature . . . . $3-$6
Goal Line art $25
3x5 index card $5
8x10 photograph $15
Mini helmet $40

Jimmy Conzelman (1898-1970) 1964
Football . . . . Unknown
Cut signature $75
Goal Line art . . . . Impossible
3x5 index card $100
8x10 photograph $350
Mini helmet . . . . Impossible

Lou Creekmur (1927-) 1996
Football $80
Cut signature $6
Goal Line art $15
3x5 index card $6
8x10 photograph $15
Mini helmet $40

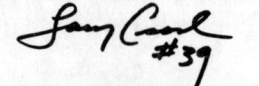

Larry Csonka (1946-) 1987
Football . . . . $75-$125
Cut signature $6
Goal Line art $35
3x5 index card . . . . $7-$10
8x10 photograph $20
Mini helmet $60

Al Davis (1929-) 1992
Football $125
Cut signature $10
Goal Line art . . . . $75-$100
3x5 index card $20
8x10 photograph . . . . $35-$50
Mini helmet $50

Willie Davis (1934-) 1981
Football $75
Cut signature . . . . $3-$7
Goal Line art $15
3x5 index card . . . . $6-$7
8x10 photograph . . . . $15-$20
Mini helmet $40

Len Dawson (1935-) 1987
Football $125
Cut signature . . . . $5-$8
Goal Line art $25
3x5 index card . . . . $7-$8
8x10 photograph $25
Mini helmet $50

Eric Dickerson (1960-) 1999
Football $90
Cut signature $5
Goal Line art $16
3x5 index card $5
8x10 photograph . . . . $20-$25
Mini helmet $50

Dan Dierdorf (1949-) 1996
Football $80
Cut signature $5
Goal Line art $15

3x5 index card $5
8x10 photograph $15
Mini helmet $40

Mike Ditka (1939-) 1988
Football ....$100-$150
Cut signature ....$10-$12
Goal Line art $20
3x5 index card ....$7-$10
8x10 photograph .....$20-$30
Mini helmet $50

Art Donovan (1925-) 1968
Football $75
Cut signature ....$3-$7
Goal Line art $20
3x5 index card $5
8x10 photograph $20
Mini helmet $40

Tony Dorsett (1954-) 1994
Football ....$125-$150
Cut signature $3
Goal Line art $40
3x5 index card $5
8x10 photograph $25
Mini helmet $60

Paddy Driscoll (1896-1968) 1965
Football ....Unknown
Cut signature $100
Goal Line art ....Impossible
3x5 index card $200
8x10 photograph ...$250-$350
Mini helmet ....Impossible

Bill Dudley (1921-) 1966
Football $75
Cut signature ....$5-$6
Goal Line art $15

3x5 index card ....$5-$7
8x10 photograph $15
Mini helmet $40

Turk Edwards (1907-1973) 1969
Football ....Unknown
Cut signature $80
Goal Line art ....Impossible
3x5 index card $125
8x10 photograph $300
Mini helmet ....Impossible

Weeb Ewbank (1907-1998) 1978
Football $75
Cut signature ....$3-$6
Goal Line art $15
3x5 index card ....$7-$10
8x10 photograph $20
Mini helmet $45

Tom Fears (1923-2000) 1970
Football $85
Cut signature ....$3-$7
Goal Line art $15
3x5 index card ....$5-$9
8x10 photograph $15
Mini helmet $45

Jim Finks (1904-1994) 1995
Football $150
Cut signature $5
Goal Line art ....Impossible
3x5 index card $10
8x10 photograph $30
Mini helmet ....Unknown

Ray Flaherty (1904-1994) 1976
Football $150
Cut signature $5
Goal Line art $40
3x5 index card $10
8x10 photograph $25
Mini helmet ....Unknown

Len Ford (1926-1972) 1976
Football ....Unknown
Cut signature ....$25-$30
Goal Line art ....Impossible
3x5 index card $50
8x10 photograph $200
Mini helmet ....Impossible

Dan Fortmann (1916-1995) 1985
Football ....Unknown
Cut signature $20
Goal Line art ....Impossible
3x5 index card $25
8x10 photograph .....$50-$75
Mini helmet ....Unknown

Dan Fouts (1951-) 1993

Football $100
Cut signature $4
Goal Line art $25
3x5 index card $7
8x10 photograph $35
Mini helmet $50

Frank Gatski (1922-) 1985
Football $75
Cut signature $3
Goal Line art $15
3x5 index card $3
8x10 photograph .....$15-$20
Mini helmet $40

Bill George (1930-1982) 1974
Football ....Unknown
Cut signature ....$40-$50
Goal Line art ....Impossible
3x5 index card $75
8x10 photograph $250
Mini helmet ....Impossible

Joe Gibbs (1940-) 1996
Football ....$100-$125
Cut signature ....$6-$7
Goal Line art $15
3x5 index card ....$7-$10
8x10 photograph $25
Mini helmet $40

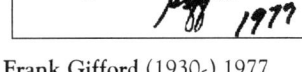

Frank Gifford (1930-) 1977
Football ....$100-$150
Cut signature ....$6-$7
Goal Line art $35
3x5 index card ....$10-$15
8x10 photograph $35
Mini helmet $45

Sid Gillman (1911-) 1983
Football $75
Cut signature ....$3-$6
Goal Line art $15
3x5 index card $6
8x10 photograph $20
Mini helmet $45

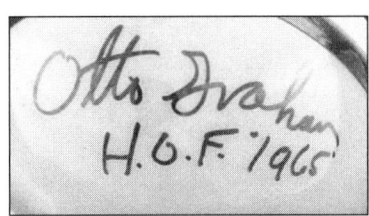

Otto Graham (1921-) 1965
Football ....$125-$150
Cut signature ....$7-$9

Goal Line art $20
3x5 index card . . . .$5-$8
8x10 photograph $20
Mini helmet . . . . .Impossible

Red Grange (1903-1991) 1963
Football . . . .$475-$600
Cut signature $35
Goal Line art $200
3x5 index card $25
8x10 photograph $125
Mini helmet . . . . .Impossible

Bud Grant (1927-) 1994
Football $85
Cut signature $3
Goal Line art $30
3x5 index $5
8x10 photograph $25
Mini helmet $40

Joe Greene (1946-) 1987
Football . . . .$75-$125
Cut signature $3
Goal Line art $25
3x5 index card $7
8x10 photograph $35
Mini helmet $45

Forrest Gregg (1933-) 1977
Football $75
Cut signature . . . .$7-$9
Goal Line art $20
3x5 index card $6
8x10 photograph $15
Mini helmet $40

Bob Griese (1945-) 1990
Football $125
Cut signature . . . .$4-$6
Goal Line art $30
3x5 index card $7
8x10 photograph $20
Mini helmet $45

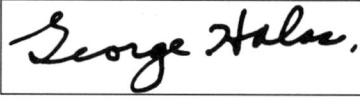

Lou Groza (1924-) 1974
Football $100
Cut signature . . . .$3-$6
Goal Line art $15
3x5 index card $6
8x10 photograph . . . .$15-$20
Mini helmet $40

Joe Guyon (1892-1971) 1966
Football . . . . .Unknown
Cut signature $35
Goal Line art . . . . .Impossible
3x5 index card $75
8x10 photograph $300
Mini helmet . . . . .Impossible

George Halas (1895-1983) 1963
Football . . . .$250-$300
Cut signature . . . .$20-$25
Goal Line art . . . . .Impossible
3x5 index card $50
8x10 photograph . . . .$175-$250
Mini helmet . . . . .Impossible

Jack Ham (1948-) 1988
Football . . . .$75-$100
Cut signature $3
Goal Line art $15
3x5 index card . . . .$7-$10
8x10 photograph . . . .$15-$20
Mini helmet $45

John Hannah (1951-) 1991
Football $75
Cut signature . . . .$3-$6
Goal Line art $20
3x5 index card . . . .$5-$8
8x10 photograph $20
Mini helmet $40

Franco Harris (1950-) 1990
Football $125
Cut signature . . . .$10-$12
Goal Line art $40
3x5 index card $8
8x10 photograph $25
Mini helmet $90

Mike Haynes (1953-) 1997
Football $75
Cut signature $7
Goal Line Art $15
3x5 index card $7
8x10 photograph . . . .$15-$18
Mini helmet $40

Ed Healey (1894-1978) 1964
Football $150
Cut signature $60
Goal Line art . . . . .Impossible
3x5 index card . . . .$50-$75
8x10 photograph $250
Mini helmet . . . . .Impossible

Mel Hein (1909-1992) 1963
Football $175
Cut signature . . . .$10-$15
Goal Line art . . . . .Impossible
3x5 index card . . . .$12-$15
8x10 photograph . . . .$40-$60
Mini helmet . . . . .Unknown

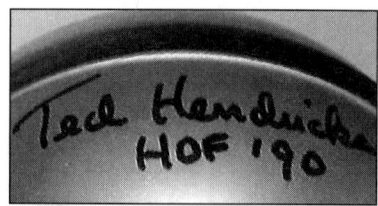

Ted Hendricks (1947-) 1990
Football $75
Cut signature . . . .$3-$6
Goal Line art $20
3x5 index card $6
8x10 photograph . . . .$15-$20
Mini helmet $40

Pete Henry (1897-1952) 1963
Football . . . . .Unknown
Cut signature $50
Goal Line art . . . . .Impossible
3x5 index card $75
8x10 photograph $275
Mini helmet . . . . .Impossible

Arnie Herber (1910-1969) 1966
Football . . . . .Unknown
Cut signature $75
Goal Line art . . . . .Impossible
3x5 index card $125
8x10 photograph . . . .$400-$500
Mini helmet . . . . .Impossible

Bill Hewitt (1909-1947) 1971
Football . . . . .Unknown
Cut signature $100
Goal Line art . . . . .Impossible
3x5 index card $200
8x10 photograph $600
Mini helmet . . . . .Impossible

Clarke Hinkle (1909-1988) 1964
Football $200
Cut signature $10
Goal Line art . . . . .Impossible
3x5 index card $30
8x10 photograph $50
Mini helmet . . . . .Impossible

Elroy Hirsch (1923-) 1968
Football $125
Cut signature $5
Goal Line art $15
3x5 index card $8
8x10 photograph $20
Mini helmet $50

Paul Hornung (1935-) 1986
Football $125
Cut signature . . . .$5-$10
Goal Line art $30
3x5 index card $8
8x10 photograph . . . .$20-$25
Mini helmet $50

Ken Houston (1944-) 1986
Football $75
Cut signature . . . .$7-$10
Goal Line art $15
3x5 index card $6
8x10 photograph . . . .$15-$20
Mini helmet $40

Cal Hubbard (1900-1977) 1963
Football . . . . .Unknown
Cut signature $25
Goal Line art . . . . .Impossible
3x5 index card $50
8x10 photograph . . . .$200-$250
Mini helmet . . . . .Impossible

Sam Huff (1934-) 1982
Football $100
Cut signature $3
Goal Line art $20
3x5 index card $6
8x10 photograph $25
Mini helmet $45

Lamar Hunt (1932-) 1972
Football $75
Cut signature . . . .$6-$8
Goal Line art $15
3x5 index card $8
8x10 photograph $20
Mini helmet $40

Don Hutson (1913-1997) 1963
Football $75
Cut signature . . . .$8-$10
Goal Line art $40
3x5 index card $10
8x10 photograph . . . .$25-$35
Mini helmet $60

Jimmy Johnson (1938-) 1994
Football $75
Cut signature $3
Goal Line art $20
3x5 index card $5
8x10 photograph $20
Mini helmet $40

John Henry Johnson (1929-) 1987
Football $75
Cut signature . . . .$6-$7
Goal Line art $20
3x5 index card . . . .$6-$8
8x10 photograph $15
Mini helmet . . . .$

Charlie Joiner (1947-) 1996
Football . . . .$75-$80
Cut signature $5
Goal Line art $15
3x5 index card $5
8x10 photograph . . . .$15-$18
Mini helmet $40

Deacon Jones (1938-) 1980
Football $100
Cut signature $3
Goal Line art $15
3x5 index card $7
8x10 photograph $15
Mini helmet $45

Stan Jones (1931-) 1991
Football $75
Cut signature . . . .$5-$6
Goal Line art $15
3x5 index card $6
8x10 photograph . . . .$12-$15
Mini helmet $40

Henry Jordan (1935-1976) 1995
Football . . . . .Unknown
Cut signature $50
Goal Line art . . . . .Impossible
3x5 index card $100
8x10 photograph $175
Mini helmet . . . . .Impossible

Sonny Jurgensen (1934-) 1983
Football $125
Cut signature $5
Goal Line art . . . .$25-$30
3x5 index card $5
8x10 photograph $20
Mini helmet $50

Leroy Kelly (1942-) 1994
Football $100
Cut signature $3
Goal Line art $15
3x5 index card $5
8x10 photograph $15
Mini helmet $40

Walt Kiesling (1903-1962) 1966
Football . . . . .Unknown
Cut signature $75
Goal Line art . . . . .Impossible
3x5 index card $150
8x10 photograph . . . .$100-$200
Mini helmet . . . . .Impossible

Frank "Bruiser" Kinard (1914-1965) 1971
Football . . . . .Unknown
Cut signature $50
Goal Line art . . . . .Impossible
3x5 index card $75
8x10 photograph $300
Mini helmet . . . . .Impossible

Paul Krause (1942-) 1998
Football $75

Cut signature $5
Goal Line art $15
3x5 index card $5
8x10 photograph ....$15-$18
Mini helmet $40

Curly Lambeau (1898-1965) 1963
Football ....Unknown
Cut signature $125
Goal Line art ....Impossible
3x5 index card $200
8x10 photograph ....$300-$400
Mini helmet ....Impossible

Jack Lambert (1952-) 1990
Football $150
Cut signature $3
Goal Line art $30
3x5 index card $6
8x10 photograph ....$22-$25
Mini helmet $60

Tom Landry (1924-2000) 1990
Football $125
Cut signature $5
Goal Line art $25
3x5 index card $7
8x10 photograph ....$25-$35
Mini helmet $50

Dick Lane (1928-) 1974
Football $75
Cut signature $3
Goal Line art $15
3x5 index card $6
8x10 photograph $15
Mini helmet $40

Jim Langer (1948-) 1987
Football ....$75-$100
Cut signature ....$5-$8
Goal Line art $15
3x5 index card ....$6-$8
8x10 photograph $15
Mini helmet $40

Willie Lanier (1945-) 1986
Football $75
Cut signature $3
Goal Line art $15
3x5 index card $6
8x10 photograph $15
Mini helmet $40

Steve Largent (1954-) 1995
Football $125
Cut signature $4
Goal Line art $15
3x5 index card $8

8x10 photograph $20
Mini helmet $45

Yale Lary (1930-) 1979
Football $75
Cut signature $3
Goal Line art $15
3x5 index card $5
8x10 photograph $15
Mini helmet $40

Dante Lavelli (1923-) 1975
Football $75
Cut signature $3
Goal Line art $15
3x5 index card $6
8x10 photograph $15
Mini helmet $40

Bobby Layne (1926-1986) 1967
Football ....$400-$500
Cut signature $15
Goal Line art ....Impossible
3x5 index card $35
8x10 photograph ....$65-$85
Mini helmet ....Impossible

Tuffy Leemans (1912-1979) 1978
Football ....Unknown
Cut signature $75
Goal Line art ....Impossible
3x5 index card $125
8x10 photograph $200
Mini helmet ....Impossible

Bob Lilly (1939-) 1980
Football $100
Cut signature $3
Goal Line art $20
3x5 index card $6
8x10 photograph $15
Mini helmet $45

Larry Little (1945-) 1993
Football $75
Cut signature $5
Goal Line art $15
3x5 index card $5
8x10 photograph $15
Mini helmet $40

Vince Lombardi (1913-1970) 1971
Football ....$1,500-$1,750
Cut signature ....$75-$100
Goal Line art ....Impossible
3x5 index card $150
8x10 photograph ....$400-$500
Mini helmet ....Impossible

Howie Long (1960-) 2000
Football $125
Cut signature $8
Goal Line art $18
3x5 index card $10
8x10 photograph $20
Mini helmet $40

Ronnie Lott (1959-) 2000
Football $100
Cut signature ....$5-$7
Goal Line art $15
3x5 index card $8
8x10 photograph $15
Mini helmet $40

Sid Luckman (1916-1998) 1965
Football $125
Cut signature $3
Goal Line art $30
3x5 index card $6
8x10 photograph ....$17-$20
Mini helmet $45

Link Lyman (1898-1972) 1964
Football ....Unknown
Cut signature $75

Goal Line art . . . . .Impossible
3x5 index card $100
8x10 photograph $200
Mini helmet . . . . .Impossible

Tom Mack (1943-) 1999
Football $75
Cut signature $4
Goal Line art $15
3x5 index card $4
8x10 photograph . . . .$14-$17
Mini helmet $40

John Mackey (1941-) 1992
Football $75
Cut signature $3
Goal Line art $15
3x5 index card $6
8x10 photograph $15
Mini helmet $40

Tim Mara (1887-1959) 1963
Football . . . . .Unknown
Cut signature $200
Goal Line art . . . . .Impossible
3x5 index card $300
8x10 photograph $700
Mini helmet . . . . .Impossible

Wellington Mara (1916-) 1997
Football $70
Cut signature $3
Goal Line art $14
3x5 index card $3
8x10 photograph $14
Mini helmet $40

Gino Marchetti (1927-) 1972
Football $75
Cut signature $3
Goal Line art $15
3x5 index card $5
8x10 photograph $15
Mini helmet $40

George Marshall (1887-1969) 1963
Football . . . . .Unknown
Cut signature $125
Goal Line art . . . . .Impossible
3x5 index card $200
8x10 photograph $400
Mini helmet . . . . .Impossible

Ollie Matson (1930-) 1972
Football $75
Cut signature $3
Goal Line art $20
3x5 index card $6
8x10 photograph $15
Mini helmet $40

Don Maynard (1935-) 1987
Football $100
Cut signature . . . .$3-$7
Goal Line art $20
3x5 index card $6
8x10 photograph $15
Mini helmet $45

George McAfee (1918-) 1966
Football $75
Cut signature $7
Goal Line art $15
3x5 index card $5
8x10 photograph $15
Mini helmet $40

Mike McCormack (1930-) 1984
Football $75
Cut signature . . . .$3-$5
Goal Line art $15
3x5 index card $5
8x10 photograph $15
Mini helmet $40

Tommy McDonald (1934-) 1998
Football $70
Cut signature $6
Goal Line art $15
3x5 index card $6
8x10 photograph . . . .$15-$19
Mini helmet $40

Hugh McElhenny (1928-) 1970
Football $100
Cut signature $10
Goal Line art $20
3x5 index card . . . .$10-$13
8x10 photograph $25
Mini helmet $40

John McNally (1903-1985) 1963
Football $500
Cut signature $25
Goal Line art . . . . .Impossible
3x5 index card $50
8x10 photograph . . . .$100-$150
Mini helmet . . . . .Impossible

Mike Michalske (1903-1983) 1964
Football $400
Cut signature $20
Goal Line art . . . . .Impossible
3x5 index card $40
8x10 photograph . . . .$150-$200
Mini helmet . . . . .Impossible

Wayne Millner (1913-1976) 1968
Football . . . . .Unknown
Cut signature $75
Goal Line art . . . . .Impossible
3x5 index card $100
8x10 photograph $300
Mini helmet . . . . .Impossible

Bobby Mitchell (1935-) 1983
Football $75
Cut signature $3
Goal Line art $20
3x5 index card $5
8x10 photograph . . . .$15-$20
Mini helmet $40

Ron Mix (1938-) 1979
Football $75
Cut signature . . . .$5-$6
Goal Line art $20
3x5 index card $6
8x10 photograph $15
Mini helmet $40

Lenny Moore (1933-) 1975
Football $75
Cut signature . . . .$6-$7
Goal Line art $20
3x5 index card . . . .$6-$9
8x10 photograph $15
Mini helmet $40

Joe Montana (1956-) 2000

Football $250
Cut signature $40
Goal Line art $65
3x5 index card $45
8x10 photograph $75
Mini helmet $100

Marion Motley (1920-1999) 1968
Football $75
Cut signature . . . . $3-$8
Goal Line art $15
3x5 index card . . . . $6-$10
8x10 photograph $15
Mini helmet $40

Anthony Munoz (1958-) 1998
Football $80
Cut signature $8
Goal Line art $16
3x5 index card $8
8x10 . . . . $18-$20
Mini helmet $40

George Musso (1910-) 1982
Football $75
Cut signature . . . . $3-$5
Goal Line art $15
3x5 index card $5
8x10 photograph $15
Mini helmet $40

Bronko Nagurski (1908-1990) 1963
Football $350
Cut signature $25
Goal Line art . . . . Impossible
3x5 index card . . . . $35-$50
8x10 photograph . . . . $100-$150
Mini helmet . . . . Impossible

Joe Namath (1943-) 1985
Football $150
Cut signature . . . . $10-$12
Goal Line art $60
3x5 index card . . . . $20-$30
8x10 photograph $40
Mini helmet $150

Earle "Greasy" Neale (1891-1973) 1969
Football . . . . Unknown

Cut signature . . . . $50-$75
Goal Line art . . . . Impossible
3x5 index card $100
8x10 photograph $300
Mini helmet . . . . Impossible

Ernie Nevers (1903-1976) 1963
Football . . . . Unknown
Cut signature $50
Goal Line art . . . . Impossible
3x5 index card $80
8x10 photograph . . . . $150-$250
Mini helmet . . . . Impossible

Ozzie Newsome (1956-) 1999
Football $75
Cut signature $5
Goal Line art $20
3x5 index card $6
8x10 photograph . . . . $15-$20
Mini helmet $40

Ray Nitschke (1936-1998) 1978
Football $100
Cut signature . . . . $3-$6
Goal Line art $25
3x5 index card $6
8x10 photograph $20
Mini helmet $60

Chuck Noll (1932-) 1993
Football $75
Cut signature $3
Goal Line art $15
3x5 index card $6
8x10 photograph $15
Mini helmet $40

Leo Nomellini (1924-) 1969
Football $75
Cut signature . . . . $3-$10
Goal Line art $20
3x5 index card $6
8x10 photograph . . . . $15-$20
Mini helmet $40

Merlin Olsen (1940-) 1982
Football . . . . $75-$100
Cut signature . . . . $5-$7
Goal Line art $20
3x5 index card $10
8x10 photograph . . . . $25-$30
Mini helmet $45

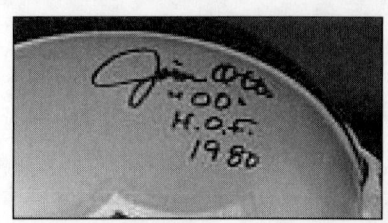

Jim Otto (1938-) 1980
Football $75
Cut signature . . . . $3-$6
Goal Line art $20
3x5 index card $6
8x10 photograph $15
Mini helmet $40

Steve Owen (1898-1964) 1966
Football . . . . Unknown
Cut signature $200
Goal Line art . . . . Impossible
3x5 index card $400
8x10 photograph $750
Mini helmet . . . . Impossible

Alan Page (1945-) 1988
Football . . . . $75-$100
Cut signature $3
Goal Line art $15
3x5 index card $6
8x10 photograph $15
Mini helmet $40

Ace Parker (1912-) 1972
Football $75
Cut signature $3
Goal Line art $15
3x5 index card $6
8x10 photograph $15
Mini helmet $40

Jim Parker (1934-) 1973
Football $75
Cut signature $3
Goal Line art $15
3x5 index card $5
8x10 photograph $15
Mini helmet $40

Walter Payton (1954-1999) 1993
Football $150
Cut signature . . . . $6-$8
Goal Line art . . . . $30-$35
3x5 index card . . . . $8-$10
8x10 photograph . . . . $25-$30
Mini helmet $150

Joe Perry (1927-) 1969
Football $100
Cut signature ....$3-$8
Goal Line art $25
3x5 index card ....$7-$8
8x10 photograph $20
Mini helmet $40

Pete Pihos (1923-) 1970
Football $75
Cut signature $3
Goal Line art $15
3x5 index card $6
8x10 photograph $15
Mini helmet $40

Hugh Ray (1884-1956) 1966
Football ....Unknown
Cut signature $200
Goal Line art ....Impossible
3x5 index card ....$350-$400
8x10 photograph $750
Mini helmet ....Impossible

Dan Reeves (1912-1971) 1967
Football ....Unknown
Cut signature ....$50-$75
Goal Line art ....Impossible
3x5 index card $100
8x10 photograph ....$300-$400
Mini helmet ....Impossible

Mel Renfro (1941-) 1996
Football $75
Cut signature $5
Goal Line art $15
3x5 index card $5
8x10 photograph $17
Mini helmet $40

John Riggins (1949-) 1992
Football $125
Cut signature ....$5-$6
Goal Line art $25
3x5 index card $8
8x10 photograph $50
Mini helmet $60

Jim Ringo (1931-) 1981
Football $75
Cut signature ....$3-$5
Goal Line art $20
3x5 index card $15
8x10 photograph $15
Mini helmet $40

Andy Robustelli (1925-) 1971
Football $100
Cut signature $3
Goal Line art $15
3x5 index card $6
8x10 photograph $15
Mini helmet $40

Art Rooney (1901-1988) 1964
Football $300
Cut signature ....$7-$10
Goal Line art ....Impossible
3x5 index card $25
8x10 photograph ....$75-$125
Mini helmet ....Impossible

Dan Rooney (1932-) 2000
Football $75
Cut signature $3
Goal Line art $15
3x5 index card $6
8x10 photograph $15
Mini helmet $40

Pete Rozelle (1926-1996) 1985
Football $125
Cut signature ....$7-$10
Goal Line art $40
3x5 index card $15
8x10 photograph $30
Mini helmet $60

Bob St. Clair (1931-) 1990
Football $75
Cut signature ....$3-$6
Goal Line art $30
3x5 index card $6
8x10 photograph $15
Mini helmet $40

Gale Sayers (1943-) 1977
Football $125
Cut signature ....$4-$7
Goal Line art $30
3x5 index card ....$7-$10
8x10 photograph $20
Mini helmet $50

Joe Schmidt (1932-) 1973
Football $75
Cut signature $3
Goal Line art $15
3x5 index card ....$6-$9
8x10 photograph $15
Mini helmet $40

Tex Schramm (1920-) 1991
Football $75
Cut signature ....$3-$6
Goal Line art $15
3x5 index card ....$6-$9
8x10 photograph $15
Mini helmet $40

Lee Roy Selmon (1954-) 1995
Football ....$70-$85
Cut signature $3
Goal Line art $16
3x5 index card $5
8x10 photograph ....$19-$21
Mini helmet $40

Billy Shaw (1938-) 1999
Football $70
Cut signature $3
Goal Line art $14
3x5 index card $3
8x10 photograph $15
Mini helmet $40

Art Shell (1946-) 1989
Football ....$75-$100
Cut signature $4
Goal Line art $15
3x5 index card $6
8x10 photograph $15
Mini helmet $40

Don Shula (1930-) 1997
Football ....$85-$100
Cut signature $6
Goal Line art $20
3x5 index card $8
8x10 photograph ....$20-$25
Mini helmet $75

O.J. Simpson (1947-) 1985
Football $250
Cut signature $25
Goal Line art ....Impossible
3x5 index card $35
8x10 photograph ....$60-$75
Mini helmet $75

Mike Singletary (1958-) 1998
Football $100
Cut signature $7
Goal Line art $25
3x5 index card $7
8x10 photograph $20
Mini helmet $45

Jackie Smith (1940-) 1994
Football $75
Cut signature $3
Goal Line art $15
3x5 index card $5
8x10 photograph $15
Mini helmet $40

Bart Starr (1934-) 1977
Football ....$100-$125
Cut signature $4
Goal Line art $30
3x5 index card $8
8x10 photograph $25
Mini helmet $60

Roger Staubach (1942-) 1985
Football $150
Cut signature ....$5-$7
Goal Line art $40
3x5 index card $8
8x10 photograph ....$25-$40
Mini helmet $60

Ernie Stautner (1925-) 1969
Football $75
Cut signature $4
Goal Line art $15
3x5 index card $7

8x10 photograph $20
Mini helmet $40

Jan Stenerud (1942-) 1991
Football $75
Cut signature ....$3-$5
Goal Line art $15
3x5 index card $6
8x10 photograph $15
Mini helmet $40

Dwight Stephenson (1957-) 1998
Football $70
Cut signature $3
Goal Line art $14
3x5 index card $3
8x10 photograph $16
Mini helmet $40

Ken Strong (1906-1979) 1967
Football ....Unknown
Cut signature $40
Goal Line art ....Impossible
3x5 index card $60
8x10 photograph $200
Mini helmet ....Impossible

Joe Stydahar (1912-1977) 1967
Football ....Unknown
Cut signature $40
Goal Line art ....Impossible
3x5 index card $60
8x10 photograph $25
Mini helmet ....Impossible

Fran Tarkenton (1940-) 1986
Football $150
Cut signature ....$5-$10
Goal Line art $40
3x5 index card $10
8x10 photograph ....$25-$30
Mini helmet $55

Charley Taylor (1941-) 1984
Football $75
Cut signature $4
Goal Line art $20
3x5 index card $6
8x10 photograph $15
Mini helmet $40

Jim Taylor (1935-) 1976
Football $75
Cut signature $4

Goal Line art $20
3x5 index card $5
8x10 photograph $15
Mini helmet $45

Lawrence Taylor (1959-) 1999
Football ....$80-$90
Cut signature ....$6-$8
Goal Line art $25
3x5 index card $7
8x10 photograph ....$20-$25
Mini helmet $60

Jim Thorpe (1888-1953) 1963
Football $6,000
Cut signature $500
Goal Line art ....Impossible
3x5 index card $700
8x10 photograph $1,500
Mini helmet ....Impossible

Y.A. Tittle (1926-) 1971
Football $100
Cut signature $4
Goal Line art $25
3x5 index card $6
8x10 photograph $25
Mini helmet $45

George Trafton (1896-1971) 1964
Football ....Unknown
Cut signature $75
Goal Line art ....Impossible
3x5 index card $125
8x10 photograph $250
Mini helmet ....Impossible

Charley Trippi (1922-) 1968
Football $75
Cut signature $3
Goal Line art $15
3x5 index card $6
8x10 photograph ....$18-$20
Mini helmet $40

Emlen Tunnell (1925-1975) 1967

Football ....Unknown
Cut signature $40
Goal Line art ....Impossible
3x5 index card $75
8x10 photograph $200
Mini helmet ....Impossible

Bulldog Turner (1919-1998) 1966
Football $100
Cut signature $4
Goal Line art $25
3x5 index card $7
8x10 photograph $20
Mini helmet $45

Johnny Unitas (1933-) 1979
Football $150
Cut signature ....$5-$10
Goal Line art ....Impossible
3x5 index card $8
8x10 photograph $20
Mini helmet $70

Gene Upshaw (1945-) 1987
Football $75
Cut signature ....$3-$7
Goal Line art $15
3x5 index card $6
8x10 photograph $15
Mini helmet $40

Norm Van Brocklin (1926-1983) 1971
Football $350
Cut signature $40
Goal Line art ....Impossible
3x5 index card $75
8x10 photograph ....$200-$225
Mini helmet ....Impossible

Steve Van Buren (1920-) 1965
Football $75
Cut signature $3
Goal Line art $20
3x5 index card $5
8x10 photograph $15
Mini helmet $40

Doak Walker (1927-1998) 1986
Football $100
Cut signature $3
Goal Line art $25
3x5 index card $5
8x10 photograph $20
Mini helmet $45

Bill Walsh (1931-) 1993
Football $125
Cut signature $5
Goal Line art $50
3x5 index card $10
8x10 photograph $25
Mini helmet $45

Paul Warfield (1942-) 1983
Football $75
Cut signature $3
Goal Line art $15
3x5 index card $6
8x10 photograph ....$15-$20
Mini helmet $40

Bob Waterfield (1920-1983) 1965
Football $350
Cut signature ....$30-$40
Goal Line art ....Impossible
3x5 index card $75
8x10 photograph ....$175-$250
Mini helmet ....Impossible

Mike Webster (1952-) 1997
Football $75
Cut signature $4
Goal Line art $15
3x5 index card $4
8x10 photograph ....$15-$20
Mini helmet $40

Arnie Weinmeister (1923-2000) 1984
Football $75
Cut signature $3
Goal Line art $15
3x5 index card $5
8x10 photograph $15
Mini helmet $40

Randy White (1953-) 1994
Football $75
Cut signature $4
Goal Line art $15

3x5 index card $4
8x10 photograph ....$16-$18
Mini helmet $45

Dave Wilcox (1942-) 2000
Football $75
Cut signature $4
Goal Line art $15
3x5 index card $4
8x10 photograph ....$16-$18
Mini helmet $40

Bill Willis (1921-) 1977
Football $75
Cut signature $3
Goal Line art $20
3x5 index card $6
8x10 photograph $15
Mini helmet $40

Larry Wilson (1938-) 1978
Football $75
Cut signature $3
Goal Line art $15
3x5 index card $6
8x10 photograph $15
Mini helmet $40

Kellen Winslow (1957-) 1995
Football $100
Cut signature $3
Goal Line art $15
3x5 index card $5
8x10 photograph $15
Mini helmet $40

Alex Wojciechowicz (1915-1992) 1968
Football $200
Cut signature $8
Goal Line art $150
3x5 index card $10
8x10 photograph ....$35-$50
Mini helmet ....Unknown

Willie Wood (1936-) 1989
Football $75
Cut signature $3
Goal Line art $15
3x5 index card $5
8x10 photograph $15
Mini helmet $40

Football Autographs
Inactive Players
* Indicates player is deceased

Dan Abramowicz
Photo $10
Football $75
Mini Helmet $40

Mike Adamle
Photo $10
Football $75
Mini Helmet $40

Julius Adams
Photo $10
Football $75
Mini Helmet $40

George Allen *
Photo $35
Football $175
Mini Helmet . . . . .Impossible

Marcus Allen
Photo $30
Football $150
Mini Helmet $75

Lyle Alzado *
Photo $50
Football $115
Mini Helmet . . . . .Impossible

Alan Ameche *
Photo $40
Football $125
Mini Helmet . . . . .Impossible

Donny Anderson
Photo $15
Football $80
Mini Helmet $45

"Flipper" Anderson
Photo $10
Football $70
Mini Helmet $40

Ken Anderson
Photo $20
Football $85
Mini Helmet $55

Neal Anderson
Photo $15
Football $75
Mini Helmet $45

Ottis Anderson
Photo $20
Football $80
Mini Helmet $50

Jon Arnett
Photo $20
Football $75
Mini Helmet $45

Coy Bacon
Photo $15
Football $75
Mini Helmet $45

Jim Bakken
Photo $20
Football $80
Mini Helmet $50

Pete Banaszak
Photo $15
Football $75
Mini Helmet $45

Tom Banks
Photo $20
Football $75
Mini Helmet $45

Steve Bartkowski
Photo $18
Football $85
Mini Helmet $45

Mark Bavaro
Photo $15
Football $70
Mini Helmet $40

Greg Bell
Photo $20
Football $80
Mini Helmet $45

Ricky Bell
Photo $40
Football $125
Mini Helmet $60

Don Beebe
Photo $20
Football $80
Mini Helmet $50

Rolf Bernirschke
Photo $20
Football $80
Mini Helmet $50

Bill Bergey
Photo $20
Football $80
Mini Helmet $50

Rod Bernstine
Photo $15
Football $70
Mini Helmet $40

Elvin Bethea
Photo $20
Football $75
Mini Helmet $45

Dean Biasucci
Photo $15
Football $70
Mini Helmet $40

Glenn Blackwood
Photo $10
Football $65
Mini Helmet $40

Verlon Biggs
Photo $12
Football $70
Mini Helmet $40

Lyle Blackwood
Photo $15
Football $75
Mini Helmet $45

Bennie Blades
Photo $15
Football $75
Mini Helmet $45

Rocky Bleier
Photo $20
Football $80
Mini Helmet $50

Mark Bortz
Photo $15
Football $70
Mini Helmet $40

Emerson Boozer
Photo $18
Football $85
Mini Helmet $45

Brian Bosworth
Photo $15
Football $75
Mini Helmet $45

Ken Bowman
Photo $20
Football $80
Mini Helmet $50

Inactive Football Player Autographs — Chapter 13

Cliff Branch
Photo $30
Football $100
Mini Helmet $65

Mike Bragg
Photo $15
Football $70
Mini Helmet $40

Zeke Bratkowski
Photo $15
Football $70
Mini Helmet $45

Jim Breech
Photo $12
Football $70
Mini Helmet $40

John Brockington
Photo $18
Football $80
Mini Helmet $50

John Brodie
Photo $35
Football $100
Mini Helmet $60

Robert Brooks
Photo $20
Football $80
Mini Helmet $50

Tom Brookshier
Photo $15
Football $75
Mini Helmet $45

Dave Brown
Photo $15
Football $75
Mini Helmet $45

Larry Brown
Photo $20
Football $80
Mini Helmet $50

Bobby Bryant
Photo $25
Football $90
Mini Helmet $55

Kelvin Bryant
Photo $20
Football $80
Mini Helmet $50

Willie Buchanon
Photo $20
Football $80
Mini Helmet $50

Norm Bulaich
Photo $15
Football $75
Mini Helmet $45

Nick Buoniconti
Photo $25
Football $85
Mini Helmet $50

Ken Burrough
Photo $15
Football $70
Mini Helmet $45

Dexter Bussey
Photo $15
Football $70
Mini Helmet $45

Kevin Butler
Photo $12
Football $70
Mini Helmet $40

Marion Butts
Photo $15
Football $70
Mini Helmet $40

Dave Butz
Photo $18
Football $75
Mini Helmet $50

Dennis Byrd
Photo $15
Football $70
Mini Helmet $45

Earnest Byner
Photo $15
Football $70
Mini Helmet $45

John Cappelletti
Photo $20
Football $80
Mini Helmet $50

Harold Carmichael
Photo $25
Football $85
Mini Helmet $55

Harry Carson
Photo $20
Football $80
Mini Helmet $50

Anthony Carter
Photo $15
Football $75
Mini Helmet $45

Dave Casper
Photo $22
Football $85
Mini Helmet $55

Bob Chandler
Photo $12
Football $70
Mini Helmet $40

Don Chandler
Photo $25
Football $85
Mini Helmet $55

Wes Chandler
Photo $12
Football $65
Mini Helmet $40

Raymond Chester
Photo $21
Football $82
Mini Helmet $53

Todd Christensen
Photo $20
Football $80
Mini Helmet $50

Dwight Clark
Photo $25
Football $85
Mini Helmet $55

Gary Clark
Photo $15
Football $75
Mini Helmet $45

Mark Clayton
Photo $15
Football $75
Mini Helmet $45

Don Cockroft
Photo $12
Football $70
Mini Helmet $40

Gail Cogdill
Photo $15

Football $75
Mini Helmet $45

Jack Concannon
Photo $15
Football $75
Mini Helmet $45

Paul Coffman
Photo $15
Football $75
Mini Helmet $45

Cris Collinsworth
Photo $20
Football $80
Mini Helmet $50

Al Cowlings
Photo $15
Football $70
Mini Helmet $45

Fred Cox
Photo $15
Football $70
Mini Helmet $45

Roger Craig
Photo $25
Football $85
Mini Helmet $55

Joe Cribbs
Photo $12
Football $72
Mini Helmet $40

Irv Cross
Photo $18
Football $80
Mini Helmet $48

Randy Cross
Photo $13
Football $73
Mini Helmet $48

John David Crow
Photo $15
Football $75
Mini Helmet $45

Sam Cunningham
Photo $12
Football $70
Mini Helmet $40

Isaac Curtis
Photo $20
Football $80
Mini Helmet $50

Mike Curtis
Photo $15
Football $75
Mini Helmet $45

Dave Dalby
Photo $15
Football $75
Mini Helmet $45

Carroll Dale
Photo $16
Football $78
Mini Helmet $48

Gary Danielson
Photo $15
Football $75
Mini Helmet $45

Ben Davidson
Photo $20
Football $80
Mini Helmet $50

Kenneth Davis
Photo $18
Football $78
Mini Helmet $55

Mouse Davis
Photo $12
Football $73
Mini Helmet $40

Joe DeLamielleure
Photo $20
Football $80
Mini Helmet $50

Tom Dempsey
Photo $25
Football $90
Mini Helmet $60

Richard Dent
Photo $20
Football $80
Mini Helmet $50

Lynn Dickey
Photo $15
Football $75
Mini Helmet $45

Conrad Dobler
Photo $20
Football $80
Mini Helmet $50

Bobby Douglass
Photo $16
Football $74
Mini Helmet $48

Boyd Dowler
Photo $16
Football $74
Mini Helmet $48

Fred Dryer
Photo $27
Football $90
Mini Helmet $55

Mark Duper
Photo $12
Football $67
Mini Helmet $44

Billy Joe DuPree
Photo $10
Football $65
Mini Helmet $40

John Dutton
Photo $15
Football $70
Mini Helmet $45

Carl Eller
Photo $25
Football $85
Mini Helmet $60

John Elway
Photo $45
Football $125
Mini Helmet $75

Steve Emtman
Photo $13
Football $73
Mini Helmet $40

Boomer Esiason
Photo $15
Football $70
Mini Helmet $45

Jim Everett
Photo $15
Football $70
Mini Helmet $50

Joe Ferguson
Photo $12
Football $67
Mini Helmet $44

Vince Ferragamo
Photo $6
Football $60
Mini Helmet $40

Pat Fischer
Photo $17
Football $67
Mini Helmet $45

Tom Flores
Photo $15
Football $75
Mini Helmet $45

Wayne Fontes
Photo $12
Football $67
Mini Helmet $44

Chuck Foreman
Photo $18
Football $78
Mini Helmet $48

Barry Foster
Photo $15
Football $75
Mini Helmet $45

Russ Francis
Photo $15
Football $70
Mini Helmet $45

Tony Franklin
Photo $7
Football $65
Mini Helmet $40

John Fuqua
Photo $9
Football $68
Mini Helmet $40

Irving Fryar
Photo $15
Football $70
Mini Helmet $45

Roman Gabriel
Photo $20
Football $75
Mini Helmet $55

Tony Galbreath
Photo $7
Football $60
Mini Helmet $40

Mike Garrett
Photo $15
Football $75
Mini Helmet $45

Walt Garrison
Photo $15
Football $75
Mini Helmet $45

Roy Gerela
Photo $15
Football $75
Mini Helmet $45

Cookie Gilchrist
Photo $20
Football $80
Mini Helmet $50

Pete Gogolak
Photo $18
Football $78
Mini Helmet $53

Bruce Gossett
Photo $17
Football $73
Mini Helmet $48

Mel Gray
Photo $17
Football $73
Mini Helmet $50

Roy Green
Photo $18
Football $74
Mini Helmet $52

Kevin Greene
Photo $15
Football $80
Mini Helmet $48

L.C. Greenwood
Photo $18

Football $73
Mini Helmet $52

Rosey Grier
Photo $18
Football $73
Mini Helmet $45

Archie Griffin
Photo $15
Football $70
Mini Helmet $45

Steve Grogan
Photo $17
Football $73
Mini Helmet $48

Ray Guy
Photo $15
Football $70
Mini Helmet $45

John Hadl
Photo $25
Football $90
Mini Helmet $55

Charles Haley
Photo $15
Football $70
Mini Helmet $45

Dan Hampton
Photo $18
Football $85
Mini Helmet $50

Dave Hampton
Photo $20
Football $85
Mini Helmet $50

Rodney Hampton
Photo $15
Football $75
Mini Helmet $45

Chris Hanburger
Photo $12
Football $68
Mini Helmet $44

Ronnie Harmon
Photo $12
Football $67
Mini Helmet $44

Alvin Harper
Photo $15
Football $75
Mini Helmet $45

Cliff Harris
Photo $13
Football $65
Mini Helmet $40

Tim Harris
Photo $15
Football $75
Mini Helmet $45

Jim Hart
Photo $20
Football $80
Mini Helmet $50

Bob Hayes
Photo $20
Football $80
Mini Helmet $50

Lester Hayes
Photo $15
Football $75
Mini Helmet $45

Mike Haynes
Photo $12
Football $70
Mini Helmet $40

Bobby Hebert
Photo $14
Football $73
Mini Helmet $46

Efren Herrera
Photo $16
Football $70
Mini Helmet $45

Calvin Hill
Photo $19
Football $78
Mini Helmet $54

Randal Hill
Photo $12
Football $67
Mini Helmet $44

Marv Hubbard
Photo $12
Football $67
Mini Helmet $44

Stan Humphries
Photo $15
Football $70
Mini Helmet $45

Michael Irvin
Photo ....$20-$25
Football ....$90-$100
Mini Helmet $75

Bo Jackson
Photo $35
Football $85
Mini Helmet $60

Keith Jackson
Photo $15
Football $75
Mini Helmet $45

Tom Jackson
Photo $25
Football $85
Mini Helmet $55

Ron Jaworski
Photo $20
Football $80
Mini Helmet $50

John Jefferson
Photo $15
Football $70
Mini Helmet $45

Roy Jefferson
Photo $15
Football $70
Mini Helmet $45

Haywood Jeffires
Photo $13
Football $71
Mini Helmet $46

Jim Jensen
Photo $12
Football $68
Mini Helmet $44

Bob Jeter
Photo $13
Football $71
Mini Helmet $46

Billy Johnson
Photo $18
Football $78
Mini Helmet $49

Charley Johnson
Photo $17
Football $77
Mini Helmet $48

Ezra Johnson
Photo $15
Football $75
Mini Helmet $45

Jimmy Johnson
Photo $25
Football $85
Mini Helmet $60

Johnny Johnson
Photo $12
Football $68
Mini Helmet $40

Norm Johnson
Photo $12
Football $67
Mini Helmet $45

Pete Johnson
Photo $15
Football $75
Mini Helmet $45

Daryl Johnston
Photo $20
Football $90
Mini Helmet $50

Brent Jones
Photo $16
Football $76
Mini Helmet $52

Bert Jones
Photo $24
Football $83

Mini Helmet $57

Ed "Too Tall" Jones
Photo $25
Football $85
Mini Helmet $60

Lee Roy Jordan
Photo $13
Football $68
Mini Helmet $44

Alex Karras
Photo $25
Football $85
Mini Helmet $60

Jim Kelly
Photo $35
Football $120
Mini Helmet $70

Jack Kemp
Photo $30
Football $100
Mini Helmet $65

Jim Kiick
Photo $24
Football $79
Mini Helmet $53

Billy Kilmer
Photo $20
Football $75
Mini Helmet $50

Joe Klecko
Photo $12
Football $67
Mini Helmet $40

David Klingler
Photo $12
Football $67
Mini Helmet $40

Chuck Knox
Photo $10
Football $65
Mini Helmet $40

Bernie Kosar
Photo $18
Football $75
Mini Helmet $50

Jerry Kramer
Photo $15
Football $75
Mini Helmet $45

Ron Kramer
Photo $13
Football $68
Mini Helmet $44

Dave Krieg
Photo $16
Football $76
Mini Helmet $52

Tim Krumrie
Photo $13
Football $68
Mini Helmet $44

Bob Kuechenberg
Photo $13
Football $68
Mini Helmet $44

Daryle Lamonica
Photo $20
Football $75
Mini Helmet $50

Greg Landry
Photo $14
Football $69
Mini Helmet $42

MacArthur Lane
Photo $18
Football $75
Mini Helmet $48

Pat Leahy
Photo $13
Football $68
Mini Helmet $44

D.D. Lewis
Photo $15
Football $75
Mini Helmet $45

Louis Lipps
Photo $12
Football $67
Mini Helmet $44

Floyd Little
Photo $22
Football $82
Mini Helmet $57

Spider Lockhart *
Photo $40
Football $125
Mini Helmet . . . . Impossible

James Lofton
Photo $20
Football $80
Mini Helmet $50

Neil Lomax
Photo $13
Football $68
Mini Helmet $47

Nick Lowery
Photo $13
Football $68
Mini Helmet $47

John Madden
Photo $35
Football $90
Mini Helmet $60

Mark Malone
Photo $10
Football $65
Mini Helmet $40

Archie Manning
Photo $15
Football $70
Mini Helmet $45

Chester Marcol
Photo $8
Football $63
Mini Helmet $40

Ed Marinaro
Photo $35
Football $90
Mini Helmet $55

Dan Marino
Photo $40
Football $125
Mini Helmet $70

Jim Marshall
Photo $19
Football $74

Mini Helmet $49

Harvey Martin
Photo $20
Football $80
Mini Helmet $50

John Matuszak *
Photo $40
Football $90
Mini Helmet . . . . Impossible

Larry McCarren
Photo $12
Football $68
Mini Helmet $42

"Wahoo" McDaniel
Photo $15
Football $75
Mini Helmet $45

Max McGee
Photo $14
Football $69
Mini Helmet $48

Reggie McKenzie
Photo $18
Football $73
Mini Helmet $50

Jim McMahon
Photo $20
Football $80
Mini Helmet $50

Steve McMichael
Photo $12
Football $67
Mini Helmet $44

Karl Mecklenberg
Photo $15
Football $75
Mini Helmet $45

Don Meredith
Photo $25
Football $90
Mini Helmet $60

Terry Metcalf
Photo $17
Football $72
Mini Helmet $45

Matt Millen
Photo $15
Football $75
Mini Helmet $45

Chris Miller
Photo $12
Football $67
Mini Helmet $43

Sam Mills
Photo $12
Football $69
Mini Helmet $40

Lydell Mitchell
Photo $15
Football $75
Mini Helmet $45

Art Monk
Photo $30
Football $90
Mini Helmet $60

Wilbert Montgomery
Photo $12
Football $69
Mini Helmet $40

Stanley Morgan
Photo $12
Football $69
Mini Helmet $40

Earl Morrall
Photo $13
Football $68
Mini Helmet $41

Bam Morris
Photo $13
Football $69
Mini Helmet $41

Joe Morris
Photo $12
Football $69
Mini Helmet $40

Mercury Morris
Photo $18
Football $78
Mini Helmet $49

Craig Morton
Photo $15
Football $75
Mini Helmet $45

Mark Moseley
Photo $13
Football $68
Mini Helmet $40

Haven Moses
Photo $12
Football $67
Mini Helmet $43

Chuck Muncie
Photo $10
Football $65
Mini Helmet $41

Brad Muster
Photo $10
Football $65
Mini Helmet $41

Browning Nagle
Photo $8
Football $63
Mini Helmet $40

Steve Nelson
Photo $8
Football $63
Mini Helmet $40

Robert Newhouse
Photo $15
Football $75
Mini Helmet $45

Nate Newton
Photo $16
Football $77
Mini Helmet $47

Tommy Nobis
Photo $17
Football $78
Mini Helmet $49

Ken O'Brien
Photo $13
Football $68
Mini Helmet $44

John Offerdahl
Photo $12
Football $67
Mini Helmet $42

Inactive Football Player Autographs — Chapter 13

Christian Okoye
Photo $12
Football $67
Mini Helmet $40

Dave Osborn
Photo $12
Football $67
Mini Helmet $40

Jim Otis
Photo $13
Football $68
Mini Helmet $43

Stephone Paige
Photo $14
Football $69
Mini Helmet $44

Lemar Parrish
Photo $15
Football $75
Mini Helmet $45

Bob Parsons
Photo $10
Football $65
Mini Helmet $41

Dan Pastorini
Photo $20
Football $80
Mini Helmet $50

Drew Pearson
Photo $15
Football $70
Mini Helmet $45

Preston Pearson
Photo $12
Football $67
Mini Helmet $43

William Perry
Photo $16
Football $77
Mini Helmet $46

Brian Piccolo *
Photo $275
Football $330
Mini Helmet ....Impossible

Jim Plunkett
Photo $28
Football $83
Mini Helmet $58

Ed Podolak
Photo $12
Football $67
Mini Helmet $41

Greg Pruitt
Photo $13
Football $68
Mini Helmet $44

Mike Pruitt
Photo $13
Football $68
Mini Helmet $42

Ahmad Rashad
Photo $25
Football $80
Mini Helmet $50

Tom Rathman
Photo $13
Football $68
Mini Helmet $40

Dan Reeves
Photo $20
Football $80
Mini Helmet $50

Frank Reich
Photo $13
Football $68
Mini Helmet $40

Ken Riley
Photo $15
Football $70
Mini Helmet $45

Dave Robinson
Photo $16
Football $77
Mini Helmet $46

Tobin Rote *
Photo $20
Football $75
Mini Helmet $50

Reggie Rucker
Photo $18
Football $73

Mini Helmet $48

Leonard Russell
Photo $10
Football $65
Mini Helmet $40

Mark Rypien
Photo $10
Football $65
Mini Helmet $40

Barry Sanders
Photo $25
Football $100
Mini Helmet $60

Charlie Sanders
Photo $13
Football $68
Mini Helmet $40

Jake Scott
Photo $17
Football $72
Mini Helmet $43

Uwe von Schamann
Photo $7
Football $62
Mini Helmet $40

Rafael Septien
Photo $10
Football $65
Mini Helmet $40

Sterling Sharpe
Photo $30
Football $90
Mini Helmet $55

Donnie Shell
Photo $15
Football $70
Mini Helmet $45

Phil Simms
Photo $15
Football $70
Mini Helmet $45

Billy Sims
Photo $13

Inactive Football Player Autographs — Chapter 13

Football $68
Mini Helmet $45

Brian Sipe
Photo $15
Football $70
Mini Helmet $45

Otis Sistrunk
Photo $18
Football $73
Mini Helmet $48

Jackie Slater
Photo $13
Football $68
Mini Helmet $45

Bubba Smith
Photo $17
Football $72
Mini Helmet $48

Norm Snead
Photo $17
Football $72
Mini Helmet $45

Matt Snell
Photo $18
Football $73
Mini Helmet $45

Jack Snow
Photo $17
Football $72
Mini Helmet $45

Chris Spielman
Photo $13
Football $68
Mini Helmet $40

Steve Spurrier
Photo $15
Football $70
Mini Helmet $48

Ken Stabler
Photo $25
Football $80
Mini Helmet $50

John Stallworth
Photo $10
Football $65
Mini Helmet $40

Darryl Stingley
Photo $75
Football $225
Mini Helmet $125

Don Strock
Photo $17
Football $72
Mini Helmet $45

Pat Sullivan
Photo $12
Football $67
Mini Helmet $40

Pat Summerall
Photo $15
Football $70
Mini Helmet $45

Pat Swilling
Photo $10
Football $65
Mini Helmet $40

Jack Tatum
Photo $15
Football $70
Mini Helmet $45

John Taylor
Photo $8
Football $63
Mini Helmet $40

Joe Theismann
Photo $20
Football $75
Mini Helmet $50

Derrick Thomas *
Photo $30
Football $100
Mini Helmet $75

Duane Thomas
Photo $25
Football $80
Mini Helmet $50

Fuzzy Thurston
Photo $13
Football $68
Mini Helmet $45

Pat Tilley
Photo $7
Football $63
Mini Helmet $40

Mick Tingelhoff
Photo $13
Football $68
Mini Helmet $45

Richard Todd
Photo $13
Football $68
Mini Helmet $40

Al Toon
Photo $15
Football $70
Mini Helmet $45

Bob Trumpy
Photo $17
Football $75
Mini Helmet $45

Bob Tucker
Photo $7
Football $63
Mini Helmet $40

Eric Turner *
Photo $20
Football $78
Mini Helmet $48

Jim Turner
Photo $15
Football $70
Mini Helmet $45

Wendall Tyler
Photo $15
Football $70
Mini Helmet $45

Rick Upchurch
Photo $15
Football $70
Mini Helmet $45

Mark Van Eeghen
Photo $13
Football $68
Mini Helmet $40

Jeff Van Note
Photo $15
Football $75

Mini Helmet $45

Brad Van Pelt
Photo $15
Football $70
Mini Helmet $45

Tommy Vardell
Photo $15
Football $70
Mini Helmet $45

Randy Vataha
Photo $15
Football $70
Mini Helmet $45

Herschel Walker
Photo $15
Football $70
Mini Helmet $45

Wesley Walker
Photo $10
Football $65
Mini Helmet $40

Andre Ware
Photo $8
Football $63
Mini Helmet $40

Curt Warner
Photo $13
Football $68
Mini Helmet $40

Gene Washington (49ers)
Photo $12
Football $67
Mini Helmet $45

Gene Washington (Vikings)
Photo $10
Football $65
Mini Helmet $40

Charles Way
Photo $15
Football $85
Mini Helmet $45

Roger Wehrli
Photo $15

Football $75
Mini Helmet $45

Ray Wersching
Photo $17
Football $78
Mini Helmet $48

Danny White
Photo $15
Football $75
Mini Helmet $45

Dwight White
Photo $14
Football $69
Mini Helmet $44

Charlie Waters
Photo $15
Football $70
Mini Helmet $45

Ed White
Photo $15
Football $75
Mini Helmet $45

Ken Willard
Photo $9
Football $64
Mini Helmet $40

Delvin Williams
Photo $12
Football $67
Mini Helmet $40

Doug Williams
Photo $15
Football $75
Mini Helmet $45

Marc Wilson
Photo $12
Football $68
Mini Helmet $40

Wade Wilson
Photo $13
Football $69
Mini Helmet $42

Ickey Woods
Photo $14
Football $70
Mini Helmet $43

Ron Yary
Photo $15
Football $75
Mini Helmet $45

Garo Yepremian
Photo $15
Football $75
Mini Helmet $45

Steve Young
Photo $40
Football $125
Mini Helmet . . . .$60-$75

Jack Youngblood
Photo $19
Football $74
Mini Helmet $49

Jim Youngblood
Photo $13
Football $70
Mini Helmet $42

Jim Zorn
Photo $15
Football $85
Mini Helmet $45

Football Autographs
Active Players

Karim Abdul Jabbar
Photo $20
Football $100
Mini Helmet $60

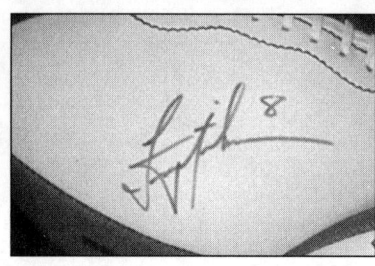

Troy Aikman
Photo $50
Football $175
Mini Helmet $100

Derrick Alexander
Photo $15
Football $75
Mini Helmet $40

Eric Allen
Photo $12
Football $70
Mini Helmet $40

Terry Allen
Photo $13
Football $75
Mini Helmet $40

Mike Alstott
Photo $30
Football $125
Mini Helmet $60

Morton Andersen
Photo $15
Football $75
Mini Helmet $40

Gary Anderson (k)
Photo $15
Football $75
Mini Helmet $40

Jamal Anderson
Photo $30
Football $150
Mini Helmet $75

LaVar Arrington
Photo $30
Football $125
Mini Helmet $60

Steve Atwater
Photo $12
Football $70
Mini Helmet $40

Tony Banks
Photo $15
Football $80
Mini Helmet $45

Ronde Barber
Photo $15
Football $80
Mini Helmet $45

Tiki Barber
Photo $12
Football $75
Mini Helmet $40

Charlie Batch
Photo $20
Football $100
Mini Helmet $60

Cornelius Bennett
Photo $18
Football $85
Mini Helmet $50

Edgar Bennett
Photo $12
Football $70
Mini Helmet $35

Jerome Bettis
Photo $25
Football $125
Mini Helmet $75

Steve Beuerlein
Photo $15
Football $85
Mini Helmet $45

Tim Biakabutuka
Photo $12
Football $75
Mini Helmet $40

Brian Blades
Photo $15
Football $85
Mini Helmet $45

Jeff Blake
Photo $15
Football $85
Mini Helmet $45

Drew Bledsoe
Photo $40
Football $175
Mini Helmet $90

David Boston
Photo $20
Football $100
Mini Helmet $60

Bubby Brister
Photo $12
Football $75
Mini Helmet $40

Reggie Brooks
Photo $12
Football $75
Mini Helmet $40

Dave Brown
Photo $12
Football $75
Mini Helmet $40

Tim Brown
Photo $20
Football $85
Mini Helmet $50

Isaac Bruce
Photo $15
Football $85
Mini Helmet $50

Mark Brunnell
Photo $50
Football $200
Mini Helmet $100

Plaxico Burress
Photo $30
Football $125
Mini Helmet $75

LeRoy Butler
Photo $20
Football $90
Mini Helmet $50

Mark Carrier
Photo $15
Football $80
Mini Helmet $45

Cris Carter
Photo $30
Football $125
Mini Helmet $75

Larry Centers
Photo $12
Football $75
Mini Helmet $40

Chris Chandler
Photo $20
Football $100
Mini Helmet $60

Mark Chmura
Photo $15
Football $80
Mini Helmet $50

Wayne Chrebet
Photo $20
Football $85
Mini Helmet $55

Ben Coates
Photo $15
Football $85
Mini Helmet $45

Kerry Collins
Photo $15
Football $85
Mini Helmet $45

Curtis Conway
Photo $12
Football $75
Mini Helmet $40

Tim Couch
Photo $30
Football $150
Mini Helmet $75

Daunte Culpepper
Photo $30
Football $100
Mini Helmet $60

Randall Cunningham

Photo $25
Football $100
Mini Helmet $55

Terrell Davis
Photo $75
Football $225
Mini Helmet $150

Ron Dayne
Photo $30
Football $150
Mini Helmet $70

Trent Dilfer
Photo $15
Football $8
Mini Helmet $50

Corey Dillon
Photo $20
Football $100
Mini Helmet $60

Jim Druckenmiller
Photo $15
Football $85
Mini Helmet $45

Rickey Dudley
Photo $12
Football $75
Mini Helmet $40

Warrick Dunn
Photo $30
Football $150
Mini Helmet $75

Quinn Early
Photo $12
Football $75
Mini Helmet $40

Robert Edwards
Photo $15
Football $80
Mini Helmet $45

Henry Ellard
Photo $15
Football $80
Mini Helmet $45

Bert Emanuel
Photo $12
Football $75
Mini Helmet $40

Bobby Engram
Photo $15
Football $75
Mini Helmet $40

Curtis Enis
Photo $18
Football $90
Mini Helmet $50

Craig Erickson
Photo $12
Football $75
Mini Helmet $40

Kevin Faulk
Photo $30
Football $125
Mini Helmet $70

Marshall Faulk
Photo $30
Football $125
Mini Helmet $70

Brett Favre
Photo $75
Football $200
Mini Helmet $120

William Floyd
Photo $15
Football $80
Mini Helmet $45

Doug Flutie
Photo $30
Football $125
Mini Helmet $70

Active Football Player Autographs — Chapter 14

Antonio Freeman
Photo $20
Football $100
Mini Helmet $60

Gus Frerotte
Photo $12
Football $75
Mini Helmet $40

Joey Galloway
Photo $20
Football $90
Mini Helmet $45

Eddie George
Photo $40
Football $175
Mini Helmet $75

Jeff George
Photo $15
Football $85
Mini Helmet $45

Terry Glenn
Photo $20
Football $100
Mini Helmet $60

Tony Gonzalez
Photo $15
Football $85
Mini Helmet $45

Elvis Grbac
Photo $15
Football $85
Mini Helmet $45

Darrell Green
Photo $15
Football $85
Mini Helmet $45

Eric Green
Photo $12
Football $75
Mini Helmet $40

Jim Harbaugh
Photo $12
Football $75
Mini Helmet $40

Marvin Harrison
Photo $20
Football $100
Mini Helmet $60

Garrison Hearst
Photo $15
Football $85
Mini Helmet $45

Ike Hilliard
Photo $12
Football $75
Mini Helmet $40

Torry Holt
Photo $20
Football $80
Mini Helmet $50

Jeff Hostetler
Photo $15
Football $85
Mini Helmet $45

Desmond Howard
Photo $15
Football $85
Mini Helmet $45

Bobby Hoying
Photo $15
Football $85
Mini Helmet $45

Rocket Ismail
Photo $15
Football $85
Mini Helmet $45

Chris Jacke
Photo $12
Football $75
Mini Helmet $40

Rickey Jackson
Photo $12
Football $75
Mini Helmet $40

Michael Jackson
Photo $15
Football $85
Mini Helmet $45

Edgerrin James
Photo $30
Football $125
Mini Helmet $70

James Jett
Photo $15
Football $75
Mini Helmet $40

Brad Johnson
Photo $20
Football $100
Mini Helmet $70

Keyshawn Johnson
Photo $25
Football $125
Mini Helmet $65

Rob Johnson
Photo $15
Football $85
Mini Helmet $45

Napolean Kaufman
Photo $20
Football $100
Mini Helmet $60

Jevon Kearse
Photo $20
Football $100
Mini Helmet $60

Eddie Kennison
Photo $18
Football $90
Mini Helmet $50

Cortez Kennedy
Photo $10
Football $65
Mini Helmet $45

Terry Kirby
Photo $8
Football $63
Mini Helmet $45

Levon Kirkland
Photo $18
Football $90
Mini Helmet $50

Jon Kitna
Photo $18
Football $90
Mini Helmet $50

Erik Kramer
Photo $15
Football $75
Mini Helmet $40

Carnell Lake
Photo $12
Football $75
Mini Helmet $40

Ryan Leaf
Photo $18
Football $90
Mini Helmet $50

Ty Law
Photo $15
Football $85
Mini Helmet $45

Dorsey Levens
Photo $20
Football $95
Mini Helmet $50

Greg Lloyd
Photo $15
Football $85
Mini Helmet $45

Peyton Manning
Photo $40
Football $150
Mini Helmet $90

Curtis Martin
Photo $30
Football $125
Mini Helmet $75

Eric Martin
Photo $12
Football $75
Mini Helmet $40

Tony Martin
Photo $15
Football $75
Mini Helmet $40

Terrance Mathis
Photo $15
Football $85
Mini Helmet $45

Bruce Matthews
Photo $12
Football $75
Mini Helmet $40

Derrick Mayes
Photo $15
Football $85
Mini Helmet $45

Ed McCaffrey
Photo $12
Football $75
Mini Helmet $40

Keenan McCardell
Photo $15
Football $85
Mini Helmet $45

Randall McDaniel
Photo $12
Football $75
Mini Helmet $40

O.J. McDuffie
Photo $15
Football $85
Mini Helmet $45

Willie McGinest
Photo $12
Football $75
Mini Helmet 40

Donovan McNabb
Photo $30
Football $125
Mini Helmet $75

Steve McNair
Photo $18
Football $95
Mini Helmet $50

Cade McNown
Photo $20
Football $100
Mini Helmet $60

Natrone Means
Photo $20
Football $100
Mini Helmet $50

Dave Meggett
Photo $12
Football $75
Mini Helmet $40

Eric Metcalf
Photo $12
Football $75
Mini Helmet $40

Ernie Mills
Photo $12
Football $75
Mini Helmet $40

Rick Mirer
Photo $12
Football $75
Mini Helmet $40

Scott Mitchell
Photo $13
Football $78
Mini Helmet $43

Warren Moon
Photo $20
Football $100
Mini Helmet $60

Herman Moore
Photo $20
Football $100
Mini Helmet $60

Rob Moore
Photo $15
Football $75
Mini Helmet $40

Johnny Morton
Photo $12
Football $75
Mini Helmet $40

Randy Moss
Photo $75
Football $250

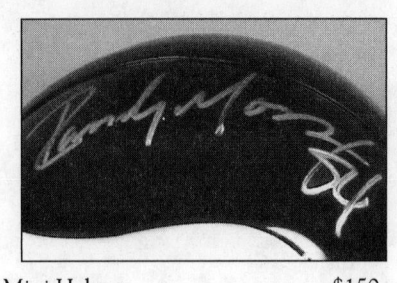

Mini Helmet $150

Eric Moulds
Photo $20
Football $110
Mini Helmet $50

Adrian Murrell
Photo $15
Football $85
Mini Helmet $45

Eddie Murray
Photo $12
Football $75
Mini Helmet $40

Tom Newberry
Photo $12
Football $75
Mini Helmet $40

Dat Nguyen
Photo $15
Football $85
Mini Helmet $45

Hardy Nickerson
Photo $15
Football $85
Mini Helmet $45

Ken Norton Jr.
Photo $15
Football $85
Mini Helmet $45

Neil O'Donnell
Photo $12
Football $75
Mini Helmet $40

Terrell Owens
Photo $20
Football $100
Mini Helmet $60

Orlando Pace
Photo $12
Football $75
Mini Helmet $40

Bryce Paup
Photo $15
Football $85
Mini Helmet $40

Rodney Peete
Photo $12
Football $75
Mini Helmet $40

Erric Pegram
Photo $12
Football $75
Mini Helmet $40

Chad Pennington
Photo $20
Football $110
Mini Helmet $50

Carl Pickens
Photo $20
Football $110
Mini Helmet $50

Jake Plummer
Photo $30
Football $120
Mini Helmet $70

Mike Pritchard
Photo $12
Football $75
Mini Helmet $40

John Randle
Photo $25
Football $120
Mini Helmet $65

Andre Reed
Photo $15
Football $85
Mini Helmet $45

Jake Reed
Photo $15
Football $85
Mini Helmet $45

Errict Rhett
Photo $15
Football $85
Mini Helmet $45

Jerry Rice
Photo $70
Football $250

Mini Helmet $135

Simeon Rice
Photo $12
Football $75
Mini Helmet $40

Andre Rison
Photo $15
Football $85
Mini Helmet $45

Willie Roaf
Photo $15
Football $85
Mini Helmet $45

Eugene Robinson
Photo $12
Football $75
Mini Helmet $40

Marcus Robinson
Photo $20
Football $100
Mini Helmet $60

Reggie Roby
Photo $12
Football $75
Mini Helmet $40

Chris Sanders
Photo $12
Football $75
Mini Helmet $40

Deion Sanders
Photo $35
Football $150
Mini Helmet $70

Frank Sanders
Photo $12
Football $75
Mini Helmet $40

Warren Sapp
Photo $20
Football $100
Mini Helmet $60

Darnay Scott
Photo $12
Football $75
Mini Helmet $40

Junior Seau
Photo $20
Football $100
Mini Helmet $60

Jason Sehorn
Photo $15

Active Football Player Autographs — Chapter 14

| Football | $85 |
| Mini Helmet | $45 |

Shannon Sharpe
Photo	$20
Football	$100
Mini Helmet	$60

Clyde Simmons
Photo	$15
Football	$85
Mini Helmet	$45

Akili Smith
Photo	$30
Football	$125
Mini Helmet	$75

Antowain Smith
Photo	$17
Football	$95
Mini Helmet	$50

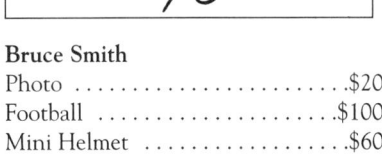

Bruce Smith
Photo	$20
Football	$100
Mini Helmet	$60

Emmitt Smith
Photo	$45
Football	$200
Mini Helmet	$130

Irv Smith
Photo	$12
Football	$75
Mini Helmet	$40

Jimmy Smith
Photo	$18
Football	$90
Mini Helmet	$45

Neil Smith
Photo	$15
Football	$85
Mini Helmet	$45

Robert Smith
Photo	$20
Football	$95
Mini Helmet	$55

James Stewart
Photo	$12
Football	$75
Mini Helmet	$40

Kordell Stewart
Photo	$30
Football	$125
Mini Helmet	$70

J.J. Stokes
Photo	$15
Football	$85
Mini Helmet	$45

Dana Stubblefield
Photo	$15
Football	$85
Mini Helmet	$45

Eric Swann
Photo	$12
Football	$75
Mini Helmet	$40

Fred Taylor
Photo	$40
Football	$150
Mini Helmet	$80

Vinny Testaverde
Photo	$30
Football	$125
Mini Helmet	$75

Yancy Thigpen
Photo	$15
Football	$85
Mini Helmet	$45

Thurman Thomas
Photo	$20
Football	$100
Mini Helmet	$60

Andre Wadsworth
Photo	$15
Football	$85
Mini Helmet	$45

Wesley Walls
Photo	$12
Football	$75
Mini Helmet	$40

Kurt Warner
| Photo | $35 |
| Football | $150 |

| Mini Helmet | $90 |

Chris Warren
Photo	$15
Football	$85
Mini Helmet	$45

Peter Warrick
Photo	$30
Football	$125
Mini Helmet	$75

Ricky Watters
Photo	$15
Football	$85
Mini Helmet	$45

Michael Westbrook
Photo	$15
Football	$85
Mini Helmet	$45

Reggie White
Photo	$35
Football	$100
Mini Helmet	$60

Ricky Williams
Photo	$40
Football	$175
Mini Helmet	$115

Charles Woodson
Photo	$20
Football	$100
Mini Helmet	$60

Hockey Hall of Famers

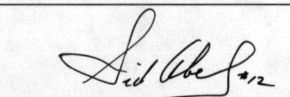

Sid Abel (1918-) 1969
Puck $30
1965-66 Topps card $15
Cut signature ....$5-$7
8x10 photograph ....$15-$20

Jack Adams (1895-1968) 1959
Puck $35
Hockey card ....Unlikely
Cut signature ....$12-$15
8x10 photograph ....$35-$50

Syl Apps (1915-1998) 1961
Puck $70
1955-56 Parkhurst card $20
Cut signature ....$5-$7
8x10 photograph $70

George Armstrong (1930-) 1975
Puck $35
1970-71 Topps card $15
Cut signature ....$5-$7
8x10 photograph $25

Ace Bailey (1903-1992) 1975
Puck $60
1955-56 Parkhurst card $30
Cut signature $10
8x10 photograph $50

Don Bain (1974-1962) 1945
Puck $75
Hockey card ....Unlikely
Cut signature ....$15-$20
8x10 photograph ....$50-$60

Hobey Baker (1892-1918) 1945
Puck ....$60-$70
Hockey card ....Unlikely
Cut signature $15
8x10 photograph $45

Bill Barber (1952-) 1990
Puck $25
1974-75 Topps card $15
Cut signature ....$7-$10
8x10 photograph ....$15-$20

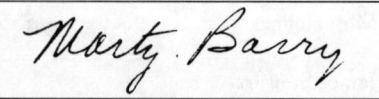

Marty Barry (1905-1969) 1965
Puck $45
Hockey card ....Unlikely
Cut signature ....$12-$15
8x10 photograph $35

Andy Bathgate (1932-) 1978
Puck ....$25-$30
1968-69 Topps card $15
Cut signature ....$6-$11
8x10 photograph ....$20-$25

Jean Beliveau (1931-) 1972
Puck ....$30-$35
1970-71 Topps card $15
Cut signature ....$6-$12
8x10 photograph ....$25-$30

Clint Benedict (1894-1976) 1965
Puck ....$60-$75
Hockey card ....Unlikely
Cut signature ....$15-$18
8x10 photograph ....$35-$45

Doug Bentley (1916-1972) 1964
Puck ....$45-$50
Hockey card ....Unlikely
Cut signature $15
8x10 photograph ....$35-$40

Max Bentley (1920-1984) 1966
Puck ....$50-$60
1953-54 Parkhurst card $25
Cut signature ....$16-$18

8x10 photograph ....$45-$50

Toe Blake (1912-1995) 1966
Puck $45
1966-67 Topps card $15
Cut signature ....$12-$15
8x10 photograph $35

Leo Boivin (1932-) 1986
Puck ....$30-$35
1964-65 Topps card $15
Cut signature ....$5-$10
8x10 photograph ....$25-$30

Dickie Boon (1878-1961) 1952
Puck $60
Hockey card ....Unlikely
Cut signature $18
8x10 photograph ....$45-$50

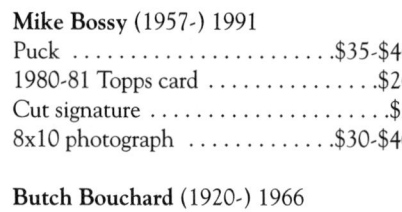

Mike Bossy (1957-) 1991
Puck ....$35-$40
1980-81 Topps card $20
Cut signature $5
8x10 photograph ....$30-$40

Butch Bouchard (1920-) 1966
Puck $25
1955-56 Parkhurst card $9
Cut signature $6
8x10 photograph $20

Frank Boucher (1901-1977) 1958
Puck $50
Hockey card ....Unlikely
Cut signature $15
8x10 photograph ....$40-$45

George Boucher (1896-1960) 1960
Puck $65
Hockey card ....Unlikely
Cut signature $18
8x10 photograph $50

John Bower (1924-) 1976
Puck ....$25-$30
1968-69 Topps card $12
Cut signature $8
8x10 photograph ....$20-$25

Dubbie Bowie (1880-1959) 1945
Puck $60
Hockey card ....Unlikely
Cut signature $18

Hockey Hall of Fame Autographs — Chapter 15

8x10 photograph $50

Frank Brimsek (1915-) 1966
Puck $25
Hockey card . . . . Unlikely
Cut signature $7
8x10 photograph . . . . $18-$20

Punch Broadbent (1892-1971) 1962
Puck $45
Hockey card . . . . Unlikely
Cut signature $17
8x10 photograph . . . . $35-$40

Turk Broda (1914-1972) 1967
Puck $45
Hockey card . . . . Unlikely
Cut signature . . . . $22-$30
8x10 photograph . . . . $35-$50

John Bucyk (1935-) 1981
Puck . . . . $25-$35
1970-71 Topps card $12
Cut signature $6
8x10 photograph . . . . $20-$25

Billy Burch (1900-1950) 1974
Puck $35
Hockey card . . . . Unlikely
Cut signature $5
8x10 photograph $20

Harry Cameron (1890-1953) 1962
Puck . . . . $60-$70
Hockey card . . . . Unlikely
Cut signature $20
8x10 photograph . . . . $50-$60

Gerry Cheevers (1940-) 1985
Puck $40
1971-72 Topps card $12
Cut signature $7

8x10 photograph . . . . $25-$30

King Clancy (1903-1986) 1958
Puck $40
Hockey card . . . . Unlikely
Cut signature $12
8x10 photograph . . . . $30-$35

Dit Clapper (1907-1978) 1947
Puck . . . . $45-$50
Hockey card . . . . Unlikely
Cut signature $6
8x10 photograph . . . . $40-$45

Bobby Clarke (1949-) 1987
Puck . . . . $35-$45
1974-75 Topps card $12
Cut signature $6
8x10 photograph . . . . $30-$35

Sprague Cleghorn (1890-1956) 1958
Puck $65
Hockey card . . . . Unlikely
Cut signature $18
8x10 photograph . . . . $55-$60

Neil Colville (1914-1987) 1967
Puck . . . . $25-$30
Hockey card . . . . Unlikely
Cut signature $5
8x10 photograph . . . . $20-$25

Charlie Conacher (1909-1967) 1961
Puck . . . . $35-$40
Hockey card . . . . Unlikely
Cut signature . . . . $6-$8
8x10 photograph . . . . $25-$30

Lionel Conacher (1900-1954) 1994
Puck $55
Hockey card . . . . Unlikely
Cut signature . . . . $10-$20
8x10 photograph . . . . $35-$45

Roy Gordon Conacher (1916-1984) 1998
Puck . . . . $35-$40
Hockey card . . . . Unlikely
Cut signature . . . . $6-$8
8x10 photograph . . . . $25-$30

Alex Connell (1902-1958) 1958
Puck $60
Hockey card . . . . Unlikely
Cut signature $18
8x10 photograph . . . . $45-$50

Bun Cook (1903-1988) 1995
Puck $40
Hockey card . . . . Unlikely
Cut signature $16
8x10 photograph . . . . $30-$35

William Cook (1896-1986) 1952
Puck $75

Hockey card . . . . Unlikely
Cut signature $25
8x10 photograph . . . . $55-$60

Art Coulter (1909-) 1974
Puck . . . . $30-$35
Hockey card . . . . Unlikely
Cut signature $6
8x10 photograph . . . . $25-$30

Yvan Cournoyer (1943-) 1982
Puck $35
1970-71 Topps card $10
Cut signature $5
8x10 photograph . . . . $25-$30

Bill Cowley (1912-) 1968
Puck $50
Hockey card . . . . Unlikely
Cut signature $7
8x10 photograph . . . . $40-$45

Rusty Crawford (1885-1971) 1962
Puck . . . . $45-$50
Hockey card . . . . Unlikely
Cut signature $16
8x10 photograph . . . . $40-$45

Jack Darragh (1890-1924) 1962
Puck . . . . $55-$60
Hockey card . . . . Unlikely
Cut signature $20
8x10 photograph . . . . $45-$50

Scotty Davidson (1890-1915) 1950
Puck $75
Hockey card . . . . Unlikely
Cut signature $25
8x10 photograph . . . . $50-$60

Hap Day (1901-1990) 1961
Puck . . . . $25-$30
Hockey card . . . . Unlikely
Cut signature $5
8x10 photograph . . . . $20-$25

Alex Delvecchio (1931-) 1977
Puck . . . . $30-$35
1973-74 Topps card $10
Cut signature $6

Hockey Hall of Fame Autographs — Chapter 15

8x10 photograph $25

Cy Denney (1897-1970) 1959
Puck $60
Hockey card ....Unlikely
Cut signature $19
8x10 photograph ....$45-$50

Marcel Dionne (1951-) 1992
Puck ....$25-$30
Hockey card ....$12-$15
Cut signature $7
8x10 photograph ....$20-$25

Gordie Drillon (1914-1986) 1975
Puck $60
Hockey card ....Unlikely
Cut signature ....$25-$30
8x10 photograph ....$45-$50

Graham Drinkwater (1875-1946) 1950
Puck ....$75-$80
Hockey card ....Unlikely
Cut signature $25
8x10 photograph ....$65-$70

Ken Dryden (1947-) 1983
Puck $65
1972-73 Topps card $40
Cut signature $8
8x10 photograph ....$50-$60

Woody Dumart (1916-) 1992

Puck $65
Hockey card ....Unlikely
Cut signature $15
8x10 photograph ....$50-$60

Thomas Dunderdale (1887-1960) 1974
Puck ....$75-$80
Hockey card ....Unlikely
Cut signature ....$25-$30
8x10 photograph ....$65-$70

Bill Durnan (1916-1972) 1964
Puck $65
Hockey card ....Unlikely
Cut signature $18
8x10 photograph ....$55-$60

Red Dutton (1898-1987) 1958
Puck ....$40-$45
Hockey card ....Unlikely
Cut signature $12
8x10 photograph ....$30-$35

Babe Dye (1898-1962) 1970
Puck ....$70-$80
Hockey card ....Unlikely
Cut signature $18
8x10 photograph ....$65-$70

Phil Esposito (1942-) 1984
Puck ....$40-$50
1973-74 Topps card $18
Cut signature $6
8x10 photograph ....$35-$40

Tony Esposito (1943-) 1988
Puck ....$30-$35
1973-74 Topps card $15

Cut signature $6
8x10 photograph ....$25-$30

Arthur Farrel (1877-1909) 1965
Puck ....$60-$65
Hockey card ....Unlikely
Cut signature ....$20-$25
8x10 photograph ....$55-$60

Fern Flaman (1927-) 1990
Puck ....$25-$30
1990-91 Score card $12
Cut signature $6
8x10 photograph ....$20-$25

Frank Foyston (1891-1966) 1958
Puck ....$65-$70
Hockey card ....Unlikely
Cut signature $25
8x10 photograph ....$55-$60

Frank Frederickson (1895-1979) 1958
Puck $65
Hockey card ....Unlikely
Cut signature ....$22-$25
8x10 photograph ....$50-$55

Bill Gadsby (1927-) 1970
Puck $25
1965-66 Topps card $12
Cut signature $6
8x10 photograph ....$20-$25

Bob Gainey (1953-) 1992
Puck $25
1979-80 Topps card $10
Cut signature $5
8x10 photograph ....$20-$25

Chuck Gardiner (1904-1934) 1945
Puck $75
Hockey card ....Unlikely

Cut signature $25
8x10 photograph . . . .$65-$70

Herb Gardiner (1891-1972) 1958
Puck . . . .$50-$60
Hockey card . . . . .Unlikely
Cut signature $18
8x10 photograph . . . .$45-$50

Jimmy Gardner (1881-1940) 1962
Puck . . . .$65-$70
Hockey card . . . . .Unlikely
Cut signature $15
8x10 photograph . . . .$50-$55

Bernie "Boom Boom" Geoffrion (1931-) 1972
Puck . . . .$25-$30
1967-68 Topps card $12
Cut signature $7
8x10 photograph . . . .$20-$25

Eddie Gerard (1890-1937) 1945
Puck . . . .$80-$90
Hockey card . . . . .Unlikely
Cut signature $35
8x10 photograph . . . .$75-$80

Eddie Giacomin (1939-) 1987
Puck . . . .$25-$30
1971-72 Topps card $12
Cut signature $7
8x10 photograph . . . .$20-$25

Rod Gilbert (1941-) 1982
Puck . . . .$25-$30
1971-72 Topps card $12
Cut signature $7
8x10 photograph $25

Billy Gilmour (1885-1959) 1962
Puck . . . .$70-$75
Hockey card . . . . .Unlikely
Cut signature $18
8x10 photograph . . . .$55-$60

Moose Goheen (1894-1979) 1952
Puck . . . .$60-$65
Hockey card . . . . .Unlikely
Cut signature $25
8x10 photograph . . . .$50-$55

Michel Goulet (1960-) 1998
Puck . . . .$25-$30
Hockey card . . . .$12-$18
Cut signature . . . .$7-$9
8x10 photograph $25

Ebbie Goodfellow (1907-1985) 1963
Puck $40
Hockey card . . . . .Unlikely
Cut signature $15
8x10 photograph . . . .$35-$40

Mike Grant (1874-1955) 1950
Puck . . . .$50-$60
Hockey card . . . . .Unlikely
Cut signature $17
8x10 photograph . . . .$45-$50

Wilf Green (1896-1960) 1962
Puck $35
Hockey card . . . . .Unlikely
Cut signature $7
8x10 photograph . . . .$25-$30

Wayne Gretzky (1961-) 1999

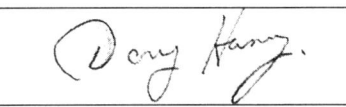

Puck . . . .$75-$80
Hockey card $35
Cut signature $25
8x10 photograph . . . .$60-$70

Si Griffis (1883-1950) 1950
Puck $90
Hockey card . . . . .Unlikely
Cut signature $35
8x10 photograph $65

George Hainsworth (1895-1950) 1961
Puck . . . .$60-$65
Hockey card . . . . .Unlikely
Cut signature $18
8x10 photograph . . . .$50-$60

Glenn Hall (1931-) 1975
Puck . . . .$30-$35
1969-70 Topps card $12
Cut signature $7
8x10 photograph . . . .$20-$30

Joe Hall (1882-1919) 1961
Puck $60
Hockey card . . . . .Unlikely
Cut signature $8
8x10 photograph . . . .$45-$55

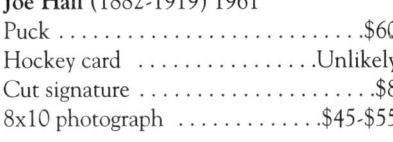

Doug Harvey (1924-1989) 1973
Puck . . . .$55-$60
1952-53 Parkhurst card $15
Cut signature $25
8x10 photograph . . . .$40-$45

George Hay (1898-1975) 1958
Puck . . . .$75-$80
Hockey card . . . . .Unlikely
Cut signature $20
8x10 photograph . . . .$65-$70

Riley Hern (1880-1929) 1962
Puck . . . .$60-$70
Hockey card . . . . .Unlikely
Cut signature $18
8x10 photograph . . . .$55-$60

Bryan Hextall (1913-1984) 1969
Puck . . . .$60-$70

Hockey card . . . . Unlikely
Cut signature $18
8x10 photograph . . . . $55-$60

Hap Holmes (1889-1940) 1972
Puck $55
Hockey card . . . . Unlikely
Cut signature $15
8x10 photograph . . . . $40-$50

Tom Hooper (1883-1960) 1962
Puck $65
Hockey card . . . . Unlikely
Cut signature $18
8x10 photograph . . . . $50-$55

Red Horner (1909-) 1965
Puck . . . . $25-$30
Hockey card . . . . Unlikely
Cut signature $6
8x10 photograph . . . . $20-$25

Tim Horton (1930-1974) 1977
Puck $300
1954-55 Parkhurst card $150
Cut signature $15
8x10 photograph $300

Gordie Howe (1928-) 1972
Puck . . . . $40-$50
1979-80 Topps card $20
Cut signature $8
8x10 photograph . . . . $35-$40

Sydney Howe (1911-1976) 1965
Puck . . . . $65-$70
Hockey card . . . . Unlikely
Cut signature $20
8x10 photograph . . . . $60-$65

Harry Howell (1932-) 1979
Puck . . . . $25-$30
1970-71 Topps card $10
Cut signature $6
8x10 photograph . . . . $20-$25

Bobby Hull (1939-) 1983
Puck . . . . $35-$40
1979-80 Topps card $15
Cut signature $7
8x10 photograph . . . . $25-$30

J.B. Hutton (1877-1962) 1962
Puck . . . . $50-$60
Hockey card . . . . Unlikely
Cut signature $18
8x10 photograph . . . . $45-$50

Harry Hyland (1889-1969) 1962
Puck . . . . $55-$60
Hockey card . . . . Unlikely
Cut signature $20
8x10 photograph . . . . $50-$55

Dick Irvin (1892-1957) 1958
Puck . . . . $60-$70
Hockey card . . . . Unlikely
Cut signature $25
8x10 photograph . . . . $55-$60

Busher Jackson (1911-1966) 1971
Puck $50
Hockey card . . . . Unlikely
Cut signature $22
8x10 photograph . . . . $45-$50

Ching Johnson (1898-1979) 1958
Puck . . . . $40-$45
Hockey card . . . . Unlikely
Cut signature $12
8x10 photograph . . . . $35-$40

Ernie Johnson (1886-1963) 1952
Puck . . . . $40-$45
Hockey card . . . . Unlikely
Cut signature $14
8x10 photograph . . . . $35-$40

Tom Johnson (1928-) 1970
Puck $45
1962-63 Parkhurst card $20
Cut signature $15
8x10 photograph . . . . $40-$45

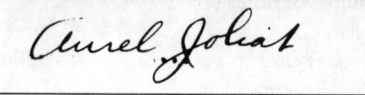

Aurel Joliat (1901-1986) 1947
Puck $95
Hockey card . . . . Unlikely
Cut signature $35
8x10 photograph . . . . $85-$90

Duke Keats (1895-1972) 1958
Puck . . . . $60-$65
Hockey card . . . . Unlikely
Cut signature $25
8x10 photograph . . . . $55-$60

Red Kelly (1927-) 1969
Puck . . . . $25-$30
1967-68 Topps card $12
Cut signature $6
8x10 photograph . . . . $20-$25

Teeder Kennedy (1925-) 1966
Puck $25
1955-56 Parkhurst card $12
Cut signature $6
8x10 photograph . . . . $20-$25

Dave Keon (1940-) 1986
Puck . . . . $25-$30
1969-70 Topps card $12
Cut signature $7
8x10 photograph . . . . $20-$25

Elmer Lach (1918-) 1966
Puck . . . .$25-$30
Hockey card . . . . .Unlikely
Cut signature $6
8x10 photograph . . . .$20-$25

Guy Lafleur (1951) 1988
Puck . . . .$45-$50
1976-77 Topps card $18
Cut signature $6
8x10 photograph . . . .$30-$35

Newsy Lalonde (1887-1971) 1950
Puck . . . .$75-$80
Hockey card . . . . .Unlikely
Cut signature $30
8x10 photograph . . . .$70-$75

Jacques Laperriere (1941-) 1987
Puck $25
1967-68 Topps card $10
Cut signature $5
8x10 photograph . . . .$20-$25

Guy LaPointe (1948-) 1993
Puck $25
Hockey card . . . .$10-$12
Cut signature $5
8x10 photograph . . . .$20-$25

Edgar LaPrade (1919-) 1993
Puck $25
Hockey card $10
Cut signature $5
8x10 photograph $20

Jack Laviolette (1879-1960) 1962
Puck . . . .$40-$50
Hockey card . . . . .Unlikely
Cut signature $12
8x10 photograph . . . .$35-$40

Hugh Lehman (1885-1961) 1958
Puck . . . .$70-$75
Hockey card . . . . .Unlikely
Cut signature $22
8x10 photograph . . . .$55-$60

Jacques Lemaire (1945-) 1984
Puck . . . .$25-$30
1969-70 Topps card $15
Cut signature $5
8x10 photograph . . . .$20-$25

Mario Lemieux (1965-) 1997
Puck . . . .$45-$50
Hockey card . . . .$20-$25
Cut signature $15
8x10 photograph . . . .$35-$40

Percy LeSueur (1881-1962) 1961
Puck . . . .$55-$60
Hockey card . . . . .Unlikely
Cut signature $20
8x10 photograph . . . .$50-$55

Herb Lewis (1907-) 1989
Puck . . . .$50-$55
Hockey card . . . . .Unlikely
Cut signature $20
8x10 photograph . . . .$45-$50

Ted Lindsay (1925-) 1966
Puck . . . .$25-$30
1959-60 Topps card $25
Cut signature $6
8x10 photograph . . . .$20-$25

Harry Lumley (1926-1998) 1980
Puck $30

Hockey card . . . . .Unlikely
Cut signature $10
8x10 photograph . . . .$25-$30

Mickey MacKay (1894-1940) 1952
Puck . . . .$70-$75
Hockey card . . . . .Unlikely
Cut signature $20
8x10 photograph . . . .$55-$60

Frank Mahovlich (1938-) 1981
Puck . . . .$40-$50
1972-73 Topps card $10
Cut signature $7
8x10 photograph . . . .$25-$30

Joe Malone (1890-1969) 1950
Puck $75
Hockey card . . . . .Unlikely
Cut signature $30
8x10 photograph . . . .$65-$70

Sylvio Mantha (1902-1974) 1960
Puck . . . .$35-$40
Hockey card . . . . .Unlikely
Cut signature $12
8x10 photograph . . . .$30-$35

Jack Marshall (1877-1965) 1965
Puck $50
Hockey card . . . . .Unlikely
Cut signature $18
8x10 photograph . . . .$40-$45

Fred Maxwell (1890-1975) 1962
Puck . . . .$55-$60
Hockey card . . . . .Unlikely
Cut signature $20
8x10 photograph . . . .$50-$55

Lanny McDonald (1953-) 1992

Hockey Hall of Fame Autographs — Chapter 15

Puck $35
1975-76 Topps card $10
Cut signature $5
8x10 photograph . . . . $30-$35

Frank McGee (?-1916) 1945
Puck $100
Hockey card . . . . Unlikely
Cut signature $40
8x10 photograph . . . . $85-$90

Billy McGimsie (1880-1968) 1962
Puck $70
Hockey card . . . . Unlikely
Cut signature $20
8x10 photograph . . . . $65-$70

George McNamara (1886-1952) 1958
Puck $60
Hockey card . . . . Unlikely
Cut signature $15
8x10 photograph $45

Stan Mikita (1940-) 1983
Puck . . . . $25-$30
1972-73 Topps card $10
Cut signature $7
8x10 photograph . . . . $20-$25

Dickie Moore (1931-) 1974
Puck $25
1962-63 Parkhurst card $10
Cut signature $5
8x10 photograph . . . . $20-$25

Paddy Moran (1877-1966) 1958
Puck $65
Hockey card . . . . Unlikely
Cut signature $18
8x10 photograph . . . . $55-$60

Howie Morenz (1902-1937) 1945

Puck $450
Hockey card . . . . Unlikely
Cut signature $200
8x10 photograph $450

Bill Mosienko (1921-1994) 1965
Puck . . . . $35-$40
Hockey card . . . . Unlikely
Cut signature $10
8x10 photograph . . . . $30-$35

Frank Nighbor (1893-1966) 1947
Puck $85
Hockey card . . . . Unlikely
Cut signature $30
8x10 photograph . . . . $75-$80

Reg Noble (1895-1962) 1962
Puck $65
Hockey card . . . . Unlikely
Cut signature $18
8x10 photograph . . . . $55-$60

Buddy O'Connor (1916-1977) 1988
Puck $50
Hockey card . . . . Unlikely
Cut signature $18
8x10 photograph $45

Harry Oliver ((1898-1985) 1967
Puck $55
Hockey card . . . . Unlikely
Cut signature $20
8x10 photograph . . . . $45-$50

Bert Olmstead (1926-) 1985
Puck . . . . $20-$25
1961-62 Parkhurst card $10
Cut signature $5
8x10 photograph . . . . $20-$25

Bobby Orr (1948-) 1979
Puck . . . . $75-$80
1973-74 Topps card $35
Cut signature $25
8x10 photograph $60

Bernie Parent (1945-) 1984
Puck . . . . $25-$30

1973-74 Topps card $12
Cut signature $6
8x10 photograph . . . . $20-$25

Brad Park (1948-) 1988
Puck . . . . $25-$35
1972-73 Topps card $12
Cut signature $6
8x10 photograph . . . . $20-$25

Lester Patrick (1883-1960) 1947
Puck . . . . $95-$100
Hockey card . . . . Unlikely
Cut signature $35
8x10 photograph . . . . $85-$90

Lynn Patrick (1912-1980) 1980
Puck . . . . $95-$100
Hockey card . . . . Unlikely
Cut signature $35
8x10 photograph . . . . $85-$90

Gil Perreault (1950-) 1990
Puck . . . . $25-$35
1973-74 Topps card $10
Cut signature $6
8x10 photograph . . . . $20-$25

Tommy Phillips (1880-1923) 1945
Puck . . . . $75-$80
Hockey card . . . . Unlikely
Cut signature $30
8x10 photograph . . . . $70-$75

Pierre Pilote (1931-) 1975
Puck ....$25-$30
1968-69 Topps card $10
Cut signature $6
8x10 photograph ....$20-$25

Didier Pitre (1883-1934) 1962
Puck $75
Hockey card ....Unlikely
Cut signature $20
8x10 photograph ....$60-$70

Jacques Plante (1929-1986) 1978
Puck $175
1958-59 Topps card $250
Cut signature $25
8x10 photograph $300

Denis Potvin (1953-) 1991
Puck ....$25-$30
1975-76 Topps card $15
Cut signature $5
8x10 photograph ....$20-$25

Babe Pratt (1916-1988) 1966
Puck $35
Hockey card ....Unlikely
Cut signature $15
8x10 photograph $35

Joe Primeau (1906-1989) 1963
Puck $50
Hockey card ....Unlikely
Cut signature $25
8x10 photograph $50

Marcel Pronovost (1930-) 1978
Puck $25
1967-68 Topps card $10
Cut signature $6
8x10 photograph ....$20-$25

Bob Pulford (1936-) 1991
Puck $50
1960-61 Parkhurst card $30
Cut signature $20
8x10 photograph $45

Harvey Pulford (1875-1940) 1945
Puck $65
Hockey card ....Unlikely
Cut signature $20

8x10 photograph ....$55-$60

Bill Quackenbush (1922-1999) 1976
Puck ....$30-$35
Hockey card ....Unlikely
Cut signature $5
8x10 photograph ....$20-$25

Frank Rankin (1889-1932) 1961
Puck ....$70-$80
Hockey card ....Unlikely
Cut signature $18
8x10 photograph $65

Jean Ratelle (1940-) 1985
Puck ....$25-$35
1969-70 Topps card $10
Cut signature $5
8x10 photograph ....$20-$25

Chuck Rayner (1920-) 1973
Puck ....$25-$30
Hockey card ....Unlikely
Cut signature $6
8x10 photograph ....$20-$25

Ken Reardon (1921-) 1966
Puck ....$35-$40
Hockey card ....Unlikely
Cut signature $5
8x10 photograph ....$25-$30

Henri Richard (1936-) 1979
Puck $25
1969-70 Topps card $10
Cut signature $6
8x10 photograph ....$20-$25

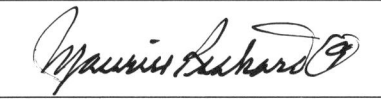

Maurice Richard (1921-2000) 1961
Puck ....$35-$40
1955-56 Parkhurst $75
Cut signature $8
8x10 photograph ....$30-$35

George Richardson (1887-1916) 1950
Puck ....$95-$100
Hockey card ....Unlikely
Cut signature $35
8x10 photograph ....$85-$90

Gordie Roberts (1891-1966) 1971
Puck $70
Hockey card ....Unlikely
Cut signature $18
8x10 photograph ....$65-$70

Larry Robinson (1951-) 1995
Puck ....$25-$30
Hockey card $10
Cut signature $5
8x10 photograph ....$20-$25

Art Ross (1886-1964) 1945
Puck ....$70-$75
Hockey card ....Unlikely
Cut signature $25

8x10 photograph ....$55-$60

Blair Russel (1880-1961) 1965
Puck ....$40-$45
Hockey card ....Unlikely
Cut signature $15
8x10 photograph ....$35-$40

Ernie Russell (1883-1963) 1965
Puck $65
Hockey card ....Unlikely
Cut signature $18
8x10 photograph ....$55-$60

Jack Ruttan (1889-1973) 1962
Puck $70
Hockey card ....Unlikely
Cut signature $25
8x10 photograph $65

Borje Salming (1951-) 1996

Puck $25
Hockey card $10
Cut signature $5
8x10 photograph ....$20-$25

Serge Savard (1946-) 1986
Puck ....$25-$30
1970-71 Topps card $10
Cut signature $5
8x10 photograph ....$20-$25

Terry Sawchuck (1929-1970) 1971
Puck $300
1953-54 Parkhurst card $250
Cut signature $30
8x10 photograph $300

Fred Scanlan (? - ?) 1965
Puck $65
Hockey card ....Unlikely
Cut signature $18
8x10 photograph ....$50-$60

Milt Schmidt (1918-) 1961
Puck $25
1965-66 Topps card $10
Cut signature $6
8x10 photograph ....$20-$25

Sweeney Schriner (1911-1990) 1962
Puck $65
Hockey card ....Unlikely
Cut signature $20
8x10 photograph ....$55-$60

Earl Seibert (1911-1990) 1963
Puck $25
Hockey card ....Unlikely
Cut signature $6
8x10 photograph ....$20-$25

Oliver Seibert (1881-1944) 1961
Puck ....$90-$100
Hockey card ....Unlikely
Cut signature $30
8x10 photograph ....$70-$75

Eddie Shore (1902-1985) 1947
Puck $200
Hockey card ....Unlikely
Cut signature $25
8x10 photograph $65

Steve Shutt (1952-) 1993
Puck $25
1975-76 Topps card $10
Cut signature $5
8x10 photograph ....$20-$25

Babe Siebert (1904-1939) 1964
Puck $65
Hockey card ....Unlikely
Cut signature $20
8x10 photograph ....$55-$60

Joe Simpson (1893-1973) 1962
Puck ....$60-$70
Hockey card ....Unlikely
Cut signature $20
8x10 photograph ....$55-$60

Darryl Sittler (1950-) 1989
Puck $25
1974-75 Topps card $10
Cut signature $5
8x10 photograph ....$20-$25

Alfred Smith (1873-1953) 1962
Puck $65
Hockey card ....Unlikely
Cut signature $20
8x10 photograph ....$55-$60

Billy Smith (1950-) 1993
Puck ....$25-$30
1974-75 Topps card $10
Cut signature $5
8x10 photograph ....$22-$25

Clint Smith (1913-) 1991
Puck $25
Hockey card ....Unlikely
Cut signature $5
8x10 photograph ....$15-$20

Hooley Smith (1903-1963) 1972
Puck $50
Hockey card ....Unlikely
Cut signature $18
8x10 photograph ....$45-$50

Tommy Smith (1885-1966) 1973
Puck $50
Hockey card ....Unlikely
Cut signature $15
8x10 photograph ....$45-$50

Allan Stanley (1926-) 1981
Puck $25
1967-68 Topps card $10
Cut signature $5
8x10 photograph ....$20-$25

Hockey Hall of Fame Autographs — Chapter 15

Barney Stanley (1893-1971) 1962
Puck ....$35-$40
Hockey card ....Unlikely
Cut signature $15
8x10 photograph ....$30-$35

Peter Stastny (1956-) 1998
Puck ....$20-$25
Hockey card $10
Cut signature $6
8x10 photograph $20

Jack Stewart (1917-1983) 1964
Puck $40
Hockey card ....Unlikely
Cut signature $15
8x10 photograph ....$35-$40

Nels Stewart (1902-1957) 1962
Puck ....$70-$75
Hockey card ....Unlikely
Cut signature $22
8x10 photograph ....$55-$60

Bruce Stuart (1882-1961) 1961
Puck $65
Hockey card ....Unlikely
Cut signature $20
8x10 photograph ....$50-$60

Cyclone Taylor (1883-1979) 1947
Puck $60
Hockey card ....Unlikely
Cut signature $18
8x10 photograph ....$50-$55

Fred Taylor (? - 1907) 1947
Puck $65
Hockey card ....Unlikely
Cut signature $18
8x10 photograph ....$50-$60

Tiny Thompson (1905-1981) 1959
Puck ....$70-$75
Hockey card ....Unlikely
Cut signature $20
8x10 photograph ....$65-$70

Vladislav Tretiak (1952-) 1989
Puck ....$65-$75
Hockey card ....Unlikely
Cut signature $22
8x10 photograph ....$60-$70

Harry Trihey (1877-1942) 1950
Puck $75
Hockey card ....Unlikely
Cut signature $30
8x10 photograph ....$65-$70

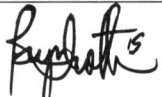

Bryan John Trottier (1956-) 1997
Puck $25
Hockey card ....$10-$12
Cut signature $6
8x10 phoptograph ....$20-$25

Norm Ullman (1935-) 1982
Puck $25
1968-69 Topps card $10
Cut signature $6
8x10 photograph ....$20-$25

Georges Vezina (1887-1926) 1945
Puck $250
Hockey card ....Unlikely
Cut signature $100
8x10 photograph $250

Jack Walker (1888-1950) 1960
Puck ....$65-$70
Hockey card ....Unlikely
Cut signature $20
8x10 photograph ....$60-$65

Marty Walsh (1883-1915) 1962
Puck $75
Hockey card ....Unlikely
Cut signature $25
8x10 photograph ....$65-$70

Harry Watson (1898-1957) 1962
Puck $75
Hockey card ....Unlikely
Cut signature $25
8x10 photograph $65

Cooney Weiland (1904-1985) 1971
Puck ....$60-$65
Hockey card ....Unlikely
Cut signature $22
8x10 photograph $55

Harry Westwick (1876-1957) 1962
Puck $75
Hockey card ....Unlikely
Cut signature $25
8x10 photograph $65

Fred Whitcroft (1882-1931) 1962
Puck $75
Hockey card ....Unlikely
Cut signature $25
8x10 photograph $65

Gordon Wilson (1895-1970) 1962
Puck ....$55-$60
Hockey card ....Unlikely
Cut signature $15
8x10 photograph ....$50-$55

Gump Worsley (1929-)1980
Puck $30
1968-69 Topps card $15
Cut signature $10
8x10 photograph ....$25-$30

Roy Worters (1900-1957) 1969
Puck ....$60-$70
Hockey card ....Unlikely
Cut signature $18
8x10 photograph ....$50-$60

Inactive Hockey Player Autographs

Glenn Anderson
Stick $35
Puck $20
Photo $8

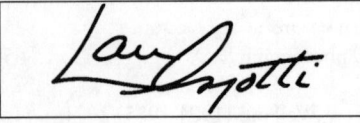

Lou Angotti
Stick $40
Puck $24
Photo $12

Al Arbour
Stick $40
Puck $24
Photo $12

Wayne Babych
Stick $35
Puck $20
Photo $8

Ralph Backstrom
Stick $40
Puck $24
Photo $12

Dave Balon
Stick $36
Puck $21
Photo $9

Murray Bannerman
Stick $38
Puck $22
Photo $10

Bobby Bauer
Stick $40
Puck $24
Photo $12

Bob Baun
Stick $40
Puck $24
Photo $12

Don Beaupre
Stick $30
Puck $20
Photo $7

Red Berenson
Stick $36
Puck $21
Photo $9

Dan Bouchard
Stick $35
Puck $20
Photo $8

Andre Boudrias
Stick $35
Puck $20
Photo $8

Neal Broten
Stick $35
Puck $20
Photo $8

Rob Brown
Stick $40
Puck $24
Photo $12

Charlie Burns
Stick $30
Puck $20
Photo $7

Jon Casey
Stick $36
Puck $21
Photo $9

Wayne Cashman
Stick $40
Puck $24
Photo $12

Guy Charron
Stick $39
Puck $23
Photo $11

Dino Ciccarelli
Stick $40
Puck $24
Photo $12

Bill Clement
Stick $35
Puck $20
Photo $8

Real Cloutier
Stick $30
Puck $20
Photo $7

Roy Conacher
Stick $48
Puck $28
Photo $18

Wayne Connelly
Stick $30
Puck $20
Photo $7

Roger Crozier
Stick $36
Puck $21
Photo $9

Clark Donatelli
Stick $36
Puck $21
Photo $9

Ted Donato
Stick $36
Puck $21
Photo $9

Gary Dornhoefer
Stick $36
Puck $21
Photo $9

Jude Drouin
Stick $30
Puck $20
Photo $7

Dick Duff
Stick $42
Puck $24
Photo $14

Don Edwards
Stick $38
Puck $22
Photo $10

Ron Ellis
Stick $42
Puck $24
Photo $14

Mike Eruzionne

Stick $40
Puck $24
Photo $12

Bill Fairbairn
Stick $35
Puck $20
Photo $8

Doug Favell
Stick $30
Puck $20
Photo $7

Bernie Federko
Stick $40
Puck $24
Photo $12

John Ferguson
Stick $38
Puck $22
Photo $10

Reggie Fleming
Stick $38
Puck $22
Photo $10

Bill Flett
Stick $35
Puck $20
Photo $8

Val Fonteyne
Stick $35
Puck $20
Photo $8

Louie Fontinato
Stick $40
Puck $24
Photo $12

Nick Fotiu
Stick $35
Puck $20
Photo $8

Emile Francis
Stick $40
Puck $24
Photo $12

Mike Gartner
Stick $42
Puck $24
Photo $14

Jean-Guy Gendron
Stick $36
Puck $21
Photo $9

Gilles Gilbert
Stick $35
Puck $20
Photo $8

Clark Gillies
Stick $38
Puck $22
Photo $10

Bill Goldsworthy
Stick $36
Puck $21
Photo $9

Butch Goring
Stick $40
Puck $24
Photo $12

Phil Goyette
Stick $40
Puck $24
Photo $12

Dirk Graham
Stick $30
Puck $20
Photo $7

Danny Grant
Stick $38
Puck $22
Photo $10

Vic Hadfield
Stick $45
Puck $25
Photo $15

Dale Hawerchuk
Stick $40
Puck $24
Photo $12

Alan Haworth
Stick $36
Puck $21
Photo $9

Andy Hebenton
Stick $40
Puck $24
Photo $12

Anders Hedberg
Stick $36
Puck $21
Photo $9

Camille Henry
Stick $40
Puck $24
Photo $12

Dennis Hextall
Stick $35
Puck $20
Photo $8

Larry Hillman
Stick $38
Puck $22
Photo $10

Ken Hodge
Stick $40
Puck $24
Photo $12

Marty Howe
Stick $25
Puck $14
Photo $6

Mark Howe
Stick $38
Puck $22
Photo $10

Dennis Hull
Stick $45
Puck $25
Photo $15

Dave Hunter
Stick $30
Puck $20

Photo $7

[Signature: Best Wishes, Tim Horton]

Tim Hunter
Stick $40
Puck $24
Photo ....$12-$15

Steve Jensen
Stick $35
Puck $20
Photo $8

Rick Kehoe
Stick $40
Puck $24
Photo $12

Orest Kindrachuk
Stick $35
Puck $20
Photo $8

Petr Klima
Stick $36
Puck $21
Photo $9

Jerry Korab
Stick $25
Puck $14
Photo $6

Jari Kurri
Stick $45
Puck $25
Photo $15

Orland Kurtenbach
Stick $36
Puck $22
Photo $9

Leo Labine
Stick $35
Puck $20
Photo $8

[Signature: Pat LaFontaine]

Pat LaFontaine
Stick $42
Puck $24
Photo $14

Guy Lapointe
Stick $36
Puck $21
Photo $9

Claude Larose
Stick $40
Puck $24
Photo $12

Pierre Larouche
Stick $42
Puck $24
Photo $14

Reggie Leach
Stick $42
Puck $24
Photo $14

Reggie Lemelin
Stick $38
Puck $22
Photo $10

Don Lever
Stick $35
Puck $20
Photo $8

Gaetz Link
Stick $35
Puck $20
Photo $8

Ken Linseman
Stick $35
Puck $20
Photo $8

Ross Lonsberry
Stick $36
Puck $21
Photo $9

Jim Lorentz
Stick $36
Puck $21
Photo $9

Rick MacLeish
Stick $38
Puck $22
Photo $10

Craig MacTavish
Stick $30
Puck $20
Photo $7

Pete Mahovlich
Stick $40
Puck $24
Photo $12

[Signature: Chico Maki]

Chico Maki
Stick $40
Puck $24
Photo $12

Wayne Maki
Stick $36
Puck $21
Photo $9

Cesare Maniago
Stick $36
Puck $21
Photo $9

Gilles Marotte
Stick $35
Puck $20
Photo $8

Pit Martin
Stick $42
Puck $24
Photo $14

Rick Martin
Stick $42
Puck $24
Photo $14

Dennis Maruk
Stick $42
Puck $24
Photo $14

Tommy McCarthy
Stick $48
Puck $30
Photo $18

Ab McDonald
Stick $38
Puck $22
Photo $10

Lanny McDonald
Stick $42
Puck $24

Photo ....$14-$18

Walt McKechnie
Stick $38
Puck $22
Photo $10

John McKenzie
Stick $39
Puck $23
Photo $11

Peter McNab
Stick $45
Puck $25
Photo $15

Basil McRae
Stick $29
Puck $19
Photo $6

Rick Meagher
Stick $35
Puck $20
Photo $8

Howie Meeker
Stick $42
Puck $24
Photo $14

Gilles Meloche
Stick $39
Puck $23
Photo $11

Rick Middleton
Stick $45
Puck $25
Photo $15

Doug Mohns
Stick $39
Puck $23
Photo $11

Joe Mullen
Stick $43
Puck $24
Photo $14

Gord Murphy
Stick $35
Puck $20
Photo $8

Lou Nanne
Stick $36
Puck $21
Photo $9

Mats Naslund
Stick $39
Puck $23
Photo $11

Cam Neely
Stick $55
Puck $45
Photo $25

Eric Nesterenko
Stick $40
Puck $24
Photo $12

Bob Nevin
Stick $40
Puck $24
Photo $12

Willie O'Ree
Stick $50
Puck $30
Photo $20

Terry O'Reilly
Stick $38
Puck $22
Photo $10

Wilf Paiement
Stick $39
Puck $23
Photo $11

Jim Pappin
Stick $36
Puck $21
Photo $9

J.P. Parise
Stick $36
Puck $21

Photo $9

Noel Picard
Stick $35
Puck $20
Photo $8

Pierre Plante
Stick $35
Puck $20
Photo $8

Willi Plett
Stick $35
Puck $20
Photo $8

Dave Poulin
Stick $35
Puck $20
Photo $8

Dean Prentice
Stick $40
Puck $24
Photo $12

Jean Pronovost
Stick $40
Puck $24
Photo $12

Claude Provost
Stick $35
Puck $20
Photo $8

Rob Ramage
Stick $25
Puck $14
Photo $6

Manon Rheaume
Stick $50
Puck $30
Photo $20

Glenn Resch
Stick $36
Puck $21
Photo $9

Jacques Richard

Stick $40
Puck $24
Photo ....$12-$15

Bobby Rousseau
Stick $35
Puck $20
Photo $8

Christian Ruuttu
Stick $35
Puck $20
Photo $8

Gary Sabourin
Stick $35
Puck $20
Photo $8

Denis Savard
Stick $43
Puck $24
Photo $14

Frank St. Marseille
Stick $35
Puck $20
Photo $8

Derek Sanderson
Stick $35
Puck $20
Photo $8

Bobby Schmautz
Stick $38
Puck $22
Photo $10

Cliff Schmautz
Stick $35
Puck $20
Photo $8

Dave Schultz
Stick $42
Puck $25
Photo ....$15-$18

Charlie Simmer
Stick $39
Puck $23
Photo $11

Glen Skov
Stick $35
Puck $20
Photo $8

Dallas Smith
Stick $35
Puck $20
Photo $8

Fred Stanfield
Stick $36
Puck $21
Photo $9

Vic Stasiuk
Stick $38
Puck $22
Photo $10

Pete Stemkowski
Stick $36
Puck $21
Photo $9

Ron Stewart
Stick $41
Puck $24
Photo ....$13-$15

Brent Sutter
Stick $38
Puck $22
Photo $10

Brian Sutter
Stick $42
Puck $24
Photo $14

Dave Taylor
Stick $41
Puck $24
Photo $13

Esa Tikkanen
Stick $35
Puck $20
Photo $8

Walt Tkaczuk
Stick $39
Puck $23
Photo $11

Gilles Tremblay
Stick $38
Puck $22
Photo $10

Mario Tremblay
Stick $40
Puck $24

Photo $12

Perry Turnbull
Stick $35
Puck $20
Photo $8

Garry Unger
Stick $45
Puck $25
Photo $15

Rogie Vachon
Stick $40
Puck $24
Photo $12

Carol Vadnais
Stick $39
Puck $23
Photo $11

John Van Boxmeer
Stick $39
Puck $23
Photo $11

Mike Walton
Stick $36
Puck $21
Photo $9

Ed Westfall
Stick $36
Puck $21
Photo $9

Kenny Wharram
Stick $39
Puck $23
Photo $11

Juha Widing
Stick $36
Puck $21
Photo $9

Active Hockey Players

Tony Amonte
Stick..........................$41
Puck..........................$23
Photo..........................$13

Dave Andreychuk
Stick..........................$35
Puck..........................$20
Photo..........................$8

Tom Barrasso
Stick..........................$35
Puck..........................$20
Photo..........................$8

Ed Belfour
Stick..........................$38
Puck..........................$22
Photo..........................$11

Brian Bellows
Stick..........................$40
Puck..........................$24
Photo..........................$12

Jeff Beukeboom
Stick..........................$38
Puck..........................$22
Photo..........................$10

Ray Bourque
Stick..........................$50
Puck..........................$30
Photo..........................$20

Daniel Briere
Stick..........................$40
Puck..........................$24
Photo..........................$12

Martin Brodeur
Stick..........................$48
Puck..........................$30
Photo..........................$18

Jan Bulis
Stick..........................$35
Puck..........................$20
Photo..........................$8

Pavel Bure
Stick..........................$50

Puck..........................$30
Photo..........................$20

Sean Burke
Stick..........................$38
Puck..........................$22
Photo..........................$10

Guy Carbonneau
Stick..........................$36
Puck..........................$21
Photo..........................$9

Bob Carpenter
Stick..........................$40
Puck..........................$24
Photo..........................$12

Chris Chelios
Stick..........................$35
Puck..........................$20
Photo..........................$8

Paul Coffey
Stick..........................$50
Puck..........................$30
Photo..........................$20

Shayne Corson
Stick..........................$28
Puck..........................$19
Photo..........................$6

Geoff Courtnall
Stick..........................$35
Puck..........................$20
Photo..........................$8

Russ Courtnall
Stick..........................$30
Puck..........................$20
Photo..........................$7

Murray Craven
Stick..........................$30
Puck..........................$20
Photo..........................$7

Adam Creighton
Stick..........................$35
Puck..........................$20
Photo..........................$8

Ulf Dahlen
Stick..........................$30
Puck..........................$20
Photo..........................$7

Alexandre Daigle
Stick..........................$55
Puck..........................$32

Photo..........................$22

Kevin Dineen
Stick..........................$28
Puck..........................$20
Photo..........................$6

Pat Falloon
Stick..........................$48
Puck..........................$28
Photo..........................$17

Sergei Fedorov
Stick..........................$40
Puck..........................$24
Photo..........................$12

Peter Forsberg
Stick..........................$40
Puck..........................$24
Photo..........................$12

Ron Francis
Stick..........................$38
Puck..........................$22
Photo..........................$10

Grant Fuhr
Stick..........................$40
Puck..........................$24
Photo..........................$12

Tony Granato
Stick..........................$41
Puck..........................$24
Photo..........................$13

Dominik Hasek
Stick..........................$50
Puck..........................$30
Photo..........................$20

Glenn Healy
Stick..........................$30
Puck..........................$20
Photo..........................$7

Ron Hextall
Stick..........................$45

Puck $25
Photo $15

Kelly Hrudey
Stick $40
Puck $24
Photo $12

Brett Hull
Stick $50
Puck $30
Photo $20

Dale Hunter
Stick $35
Puck $20
Photo $8

Al Iafrate
Stick $40
Puck $24
Photo $12

Jaromir Jagr
Stick $80
Puck $40
Photo $25

Olli Jokinen
Stick $38
Puck $22
Photo $10

Paul Kariya
Stick $50
Puck $30
Photo $20

Saku Koivu
Stick $30
Puck $20
Photo $7

Curtis Joseph
Stick $50
Puck $30
Photo $20

Vincent Lecavalier
Stick $30
Puck $20
Photo $7

John LeClair
Stick $28
Puck $20
Photo $6

Claude Lemieux
Stick $38
Puck $22
Photo $10

Nicklas Lidstrom
Stick $40
Puck $24
Photo $12

Eric Lindros
Stick $60
Puck $50
Photo $30

Al MacInnis
Stick $30
Puck $20
Photo $7

John MacLean
Stick $36
Puck $21
Photo $9

Patrick Marleau
Stick $36
Puck $21
Photo $9

Marty McSorley
Stick $30
Puck $20
Photo $7

Mark Messier
Stick $60
Puck $50
Photo $30

Alexander Mogilny
Stick $58
Puck $48
Photo $28

Mike Modano
Stick $38
Puck $22
Photo $10

Andy Moog
Stick $45
Puck $25
Photo $15

Joey Mullin
Stick $35
Puck $20
Photo $8

Kirk Muller
Stick $36
Puck $21
Photo $9

Bernie Nicholls
Stick $43
Puck $24
Photo $14

Joe Nieuwendyk
Stick $48
Puck $28
Photo $17

Adam Oates
Stick $46
Puck $25
Photo $15

Mattias Ohlund
Stick $35
Puck $20
Photo $8

Felix Potvin
Stick $36
Puck $21
Photo $9

Active Hockey Player Autographs — Chapter 17

Bob Probert
Stick $35
Puck $20
Photo $8

Mark Recchi
Stick $40
Puck $24
Photo $12

Mike Richter
Stick $30
Puck $20
Photo $7

Luc Robitaille
Stick $45
Puck $25
Photo $15

Jeremy Roenick
Stick $50
Puck $30
Photo $20

Patrick Roy
Stick $50
Puck $30
Photo $20

Joe Sakic
Stick $48
Puck $28
Photo $17

Tomas Sandstrom
Stick $43
Puck $24
Photo $14

Sergei Samsonov

Stick $29
Puck $19
Photo $6

Philippe Sauve
Stick $29
Puck $19
Photo $6

Teemu Selanne
Stick $45
Puck $25
Photo $15

Brendan Shanahan
Stick $50
Puck $30
Photo $20

Kevin Stevens
Stick $35
Puck $20
Photo $8

Marty Straka
Stick $38
Puck $22
Photo . . . . $10-$12

Marco Sturm
Stick $28
Puck $19
Photo $6

Mats Sundin
Stick $35
Puck $20
Photo $8

Gary Suter
Stick $38
Puck $22
Photo . . . . $10-$12

Mark Tinordi
Stick $29
Puck $19
Photo $6

Joe Thornton
Stick $29
Puck $19
Photo $6

Keith Tkachuk
Stick $38
Puck $22
Photo $10

Rick Tocchet
Stick $45
Puck $25
Photo $15

Darren Turcotte
Stick $40
Puck $24
Photo $12

Pierre Turgeon
Stick $38
Puck $22
Photo $10

John Vaniesbrouck
Stick $45
Puck $25
Photo $15

Mike Vernon
Stick $38
Puck $22
Photo $10

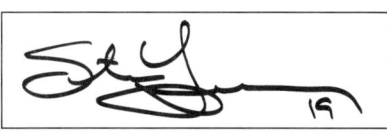

Steve Yzerman
Stick $55
Puck $45
Photo $25

Wrestling Autographs
* Indicates wrestler is deceased

Adrian Adonis *
Cut signature $10
Photo $25

Captain Lou Albano
Cut signature $6
Photo $15

Andre The Giant *
Cut signature $45
Photo $120

Tony Atlas
Cut signature $5
Photo $12

"Stone Cold" Steve Austin
Cut signature $10
Photo $40

Bob Backlund
Cut signature $8
Photo $20

Buff Bagwell
Cut signature $8
Photo $20

Paul Bearer
Cut signature $5
Photo $10

Brutus Beefcake
Cut signature $8
Photo $20

Chris Benoit
Cut signature $8
Photo $20

Bam Bam Bigelow
Cut signature $7
Photo $15

Eric Bischoff
Cut signature $8
Photo $20

Steve Blackman
Cut signature $5
Photo $12

Jerry Blackwell
Cut signature $6
Photo $15

Tully Blanchard
Cut signature $6
Photo $15

The Blue Meanie
Cut signature $5
Photo $12

Nick Bockwinkel
Cut signature $8
Photo $20

Booker T. (G.I Bro)
Cut signature $8
Photo $20

Boss Man
Cut signature $6
Photo $15

D 'Lo Brown
Cut signature $6
Photo $15

King Kong Bundy
Cut signature $6
Photo $15

Jumpin' Jim Brunsell
Cut signature $4
Photo $10

Christian
Cut signature $5
Photo $10

Brian Christopher
Cut signature ....$10-$15
Photo $25

The Chrusher
Cut signature $12
Photo $25

Chyna
Cut signature $8
Photo $20

Debra
Cut signature ....$10-$15
Photo $25

Ted Dibiase
Cut signature $6
Photo $15

Dick the Bruiser *
Cut signature ....$12-$15
Photo ....$35-$40

Disco Inferno
Cut signature $6
Photo $15

Droz
Cut signature $5
Photo $12

Hacksaw Jim Duggan
Cut signature $5
Photo $11

Edge
Cut signature $6
Photo $15

Miss Elizabeth
Cut signature $10
Photo $25

Ric Flair
Cut signature $12
Photo $35

Mick Foley
(Mankind/Dude Love/Cactus Jack)
Cut signature $10
Photo $25

Terry Funk
Cut signature $6
Photo $15

Greg Gagne
Cut signature ....$4-$6
Photo ....$10-$12

Verne Gagne
Cut signature $10
Photo $25

Gangrel
Cut signature $5

Photo $10

Gorgeous George
Cut signature $25
Photo $60

The Godfather
Cut signature $6
Photo $15

Bill Goldberg
Cut signature $12
Photo $35

Goldust
Cut signature $6
Photo $15

Eddy Guerrero
Cut signature $8
Photo $20

Bart Gunn
Cut signature $5
Photo $10

B.A. Billy Gunn
Cut signature $8
Photo $20

Scott Hall
Cut signature $12
Photo $30

Hardcore Holly
Cut signature $5
Photo $10

Brett Hart

Cut signature $10
Photo $25

Jimmy Hart
Cut signature $6
Photo $15

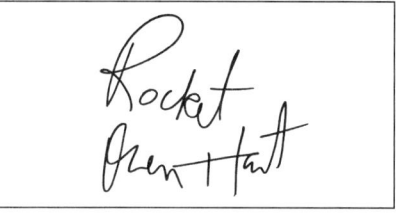

Owen Hart *
Cut signature $15
Photo $30

Curt Hennig
Cut signature $10
Photo $25

Larry "The Axe" Hennig
Cut signature $6
Photo $15

Bobby Heenan
Cut signature $8
Photo $20

Mark Henry
Cut signature $6
Photo $15

Hunter Hearst Hemsley
Cut signature $10
Photo $25

Hulk Hogan
Cut signature $15
Photo $40

Iron Sheik
Cut signature $8
Photo $20

"Road Dog" Jesse James
Cut signature $8
Photo $20

Jeff Jarrett
Cut signature $8
Photo $20

Chris Jericho
Cut signature $8
Photo $20

Kamala
Cut signature $12
Photo $30

Kane
Cut signature $10
Photo $25

Konnan
Cut signature $6
Photo $15

Kurrgan
Cut signature $5
Photo $10

Jerry "The King" Lawler
Cut signature $10
Photo $25

Lex Luger
Cut signature $10
Photo $25

Rocky Maivia
Cut signature $12
Photo $30

Dean Malenko
Cut signature $8
Photo $20

Vince McMahon
Cut signature $8
Photo $20

Shawn Michaels
Cut signature $12
Photo $30

Midian
Cut signature $5
Photo $12

Gorilla Monsoon *
Cut signature $15
Photo $40

Rey Mysterio Jr.
Cut signature $7
Photo $17

Kevin Nash
Cut signature $15
Photo $40

Mean Gene Okerlund
Cut signature $4
Photo $10

Diamond Dallas Page
Cut signature $12
Photo $30

Ken Patera
Cut signature $8
Photo $20

"Rowdy" Roddy Piper
Cut signature $10
Photo $25

"Leaping Lanny" Poffo
Cut signature $7
Photo $18

Ivan Putski
Cut signature $8
Photo $20

Raven
Cut signature $8
Photo $20

Harley Race
Cut signature $10
Photo $25

Stevie Ray
Cut signature $8
Photo $20

Dustin Rhodes
Cut signature $7
Photo $18

Dusty Rhodes
Cut signature $8
Photo $20

Billy Robinson
Cut signature $15
Photo $40

Jake "The Snake" Roberts
Cut signature $8
Photo $20

Jim Ross
Cut signature $5
Photo $10

Ravashing Rick Rude
Cut signature $20
Photo $60

Terri Runnels

Cut signature $6
Photo $15

Sable (Rena Mero)
Cut signature $15
Photo $40

Bruno Samartino
Cut signature $10
Photo $25

Tito Santana
Cut signature $6
Photo $15

Saturn
Cut signature $5
Photo $10

Randy "Macho Man" Savage
Cut signature $14
Photo $30

Scotty 2 Hotty
Cut signature $8
Photo $20

Ken Shamrock
Cut signature $8
Photo $20

Tiger Ali Singh
Cut signature $6
Photo $15

Sergeant Slaughter
Cut signature $10
Photo $25

Al Snow
Cut signature $6
Photo $15

Jimmy "Superfly" Snuka
Cut signature $8
Photo $20

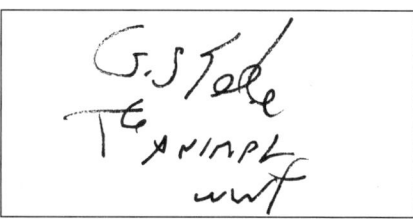

George "The Animal" Steele
Cut signature $6
Photo $15

Rick Steiner
Cut signature $8
Photo $20

Scott Steiner
Cut signature $8
Photo $20

Wrestling Autographs — Chapter 18

Sting
Cut signature $12
Photo $30

Big John Studd *
Cut signature $20
Photo $50

Sunny
Cut signature $8
Photo $20

Test
Cut signature $6
Photo $15

The Undertaker
Cut signature $10
Photo $25

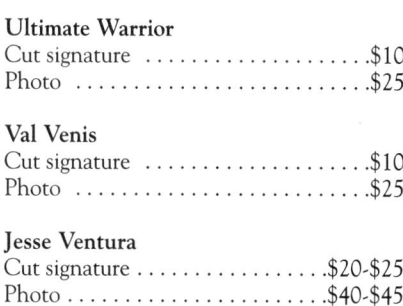

Ultimate Warrior
Cut signature $10
Photo $25

Val Venis
Cut signature $10
Photo $25

Jesse Ventura
Cut signature ....$20-$25
Photo ....$40-$45

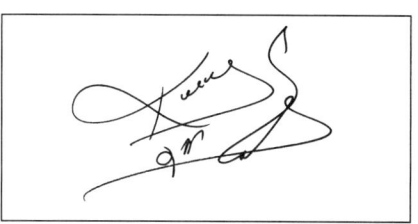

Kerry Von Erich
Cut signature $10
Photo $25

Baron Von Raschke
Cut signature $10
Photo $25

Paul Wight
Cut signature $8
Photo $20

X-Pac
Cut signature $8
Photo $20

Larry Zbyzsko
Cut signature $9
Photo $20

Boxing Autographs

Charles Adkins
Cut Signature $5
Photo $19
Glove $45

Virgil Akins
Cut Signature $15
Photo $35
Glove $145

Muhammad Ali
Cut Signature $15
Photo $35
Glove $130
(as Cassius Clay)
Cut Signature $100
Photo $250
Glove ....$(varies)

Lou Ambers *
Cut Signature $10
Photo $30
Glove $125

Fred Apostoli *
Cut Signature $35
Photo $90
Glove $390

Art Aragon
Cut Signature $5
Photo $10
Glove $45

Alexis Arguello
Cut Signature $7
Photo $15
Glove $65

Henry Armstrong *
Cut Signature $75
Photo $175
Glove $755

Abe Attell *
Cut Signature $60
Photo $160
Glove $690

Buddy Baer *
Cut Signature $12
Photo $40
Glove $175

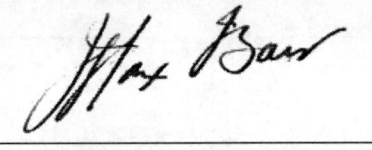

Max Baer *
Cut Signature $110
Photo $300
Glove $1,250

Carmen Basilio
Cut Signature $8
Photo $15
Glove $65

Nino Benvenuti
Cut Signature $15
Photo $65
Glove $265

Kid Berg *
Cut Signature $25
Photo $60
Glove $260

Paul Berlenbach *
Cut Signature $30
Photo $60
Glove $270

Melio Bettina *
Cut Signature $8
Photo $20
Glove $85

Riddick Bowe
Cut Signature $8
Photo ....$15-$20
Glove $90

James J. Braddock *
Cut Signature $65
Photo $250
Glove $1,200

Mark Breland
Cut Signature $6
Photo $15
Glove $60

Teddy Brenner
Cut Signature $5
Photo $10
Glove $40

Joe Brown
Cut Signature $6
Photo $15
Glove $60

Frank Bruno
Cut Signature $5
Photo $10
Glove $40

Ken Buchanan
Cut Signature $6
Photo $17
Glove $60

Tommy Burns *
Cut Signature $275
Photo $750
Glove $2,500

Mushy Callahan
Cut Signature $12
Photo $25
Glove $100

Hector Camacho
Cut Signature $10
Photo $20
Glove $65

Tony Canzoneri *
Cut Signature $60
Photo $130
Glove $570

Michael Carbajal
Cut Signature $7
Photo $15
Glove $75

Primo Carnera *
Cut Signature $225
Photo $500
Glove $2,150

Georges Carpentier *
Cut Signature $110
Photo $225
Glove $975

Jimmy Carter *
Cut Signature $12
Photo $25
Glove $100

Rubin "Hurricane" Carter
Cut Signature $10
Photo . . . . $15-$20
Glove . . . . $50-$60

Rocky Castellani
Cut Signature $5
Photo $15
Glove $60

Marcel Cerdan *
Cut Signature $280
Photo $775
Glove $3,200

Bobby Chacon
Cut Signature $10
Photo $20
Glove $85

Jeff Chandler
Cut Signature $5
Photo $10
Glove $40

Ezzard Charles *
Cut Signature $110
Photo $225
Glove $975

Julio Cesar Chavez
Cut Signature $12
Photo $32
Glove $125

George Chuvalo
Cut Signature $5
Photo $10
Glove $40

Gil Clancy
Cut Signature $5
Photo $10
Glove $40

Randal "Tex" Cobb
Cut Signature $8
Photo $15
Glove $50

Gerrie Coetzee
Cut Signature $5
Photo $10
Glove $40

Curtis Cokes
Cut Signature $4
Photo $8
Glove $35

Billy Conn *
Cut Signature $20
Photo $65
Glove $260

Gerry Cooney
Cut Signature $5
Photo $10
Glove $40

James J. Corbett *
Cut Signature $400
Photo $800
Glove $3,500

Johnny Coulon *
Cut Signature $45
Photo $100
Glove $425

Bobby Czyz
Cut Signature $5
Photo $10
Glove $45

Chuck Davey
Cut Signature $4
Photo $8
Glove $35

Oscar De La Hoya
Cut Signature $15
Photo $35
Glove $125

Paddy DeMarco
Cut Signature $6
Photo $13
Glove $50

Tony DeMarco
Cut Signature $6
Photo $13
Glove $50

Jack Dempsey
Cut Signature $75

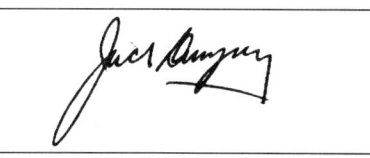

Photo $165
Glove $730

Michael Dokes
Cut Signature $5
Photo $13
Glove $50

Angelo Dundee
Cut Signature $6
Photo $12
Glove $50

Chris Dundee
Cut Signature $12
Photo $30
Glove $100

Johnny Dundee *
Cut Signature $45
Photo $100
Glove $400

Don Dunphy
Cut Signature $5
Photo $10
Glove $40

Roberto Duran
Cut Signature $15
Photo $35
Glove $125

Flash Elorde
Cut Signature $25
Photo $55
Glove $240

Jimmy Ellis
Cut Signature $5
Photo $10
Glove $40

Alfredo Escalera
Cut Signature $6
Photo $14
Glove $55

Johnny Famechon
Cut Signature $6
Photo $14
Glove $55

Tommy Farr
Cut Signature $25
Photo $60
Glove $250

Jeff Fenech
Cut Signature $8
Photo $17
Glove $70

Jackie Fields
Cut Signature $8
Photo $14
Glove $50

Bob Fitzsimmons *
Cut Signature $2,200
Photo $6,000
Glove $13,000

Nat Fleischer
Cut Signature $15
Photo $30
Glove $120

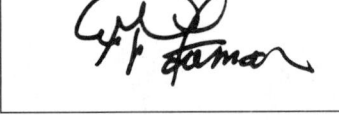

George Foreman
Cut Signature $10
Photo $20
Glove $80

Bob Foster
Cut Signature $8
Photo $15
Glove $65

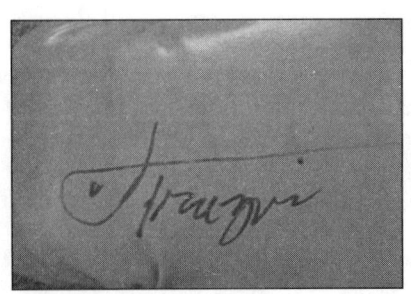

Joe Frazier
Cut Signature $9
Photo $20
Glove $85

Gene Fullmer

Cut Signature $8
Photo $15
Glove $65

Charlie Fusari
Cut Signature $5
Photo $10
Glove $40

Eddie Futch
Cut Signature $8
Photo $15
Glove $65

Tony Galento
Cut Signature $45
Photo $95
Glove $390

Ceferino Garcia
Cut Signature $5
Photo $10
Glove $40

Kid Gavilan
Cut Signature $12
Photo $25
Glove $90

Joey Giambra
Cut Signature $5
Photo $10
Glove $40

Joey Giardello
Cut Signature $6
Photo $15
Glove $65

Abe Goldstein *
Cut Signature $45
Photo $90
Glove $390

Wilfredo Gomez
Cut Signature $6
Photo $15

Glove $65

Rocky Graziano *
Cut Signature $30
Photo $55
Glove $240

Emile Griffith
Cut Signature $6
Photo $15
Glove $45

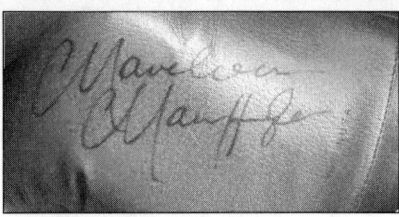

Marvin Hagler
Cut Signature $12
Photo $30
Glove $100

Marvin Hart *
Cut Signature $800
Photo $1,700
Glove $7,325

Thomas Hearns
Cut Signature $10
Photo $30
Glove $95

Larry Holmes
Cut Signature $11
Photo $25
Glove $65

Evander Holyfield
Cut Signature $22
Photo $45
Glove $60

Al Hostak
Cut Signature $15
Photo $30
Glove $125

Beau Jack *
Cut Signature $12
Photo $20
Glove $55

James J. Jeffries *
Cut Signature $370
Photo $750

Glove $3,225

Lew Jenkins
Cut Signature $5
Photo $10
Glove $40

Eder Jofre
Cut Signature $10
Photo $22
Glove $70

Ingemar Johansson
Cut Signature $15
Photo $30
Glove $110

Harold Johnson
Cut Signature $8
Photo $15
Glove $50

Jack Johnson *
Cut Signature $775
Photo $1,400
Glove $6,100

Ralph Jones
Cut Signature $7
Photo $20
Glove $55

Roy Jones
Cut Signature $8
Photo $20
Glove $80

Jack Kearns
Cut Signature $30
Photo $60
Glove $250

Don King
Cut Signature $5
Photo $10

Glove $40

Fidel LaBarba
Cut Signature $10
Photo $20
Glove $75

Jake LaMotta
Cut Signature $12
Photo $20
Glove $75

Roland Lastarza
Cut Signature $5
Photo $10
Glove $40

Benny Leonardm *
Cut Signature $40
Photo $100
Glove $450

Sugar Ray Leonard
Cut Signature $20
Photo $35
Glove $150

Gus Lesnevich
Cut Signature $25
Photo $50
Glove $215

John Henry Lewis *
Cut Signature $65
Photo $160
Glove $690

Lennox Lewis
Cut Signature $10
Photo $30
Glove $110

Sonny Liston *
Cut Signature $250
Photo $750
Glove $3,250

Danny Lopez
Cut Signature $5
Photo $10
Glove $40

Tommy Loughran *
Cut Signature $35
Photo $80
Glove $345

Joe Louis *
Cut Signature $175
Photo $325
Glove $1,400

Ray Mancini
Cut Signature $10
Photo $24
Glove $80

Sammy Mandell
Cut Signature $10
Photo $20
Glove $85

Rocky Marciano *
Cut Signature $300
Photo $700
Glove $2,100

Buster Mathis Sr.*
Cut Signature $15
Photo . . . . $25-$30
Glove $90

Joey Maxim
Cut Signature $8
Photo $20
Glove $75

Boxing Autographs — Chapter 19

Jimmy McLarnin
Cut Signature $15
Photo $30
Glove $100

Ray Mercer
Cut Signature $7
Photo $15
Glove $60

Freddie Mills
Cut Signature $20
Photo $50
Glove $215

Charles Mitchell
Cut Signature $20
Photo $50
Glove $215

Carlos Monzon *
Cut Signature $40
Photo $110
Glove $260

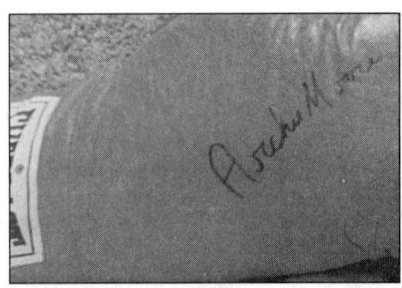

Archie Moore *
Cut Signature $9
Photo $20
Glove $90

Michael Moorer
Cut Signature $10
Photo $20
Glove $70

Tommy Morrison

Cut Signature $10
Photo $25
Glove $75

Eddie M. Muhammad
Cut Signature $5
Photo $13
Glove $55

Matthew S. Muhammad
Cut Signature $5
Photo $13
Glove $55

Jose Napoles
Cut Signature $11
Photo $25
Glove $75

Battling Nelson *
Cut Signature $80
Photo $175
Glove $760

Terry Norris
Cut Signature $7
Photo $15
Glove $60

Ken Norton
Cut Signature $10
Photo $25
Glove $75

Lou Nova
Cut Signature $5
Photo $10
Glove $45

Ruben Olivares
Cut Signature $8
Photo $18
Glove $60

Carl Olson
Cut Signature $7
Photo $15
Glove $60

Carlos Ortiz
Cut Signature $7
Photo $16
Glove $55

Carlos Palmino
Cut Signature $5
Photo $10
Glove $45

Bob Montgomery
Cut Signature $6
Photo $13
Glove $55

Billy Papke *
Cut Signature $245
Photo $500
Glove $2,150

Willie Pastrano
Cut Signature $5
Photo $10
Glove $45

Floyd Patterson
Cut Signature $10
Photo $20
Glove $85

Eusebio Pedroza
Cut Signature $5
Photo $10
Glove $40

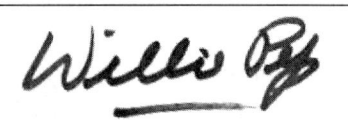

Willie Pep
Cut Signature $6
Photo $15
Glove $60

Aaron Pryor
Cut Signature $5
Photo $15
Glove $55

Dwight Qawi
Cut Signature $5
Photo $10
Glove $40

Jerry Quarry *
Cut Signature $9
Photo $20
Glove $75

Sugar Ramos
Cut Signature $7
Photo $18
Glove $70

Tex Rickard *
Cut Signature $170
Photo $360
Glove $1,600

Eddie Risko
Cut Signature $10
Photo $25
Glove $85

Willie Ritchie *
Cut Signature $20
Photo $40
Glove $170

Sugar Ray Robinson *
Cut Signature $40
Photo $175
Glove $750

Louis Rodriguez
Cut Signature $10
Photo $25
Glove $100

Edwin Rosario
Cut Signature $7
Photo $18
Glove $60

Maxie Rosenbloom *
Cut Signature $40
Photo $80
Glove $350

Barney Ross *
Cut Signature $40
Photo $80
Glove $350

Sandy Saddler
Cut Signature $10
Photo $28
Glove $80

Johnny Saxton
Cut Signature $8
Photo $19
Glove $80

Max Schmeling *
Cut Signature $20
Photo $40
Glove $175

Marty Servo
Cut Signature $5
Photo $10
Glove $40

Jack Sharkey *
Cut Signature $75

Photo $150
Glove $600

Earnie Shavers
Cut Signature $5
Photo $12
Glove $45

Leon Spinks
Cut Signature $6
Photo $12
Glove $45

Michael Spinks
Cut Signature $10
Photo $20
Glove $75

John L. Sullivan *
Cut Signature $500
Photo $950
Glove $4,100

John Tate
Cut Signature $8
Photo $18
Glove $65

Ernie Terrell
Cut Signature $6
Photo $13
Glove $55

Pinklon Thomas
Cut Signature $6
Photo $13
Glove $55

Dick Tiger *
Cut Signature $75
Photo $200
Glove $850

Gene Tunney *
Cut Signature $80
Photo $180
Glove $775

Randy Turpin *
Cut Signature $110
Photo $175

Glove $800

Mike Tyson
Cut Signature $30
Photo $65
Glove $150

Jersey Joe Walcott *
Cut Signature $25
Photo $65
Glove $275

Mickey Walker *
Cut Signature $50
Photo $160
Glove $650

Mike Weaver
Cut Signature $5
Photo $10
Glove $45

Sweet Pea Whitaker
Cut Signature $5
Photo $9
Glove $40

Jess Willard *
Cut Signature $220
Photo $450
Glove $2,000

Cleveland Williams
Cut Signature $6
Photo $13
Glove $50

Ike Williams *
Cut Signature $12
Photo $25
Glove $125

Tony Zale *
Cut Signature $9
Photo $18
Glove $65

Alfonso Zamora
Cut Signature $5
Photo $12
Glove $50

Auto Racer Autographs
Active and retired

Bobby Allison
Cut signature $11
8x10 photo $19

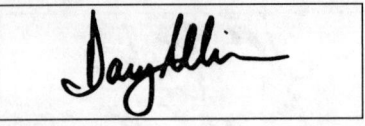

Davey Allison *
Cut signature $54
8x10 photo $90

Mario Andretti
Cut signature $21
8x10 photo $35

Michael Andretti
Cut signature $13
8x10 photo $22

Buddy Baker
Cut signature $12
8x10 photo $25

Johnny Benson
Cut signature $13
8x10 photo $20

Joe Bessey
Cut signature $10
8x10 photo $15

Tony Bettenhausen
Cut signature $11
8x10 photo $18

Brett Bodine
Cut signature $10
8x10 photo $16

Geoff Bodine
Cut signature $13
8x10 photo $21

Todd Bodine
Cut signature $12
8x10 photo $25

Neil Bonnett
Cut signature $30
8x10 photo $50

Jeff Burton
Cut signature $14
8x10 .... $24

Ward Burton
Cut signature $14
8x10 .... $24

Eddie Cheever
Cut signature $11
8x10 photo $18

Derrick Cope
Cut signature $7
8x10 photo $12

Wally Dallenbach
Cut signature $15
8x10 photo $25

Dale Earnhardt Sr.
Cut signature $25
8x10 photo $45

Dale Earnhardt Jr.
Cut signature $15
8x10 photo $25

Bill Elliot
Cut signature $20
8x10 photo $30

Tim Fedewa
Cut signature $15
8x10 photo $25

Adrian Fernandez
Cut signature $14
8x10 photo $22

Emerson Fittipaldi
Cut signature $16
8x10 photo $25

A.J. Foyt
Cut signature $15
8x10 photo $25

Dario Francitti
Cut signature $14
8x10 photo $22

Jeff Fuller
Cut signature $15
8x10 photo $25

Harry Gant
Cut signature $15
8x10 photo $27

Scott Goodyear
Cut signature $14
8x10 photo $24

Jeff Gordon
Cut signature $25
8x10 photo $40

David Green
Cut signature $10
8x10 photo $15

Roberto Guerrero
Cut signature $12
8x10 photo $24

Bobby Hamilton
Cut signature $10
8x10 photo $15

Jimmy Hensley
Cut signature $10

8x10 photo $15

Damon Hill
Cut signature $14
8x10 photo $22

Ernie Irvan
Cut signature $18
8x10 photo $30

Kenny Irwin
Cut signature $10
8x10 photo $12

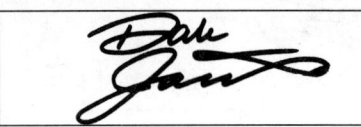

Dale Jarrett
Cut signature $18
8x10 photo $30

Jason Jarrett
Cut signature $12
8x10 photo $25

Ned Jarrett
Cut signature $12
8x10 photo $25

Gordon Johncock
Cut signature $14
8x10 photo $25

Parnelli Jones
Cut signature $13
8x10 photo $25

Steve Knapp
Cut signature $14
8x10 photo $22

Benny Parsons
Cut signature $10
8x10 photo $15

Matt Kenseth
Cut signature $10
8x10 photo $15

Alan Kulwicki *
Cut signature $50
8x10 photo $90

Bobby Labonte
Cut signature $14
8x10 photo $24

Terry Labonte
Cut signature $16
8x10 photo $27

Randy LaJoie
Cut signature $10

Racing Autographs — Chapter 20

8x10 photo $15

Kevin Lepage
Cut signature $10
8x10 photo $15

Chad Little
Cut signature $10
8x10 photo $15

Arie Luyendyk
Cut signature $12
8x10 photo $20

Jimmy Makar
Cut signature $10
8x10 photo $15

Nigel Mansell
Cut signature $20
8x10 photo $25

Dave Marcis
Cut signature $12
8x10 photo $15

Sterling Marlin
Cut signature $13
8x10 photo $20

Mark Martin
Cut signature $18
8x10 photo $30

Jeremy Mayfield
Cut signature $14
8x10 photo $24

Mike McLaughlin
Cut signature $10
8x10 photo $15

Ralph Moody Jr.
Cut signature $8
8x10 photo $15

Rob Moroso *
Cut signature $15
8x10 photo $25

Sterling Moss
Cut signature $20
8x10 photo $25

Ted Musgrave
Cut signature $14
8x10 photo $25

Rick Mears
Cut signature $16
8x10 photo $27

Juan Montoya
Cut signature $15
8x10 photo $25

Jerry Nadeau
Cut signature $10
8x10 photo $15

Joe Nemechek
Cut signature $10
8x10 photo $15

Steve Park
Cut signature $12
8x10 photo $15

Todd Parrot
Cut signature $12
8x10 photo $24

Benny Parsons
Cut signature $12
8x10 photo $24

Phil Parsons
Cut signature $12
8x10 photo $18

David Pearson
Cut signature $8
8x10 photo $12

Roger Penske
Cut signature $20
8x10 photo $25

Andy Petree
Cut signature $8
8x10 photo $15

Adam Petty *
Cut signature $20
8x10 photo $30

Kyle Petty
Cut signature $17
8x10 photo $21

Richard Petty
Cut signature $20
8x10 photo $35

Bobby Rahal
Cut signature $15
8x10 photo $25

Tim Richmond *
Cut signature $12
8x10 photo $24

Ricky Rudd
Cut signature $11
8x10 photo $19

Johnny Rutherford
Cut signature $12
8x10 photo $20

Elliot Sadler
Cut signature $8
8x10 photo $15

Elton Sawyer
Cut signature $10
8x10 photo $15

Ken Schrader
Cut signature $12
8x10 photo $19

Morgan Shepherd
Cut signature $10
8x10 photo $15

Mike Skinner
Cut signature $10
8x10 photo $14

Tom Sneva
Cut signature $13
8x10 photo $21

Jimmy Spencer
Cut signature $12
8x10 photo $20

Jackie Stewart
Cut signature $12
8x10 photo $20

Tony Stewart
Cut signature $13
8x10 photo $22

Hut Strickland
Cut signature $10
8x10 photo $17

Danny Sullivan
Cut signature $16
8x10 photo $24

Dick Trickle
Cut signature $14
8x10 photo $22

Al Unser
Cut signature $12
8x10 photo $20

Al Unser Jr.
Cut signature $14
8x10 photo $25

Jimmy Vasser
Cut signature $12
8x10 photo $20

Kenny Wallace
Cut signature $13
8x10 photo $21

Rusty Wallace
Cut signature $19
8x10 photo $32

Darrell Waltrip
Cut signature $17
8x10 photo $27

Michael Waltrip
Cut signature $10
8x10 photo $15

Cale Yarborough
Cut signature $14
8x10 photo $22

Tennis Autographs

Andre Agassi
Photo $50
Ball $55
3x5 index card $12

Arthur Ashe*
Photo ....$90-$100
Ball ....$100-$120
3x5 index card ....$15-$18

Boris Becker
Photo $25
Ball $30
3x5 index card $6

Jonas Bjorkman
Photo $15
Ball $20
3x5 index card $5

Bjorn Borg
Photo $20
Ball $25
3x5 index card $6

Sergi Bruguera
Photo $15
Ball $20
3x5 index card $5

Jennifer Capriati
Photo $20
Ball $25
3x5 index card $6

Michael Chang
Photo $25
Ball $30
3x5 index card $6

Amanda Coetzer
Photo $15
Ball $20
3x5 index card $5

Jimmy Connors
Photo $30
Ball $35
3x5 index card $7

Jim Courier
Photo $30
Ball $35
3x5 index card $7

Margaret Court
Photo $20
Ball $25
3x5 index card $6

Lindsay Davenport
Photo $25
Ball $30
3x5 index card $7

Stefan Edberg
Photo $25
Ball $30
3x5 index card $7

Chris Evert
Photo $20
Ball $25
3x5 index card $6

Mary Joe Fernandez
Photo $15
Ball $20
3x5 index card $5

Vitas Gerulaitis*
Photo $75
Ball $90
3x5 index card $15

Pancho Gonzalez *
Photo $60
Ball $80
3x5 index card ....$12-$14

Steffi Graf
Photo $35
Ball $45
3x5 index card ....$7-$8

Martina Hingis
Photo $30
Ball $40
3x5 index card $10

Goran Ivanisevic
Photo $25

Ball $30
3x5 index card $7

Yevgeny Kafelnikov
Photo $15
Ball $20
3x5 index card $5

Billie Jean King
Photo $20
Ball $25
3x5 index card $6

Petr Korda
Photo $20
Ball $25
3x5 index card $6

Anna Kournikova
Photo $30
Ball $40
3x5 index card $10

Richard Krajicek
Photo $15
Ball $20
3x5 index card $5

Rod Laver
Photo $20
Ball $25
3x5 index card $6

Ivan Lendl
Photo $20
Ball $25
3x5 index card $6

Conchita Martinez
Photo $15
Ball $20
3x5 index card $5

John McEnroe
Photo $60
Ball $80
3x5 index card ....$15-$18

Thomas Muster
Photo $20
Ball $25
3x5 index card $6

Ilie Nastase
Photo $35
Ball $40
3x5 index card ....$10-$12

Martina Navratilova
Photo $30

Ball $40
3x5 index card $8

John Newcombe
Photo $20
Ball $25
3x5 index card $6

Jana Novotna
Photo $15
Ball $20
3x5 index card $5

Mary Pierce
Photo $20
Ball $25
3x5 index card $6

Patrick Rafter
Photo $15
Ball $20
3x5 index card $5

Bobby Riggs*
Photo $50
Ball $60
3x5 index card $10

Carlos Rios
Photo $20
Ball $25
3x5 index card $6

Gabriela Sabatini
Photo $20
Ball $25
3x5 index card $6

Pete Sampras
Photo $50
Ball $60
3x5 index card $10

Vicario A. Sanchez
Photo $15

Ball $20
3x5 index card $5

Monica Seles
Photo $25
Ball $30
3x5 index card $6

Pam Shriver
Photo $15
Ball $20
3x5 index card $5

Michael Stich
Photo $15
Ball $20
3x5 index card $5

Bill Tilden*
Photo $250
Ball $300
3x5 index card ....$90-$100

Malivai Washington
Photo $20
Ball $25
3x5 index card $6

Mats Wilander
Photo $20
Ball $25
3x5 index card $6

Venus Williams
Photo $25
Ball $30
3x5 index card $7

Serena Williams
Photo $25
Ball $30
3x5 index card $7

Helen Wills-Moody
Photo $20
Ball $25
3x5 index card $6

Golf Autographs

Tommy Aaron
Photo $20
Ball $25

Amy Alcott
Photo $15
Ball $20

George Archer
Photo $20
Ball $25

Paul Azinger
Photo $20
Ball $25

Seve Ballesteros
Photo $25
Ball $30

Butch Baird
Photo $15
Ball $20

Miller Barber
Photo $20
Ball $25

Andy Bean
Photo $15
Ball $20

Chip Beck
Photo $15
Ball $20

Patti Berg
Photo $25
Ball $30

Tommy Bolt
Photo $20
Ball $25

Julius Boros
Photo $30
Ball $40

Jack Burke
Photo $15
Ball $20

Gay Brewer
Photo $15
Ball $20

Billy Casper
Photo $20
Ball $25

Jim Colbert
Photo $15
Ball $20

Fred Couples
Photo $25
Ball $30

Ben Crenshaw
Photo $25
Ball $30

John Daly
Photo $25
Ball $30

Jimmy Demaret
Photo $30
Ball $50

David Duval
Photo $30
Ball $50

Lee Elder
Photo $15
Ball $20

Steve Elkington
Photo $15
Ball $20

Ernie Els
Photo $25
Ball $30

Nick Faldo
Photo $30
Ball $40

Ray Floyd
Photo $25
Ball $30

Sergio Garcia
Photo $15
Ball $20

Hubert Green
Photo $15
Ball $20

Jay Hebert
Photo $15
Ball $20

Ben Hogan *
Photo $200
Ball $250

Juli Inkster
Photo $15
Ball $20

Hale Irwin
Photo $20
Ball $25

Lee Janzen
Photo $20
Ball $25

Tony Jacklin
Photo $15
Ball $20

Don January
Photo $25
Ball $30

Bobby Jones *
Photo $2,000
Ball $2,500

Betsy King
Photo $30
Ball $50

Tom Kite
Photo $20
Ball $25

Bernard Langer
Photo $20
Ball $25

Tom Lehman
Photo $20
Ball $25

Justin Leonard
Photo $20
Ball $25

Gene Littler
Photo $25
Ball $30

Nancy Lopez
Photo $20
Ball $25

Davis Love III
Photo $25
Ball $30

Casey Martin
Photo $15
Ball $20

Phil Mickelson
Photo $25
Ball $30

Johnny Miller

Golf Autographs — Chapter 22

Photo	$20
Ball	$25

Larry Mize
Photo $15
Ball $20

Colin Montgomerie
Photo $20
Ball $25

Orville Moody
Photo $15
Ball $20

Bob Murphy
Photo $20
Ball $25

Byron Nelson
Photo $35
Ball $40

Larry Nelson
Photo $15
Ball $20

Jack Nicklaus
Photo $75
Ball $100

Greg Norman
Photo $30
Ball $40

Mark O'Meara
Photo $25
Ball $30

Arnold Palmer
Photo $75
Ball $100

Se Ri Pak
Photo $25
Ball $30

Jesper Parnevik
Photo $15
Ball $20

Steve Pate
Photo $15
Ball $20

Corey Pavin
Photo $20
Ball $25

Gary Player

Photo $25
Ball $30

Nick Price
Photo $25
Ball $30

Betsy Rawls
Photo $20
Ball $25

Chi Chi Rodriguez
Photo $25
Ball $30

Gene Sarazen *
Photo $30
Ball $35

Scott Simpson
Photo $15
Ball $20

Charles Sifford
Photo $25
Ball $30

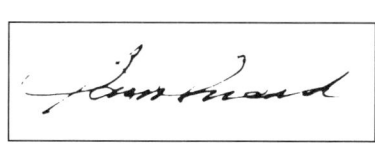

Vijay Singh
Photo $20
Ball $25

J.C. Snead
Photo $20
Ball $25

Sam Snead
Photo $30
Ball $35

Annika Sorenstam
Photo $15
Ball $20

Craig Stadler
Photo $25
Ball $30

Payne Stewart *
Photo $50
Ball $70

Dave Stockton
Photo $15
Ball $20

Curtis Strange
Photo $25
Ball $30

Hal Sutton
Photo $20
Ball $25

Lee Trevino
Photo $30
Ball $35

Ken Venturi
Photo $25
Ball $30

Lanny Wadkins
Photo $20
Ball $25

Tom Watson
Photo $25
Ball $30

Tom Weiskopf
Photo $20
Ball $25

Lee Westwood
Photo $15
Ball $20

Tiger Woods
Photo ....$125-$150
Ball ....$350-$400

Babe Didrikson Zaharias *
Photo $150
Ball $200

Larry Ziegler
Photo $15
Ball $20

Fuzzy Zoeller
Photo $25
Ball $30

Sources

The following sources have been utilized for information or to help determine prices:

Baker, Mark Allen. *Advanced Autograph Collecting*, Krause Publications, Iola, Wis. 2000
Baker, Mark Allen. *Collector's Guide to Celebrity Autographs*, Krause Publications, Iola, Wis. 2000
Baker, Mark Allen. *Sports Collectors Digest's All Sport Autograph Guide*, Krause Publications, Iola, Wis. 1994
Baker, Mark Allen. *Sports Collectors Digest's Baseball Autograph Handbook*, Krause Publications, Iola, Wis. second edition, 1991
Baker, Mark Allen. *Sports Collectors Digest's Complete Guide to Boxing Collectibles*, Krause Publications, Iola, Wis. 1995
Baker, Mark Allen. *Sports Collectors Digest's Team Baseballs, A Comprehensive Guide to Autographed Team Baseballs*, Krause Publications, Iola, Wis. 1992
Baker, Mark Allen. *Standard Guide to Collecting Autographs*, Krause Publications, Iola, Wis. 1999
Keating, Kevin and Kolleth, Michael. *The Negro Leagues Autograph Guide*, Tuff Stuff Books, Richmond, Va. 1999
Larsen, Mark K. *Sports Collectors Digest's Complete Guide to Baseball Memorabilia*, third edition, Krause Publications, Iola, Wis. 1996
Larsen, Mark K. *Sports Collectors Digest's Complete Guide to Football, Basketball & Hockey Memorabilia*, Krause Publications, Iola, Wis. 1995
Malloy, Roderick A. *Malloy's Sports Collectibles Value Guide*, Wallace-Homestead Book Co. Radnor, Pa. 1993
Martin, Kevin. *Signatures of the Stars*, Antique Trader Books, Norfolk, Va. 1998
Mortenson, Thomas G. *Sports Collectors Digest's Standard Catalog of Sports Memorabilia*, Krause Publications, Iola, Wis. 1999
Pope, Kristian; Whebbe Jr., Ray. *Professional Wrestling Collectibles*, Krause Publications, Iola, Wis. 2000
Warren, Jim; Haynie, Melanie; Shaver, Jerry and Madigan, Dennis. *Tuff Stuff's Baseball Memorabilia Price Guide*, Tuff Stuff Books, Richmond, Va. 1998

Also, back issues of *Sports Collectors Digest* and *Tuff Stuff*, along with various internet auctions and numerous sports memorabilia auction company catalogs have been used for reference, identification and pricing determination.

WHATEVER YOUR GAME, WE'VE GOT SOMETHING FOR YOU!

13 issues only $12.95
Details the sports memorabilia collecting hobby - trading cards, uniforms, autographs, and equipment.

12 issues only $29.95
The most trusted guide in the sports card and collectibles hobby.

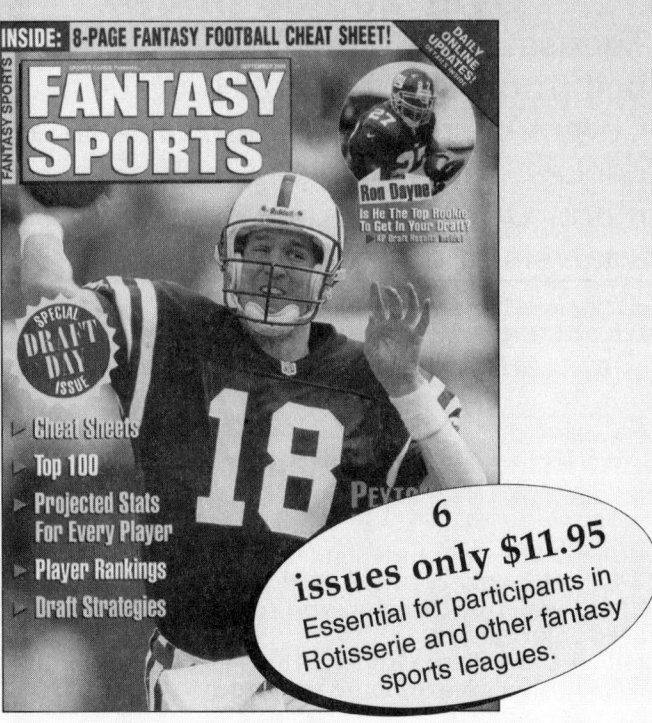

6 issues only $11.95
Essential for participants in Rotisserie and other fantasy sports leagues.

6 issues only $9.95
Covers all aspects of sports collecting, esp. trading cards for the major sports.

Keep Up With Today's Collectors ▪ SUBSCRIBE TODAY!

Credit Card Customers Call Toll-free

800-258-0929 ABA1MC

M-F, 7 am - 8 pm • Sat, 8 am - 2 pm, CST
To subscribe by mail: Krause Publications Dept. ABA • 700 E. State Street • Iola, WI 54990-0001

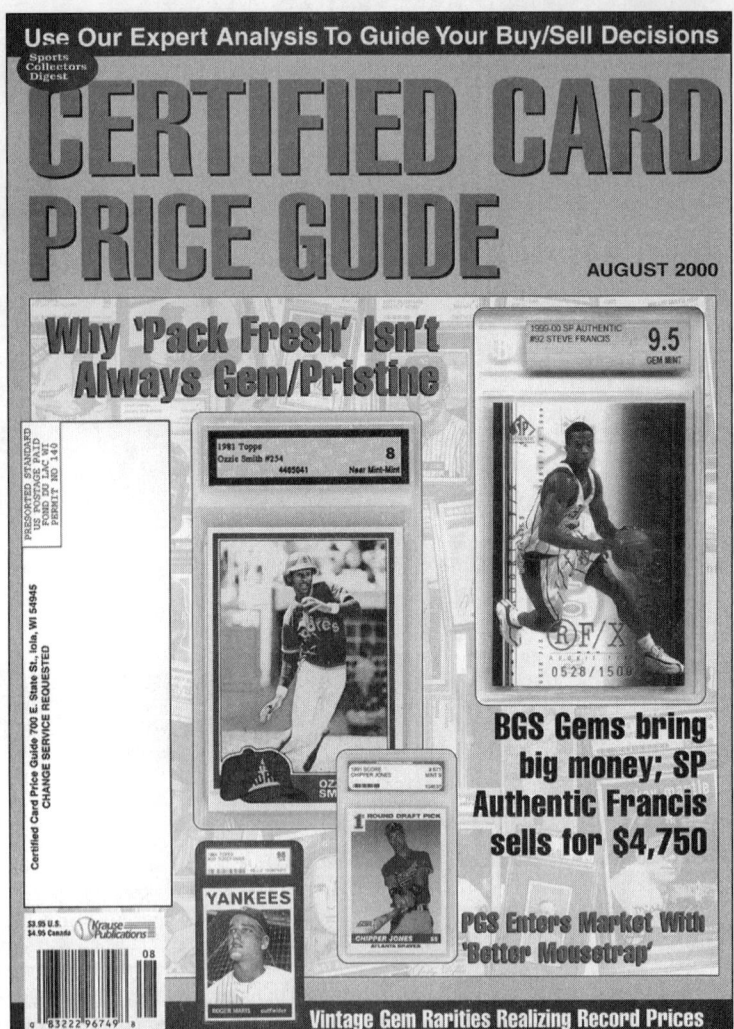

VITAL SPORTS REFERENCE BOOKS

2001 Standard Catalog™ of Basketball Cards
4th Edition
by Price Guide Editors of Sports Collectors Digest
Over 125,000 cards from 1948 - 2000 are checklisted and priced. More than 900 sets from all the top manufacturers are listed including Topps, Fleer, Score, Pacific, Upper Deck, SkyBox, Hoops and more. NBA, WNBA, CBA, college, regional, Olympic, food sets and more are covered. Includes a certified card price guide, autograph price guide and complete pricing for Kenner Starting Lineup and other figurines.
Softcover • 8-1/2 x 11 • 368 pages
1,500+ b&w photos
Item# SCBC4 • $21.95

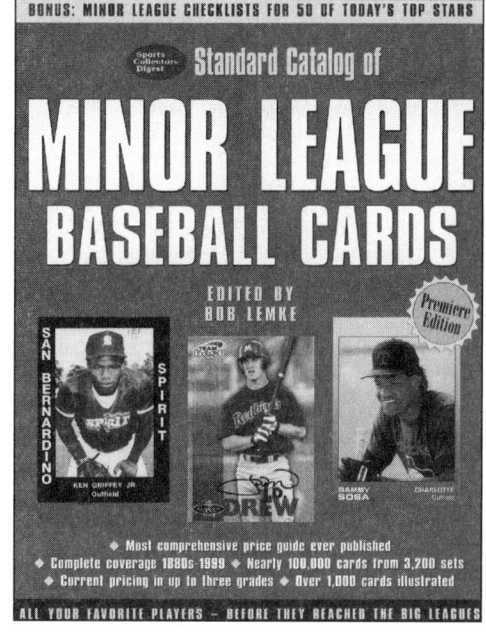

Standard Catalog™ of Minor League Baseball Cards
edited by Bob Lemke
Trace the careers of your favorite stars from before Ty Cobb to today's starters in the most complete source for Minor League baseball cards ever published. Information on card quantities and rare issues are only found in this volume. Included are more than 40,000 players and 3,200 team sets, some going back to the 1880s. Listings are priced in up to three different grades. Special sections list all minor league cards for 50 of today's top major league stars. A great guide for baseball fans of all ages.
Softcover • 8-1/2 x 11
480 pages • 400 bw photos
Item# SG02 • $24.95

2001 Standard Catalog™ of Baseball Cards
10th Edition
edited by Bob Lemke
Over 425,000 cards from 1869 - early 2000 releases. More than 600,000 accurate, real-world prices for making crucial buying and selling decisions (each individually reviewed, updated and reverified for accuracy). Over 12,000 large clear photos of card fronts and backs to help you identify and grade your own cards.
Softcover • 8-1/2 x 11 • 1,664 pages
12,000+ b&w photos
Item# SB10 • $39.95

2000 Standard Catalog™ of Sports Memorabilia
by Tom Mortenson
This is the largest, most comprehensive catalog of football, baseball, basketball, hockey and other sport memorabilia ever compiled. Accurate market pricing for thousands of items including autographs, uniforms, equipment, ticket stubs, press pins, publications, pennants, books, figurines and much more.
Softcover • 8-1/2 x 11 • 496 pages
2,000 b&w photos
Item# SMEM1 • $21.95

Bobbing Head Dolls
1960-2000
by Tim Hunter
This first-ever price and identification guide features hundreds of dolls, including: baseball, football, basketball, hockey, TV stars, advertising icons, political figures and cartoon characters. Learn how to identify which series a doll is from, if it's a rare variation, and how much it's worth. Do you have the common Houston Astros doll worth $80 or the scarce Astros version with the shooting star decal priced at $700? With over 250 photos and 700 individual listings, you're sure to find values for the dolls in your collection.
Softcover • 8-1/2 x 11
160 pages • 250+ bw photos
30+ color photos
Item# BOBHD • $19.95

2001 Standard Catalog™ of Football Cards
4th Edition
by Price Guide Editors of SCD
Includes over 325,000 cards from 2,300 sets. NFL, CFL, USFL, WLAF, college and food issues are all here. Plus you'll get a certified card price guide, an autograph price guide and a complete listing with prices for Kenner Starting Lineup and other figurines. Cards from 1894 to present from Topps, Fleer, SkyBox, Upper Deck, Pinnacle, Score, Pacific, Press Pass, Bowman, Sage and many more.
Softcover • 8-1/2 x 11 • 592 pages
2,200+ b&w photos
Item# SCFC4 • $22.95

To place a credit card order or for a FREE all-product catalog call

800-258-0929 Offer SPBR

M-F, 7 am - 8 pm • Sat, 8 am - 2 pm, CST

Krause Publications, Offer SPBR

P.O. Box 5009, Iola, WI 54945-5009

www.krausebooks.com

Shipping and Handling: $3.25 1st book; $2 ea. add'l. Foreign orders $20.95 1st item, $5.95 each add'l.
Sales tax: CA, IA, IL, PA, TN, VA, WA, WI residents please add appropriate sales tax.
Satisfaction Guarantee: If for any reason you are not completely satisfied with your purchase, simply return it within 14 days and receive a full refund, less shipping.
Retailers call toll-free 888-457-2873 ext 880, M-F, 8 am - 5 pm

INFORMATION EVERY SUCCESSFUL COLLECTOR NEEDS

Professional Wrestling Collectibles
by Kristian Pope & Ray Whebbe Jr.
Packed with 400 color photos and hundreds of wrestling-related items including dolls and figures, autographs, photographs, games, videos, and more-all identified and valued for the first time in one book. Along with the major stars of the World Wrestling Federation and World Championship Wrestling-Goldberg, "Stone Cold" Steve Austin, Kevin Nash and Hulk Hogan-the book also features international stars of the ring.
Softcover • 8-1/4 x 10-7/8 • 160 pages
400+ color photos
Item# PWRES • $21.95

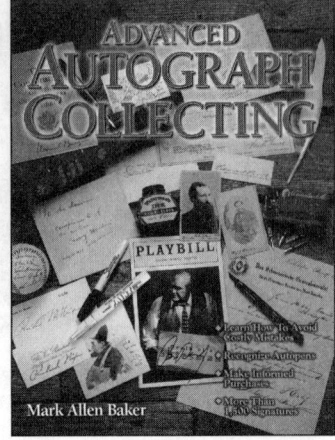

Advanced Autograph Collecting
by Mark Allen Baker
Expand your autograph collecting knowledge with Mark Allen Baker's latest book, Advanced Autograph Collecting. It covers many important collecting topics including the impact of technology on the rare document market, and what you need to know to avoid costly mistakes. Some of the best autograph and manuscript hoaxes are detailed. All advanced autograph enthusiasts will benefit from this book.
Softcover • 8-1/2 x 11 • 352 pages
300 b&w photos
1,500 facsimile signatures
Item# ADAC • $24.95

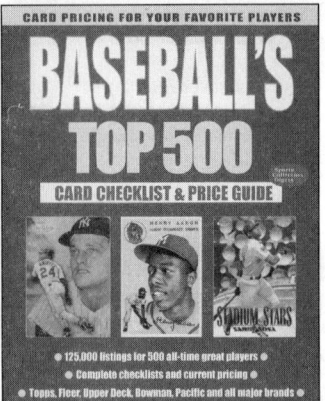

Baseball's Top 500
Card Checklist & Price Guide
by Price Guide Editors of Sports Collectors Digest
All the top baseball players are listed alphabetically with each of their cards listed in chronological order for easy reference. More than 125,000 listings and 500 photos make this the perfect reference guide for beginners or veteran card collectors.
Softcover • 8-1/2 x 11 • 400 pages
500 b&w photos
Item# BBT • $19.95

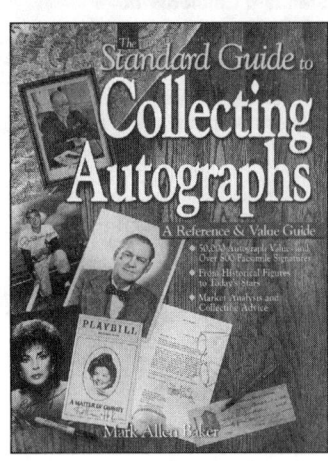

Standard Guide to Collecting Autographs
A Reference & Value Guide
by Mark Allen Baker
You will find everything from the basics to the big-time in dozens of categories and will refer to this volume again and again for easy, quick identification. Filled with facts and more than 50,000 autograph values-15,000 names-this is the most comprehensive book of its kind.
Softcover • 8-1/2 x 11 • 608 pages
1,000 illustrations
Item# CA01 • $24.95

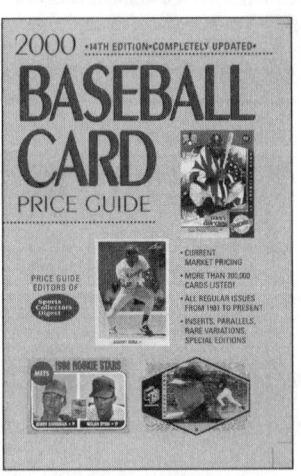

2000 Baseball Card Price Guide
14th Edition
by the Price Guide Editors of Sports Collectors Digest
This is the volume you will need to buy, sell and trade baseball cards smarter. This is the most comprehensive checklist available for cards issued from 1981 - 2000. 175,000+ cards and over 1,500 more sets than the previous edition. All values are based on the latest actual card transactions from coast to coast. Plus, there are more than 2,000 clear crisp photos to make identifying cards easy.
Softcover • 6 x 9 • 832 pages
2,000 b&w photos
Item# BP14 • $16.95

2000 Sports Collectors Almanac
From the Editors of Sports Collectors Digest
The complete one-stop sourcebook for all new-issue cards in football, basketball, baseball, hockey and motor sports You will find vital statistics, up-to-date values and clean, crisp photos to make identifying cards fun and easy. Plus, you get bonus listings of Starting Lineup products and recently produced sports figurines. Complete coverage of 250 recent issue card sets and 125,000 value listings in mint condition, make this a vital addition to any sports card collector's reference library.
Softcover • 8-1/2 x 11 • 272 pages
1,500 b&w photos
Item# SCA00 • $21.95

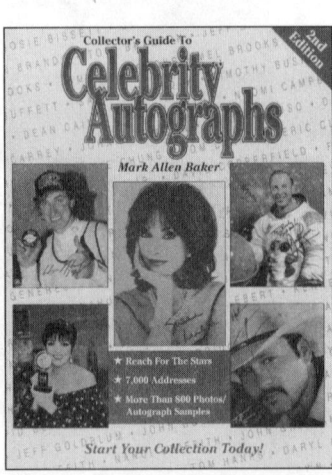

Collector's Guide to Celebrity Autographs
2nd Edition
by Mark Allen Baker
Mark Allen Baker packs more than 30 years of autograph collecting experience into the second edition of this best-selling guide. With more than 7,000 listings and updated addresses, this new edition features a reader-friendly checklist and an author's choice symbol to guide you to great responders. Addresses include stars of the screen, stage and TV, heads of state, sports stars and other people of cultural significance.
Softcover • 8-1/2 x 11 • 352 pages
900+ b&w photos
Item# CAU2 • $24.95

To place a credit card order or for a FREE all-product catalog call

800-258-0929 Offer SPBR

M-F, 7 am - 8 pm • Sat, 8 am - 2 pm, CST

Krause Publications, Offer SPBR
P.O. Box 5009, Iola, WI 54945-5009
www.krausebooks.com

Shipping and Handling: $3.25 1st book; $2 ea. add'l. Foreign orders $20.95 1st item, $5.95 each add'l.
Sales tax: CA, IA, IL, PA, TN, VA, WA, WI residents please add appropriate sales tax.
Satisfaction Guarantee: If for any reason you are not completely satisfied with your purchase, simply return it within 14 days and receive a full refund, less shipping.
Retailers call toll-free 888-457-2873 ext 880, M-F, 8 am - 5 pm